Praise for *The Loop*

"It is an odd paradox that few Chicagoans would call the 'L' beautiful, yet we're quite sure and happy that it defines the very essence of our town. It is a set of trains screeching overhead, yet also a place—the Loop!—and a state of mind. Now a superb reporter, Patrick T. Reardon, tells the full and fascinating story of how Chicago built the 'L' and how the 'L' built Chicago. Read this book on the 'L' and you might miss your stop."
       —**Tom McNamee**, editorial page editor of the *Chicago Sun-Times*

"Reardon, Chicago's preeminent urban affairs journalist, has written a fascinating and indispensable history of one of the nation's most distinctive public works projects. It's the rare Chicagoan that hasn't ridden the tracks that gave the downtown area its famous name. I once lived on the third floor of a Chicago walkup that sat hard against the 'L' tracks, and could not only see and hear but also *feel* the trains that lumbered past on their infinite travels in and out of the Loop. But Pat's deep and detailed reporting reveals so much we didn't know about the life (and near death) of those elevated tracks and the colorful cast of Chicagoans—from Pulitzer-winning reporters to corrupt politicians—who secured the Loop's legacy. Given the city's famous architectural riches, it's pretty brazen to crown anything "the single most important structure in the history of Chicago." But that's what Pat concludes about these historic tracks. And damn if he isn't right."
       —**Ann Marie Lipinski**, winner of the Pulitzer Prize
       for investigative reporting and head of the Nieman
       Foundation for Journalism at Harvard University

"Reardon examines how the visual dominance of the Union Elevated Railroad's 'downtown loop structure' became so intertwined with the identity and fortunes of Chicago's growing downtown that its citizens began referring to the city's central business district as 'the Loop.' More important, he documents how the term 'Loop' as a proper-noun place name came into common use. Reardon's thoughtful and reasoned research is both groundbreaking and long overdue. Not content with simply documenting the origin of the term, he also examines how this unique transit infrastructure has maintained its relevancy through changing times."

—**Bruce G. Moffat**, author of *The Chicago*
"L's" Great Steel Fleet: The Baldies

"A dean among Chicago's estimable cadre of historians and journalists, Reardon has revealed all the drama and corruption as well as the genius and triumph that created a structure dubbed "the city's rusty heart," the squeaky elevated public transit train tracks that encircle downtown. Usually seen as prosaic and functional, if not a noisy atavism, the "L" tracks are transformed through Reardon's brilliant storytelling into the focus of a century-long, zero-sum contest to define the iconic center of the great American metropolis, with a cast of complex characters, mayors and urban planners, writers and architects, dreamers and schemers all."

—**Ethan Michaeli**, author of *The Defender: How the*
Legendary Black Newspaper Changed America, from the
Age of the Pullman Porters to the Age of Obama

"This fascinating book lays out a strong case for why the 'L' is the most important structure ever built in Chicago. Although noisy and rusty, that unique ribbon of riveted steel solidified the downtown and kept the city vibrant. Reardon describes how—despite umpteen plans to tear it down—the Loop 'L' defines Chicago."

—**Greg Borzo**, author of *The Chicago "L"* and *Chicago Cable Cars*

The Loop →

The Loop

The "L" Tracks That Shaped and Saved Chicago

Patrick T. Reardon

Southern Illinois University Press   *Carbondale*

Southern Illinois University Press
www.siupress.com

24 23 22 21   4 3 2 1

Cover illustration: Steve Kagan

Library of Congress Cataloging-in-Publication Data
Names: Reardon, Patrick T., author.
Title: The Loop : the "L" tracks that shaped and saved Chicago /
  Patrick T. Reardon.
Description: First. | Carbondale : Southern Illinois University Press, 2021.
  | Includes bibliographical references and index.
Identifiers: LCCN 2020011486 (print) | LCCN 2020011487 (ebook)
  | ISBN 9780809338108 (paperback) | ISBN 9780809338115 (ebook)
Subjects: LCSH: Loop (Chicago, Ill.)—Economic conditions.
  | Loop (Chicago, Ill.)—Social conditions. | Economic development—
  Illinois—Chicago. | Central business districts—Illinois—Chicago—Planning.
  | City planning—Illinois—Chicago.
Classification: LCC HC108.C4 R43 2021 (print) | LCC HC108.C4 (ebook)
  | DDC 330.9773/11—dc23
LC record available at https://lccn.loc.gov/2020011486
LC ebook record available at https://lccn.loc.gov/2020011487

Printed on recycled paper ♻

This paper meets the requirements of ANSI/NISO Z39.48-1992 (Permanence of
  Paper). ∞

To Sarah, John, Tara, David,
and Emmaline
and, as always,
Cathy

Contents

Galleries of illustrations beginning on pages 67 and 143

Table, "Use of the Word 'Loop' in Chicago Tribune *Headlines,
    1882–96"   66*

*Each note in the back of the book is keyed to the main text by a page
    number, followed by the word or phrase being annotated.*

Maps by Dennis McClendon

The Loop ➔

⬅ Introduction

> One of my most astute Chicago friends . . . loves that grim rectangle,
> bounded in its iron crown of elevated-railroad tracks, and says that
> during the war, when he was overseas and he thought of Chicago, it
> was always of the Loop in the rain, with the sound of the low-pitched,
> bisyllabic police whistles, like sea birds' cries.
> —A. J. Liebling, *Chicago: The Second City*

From its completion in 1883, the majestic 1.1-mile-long Brooklyn
Bridge, linking Manhattan with its cousin borough, has been a dominant
element on the New York scene. In *Brooklyn Bridge: Fact and Symbol*, Alan
Trachtenberg notes that the suspension bridge's designer, John Roebling,
predicted that it would be ranked as a national monument and as "a great
work of art," adding, "Roebling's claims were far from modest, but history
has borne them out. There is no more famous bridge in all the world. And
in 1964, almost a hundred years later, the American government proclaimed
the structure an official national monument."

By contrast, Chicago's elevated Loop is a stumpy 2.1-mile-long rectangle of
railroad tracks that run twenty feet or so above four downtown streets. It is a
structure that is woven so deeply into the physical fabric of Chicago's central
business district, woven so deeply into a cityscape of towering skyscrapers, that,
unlike the Brooklyn Bridge, it can't ever be seen in its entirety. Try to take a
photograph, whether from ground level or some high vantage point, and you'll
capture only a portion of the elevated Loop, at best one of its four sections.

As for being honored, the only recognition that has been granted to the
elevated Loop has been its inclusion, as a seeming afterthought, in the Loop
Retail District when that area was placed on the National Register of Historic
Places in 1998. Many of the structures in the thirty-nine city blocks enclosed
by its tracks have been designated National Historic Landmarks and official
Chicago landmarks. Not the elevated Loop.

Yet, as this book argues, the elevated Loop—disregarded, denigrated, and
often unloved for much of a century—has been the single most important
structure in the history of Chicago.

1

Outwardly, the elevated Loop and the Brooklyn Bridge seem very different. Nonetheless, they are both transportation structures that have played important roles in shaping their cities in physical and symbolic ways.

Throughout much of its history, Chicago's steel-and-wood elevated structure was thought of as the antithesis of anything artful. It was viewed as something ugly and grungy but, like a sewer, needed. Nothing elegant, like the Brooklyn Bridge, majestically rising 276.5 feet and spanning the East River, "vaulting the sea," as Hart Crane writes.

Trachtenberg's book on the bridge looks at how and why it was built and also what it was seen to mean, its role as a symbol: "Coming into existence at a time of change—change from a predominately rural to an overwhelmingly urban and industrial society—Brooklyn Bridge seemed to represent that change. . . . A symbol serves a culture by articulating in objective form the important ideas and feelings of that culture. . . . Brooklyn Bridge symbolized and enhanced modern America."

As a monumental, free-standing structure, the bridge was initially the most visible of landmarks in the nation's largest, most powerful, and most congested city. Today it competes with Manhattan's gleaming forest of skyscrapers, but most views of those towers reveal only the upper floors. By contrast, the Brooklyn Bridge can be seen in its full glory from many vantage points.

When the bridge was built, it linked two cities, but in 1898, Brooklyn and three other boroughs were consolidated with Manhattan to create a much larger and even more dominant New York City. The Brooklyn Bridge became a metaphor of that greater municipality—and of the fast-growing United States. It seemed to embody in its steel, limestone, granite, and cement a heady mix of strength and beauty that was catnip to local and national boosters.

A Visceral Experience

While the bridge is best viewed from afar, the elevated Loop in Chicago is a much more visceral experience, felt and heard as much as seen. The office worker or shopper or tourist who, on a sunny day, walks from State Street across Lake Street enters, for that short time, a world of sharp-edged, patterned shadows. The lattice steel girders are a forest through which cars, trucks, and pedestrians dart while, overhead, a train rumbles, overwhelming most other street sounds and halting conversations, even though the screeching of metal wheels on metal tracks during turns has been greatly dampened in recent years.

Even before the elevated Loop was finished, there were calls for it to be razed. Over the next eight decades, that chorus continued. The only way to beautify the downtown, the argument went, was to get rid of the inelegant structure. The last push to tear it down came in 1978.

During those years, Chicago's public officials, business leaders, and promoters never entertained the idea of the elevated Loop as any kind of symbol. It got people into and out of downtown, and that was that. Yet, without anyone paying much attention, the elevated Loop came to "symbolize and enhance" Chicago in a way that was as significant locally as the Brooklyn Bridge's impact was nationally.

Just as the bridge linked Brooklyn and Manhattan, the elevated Loop linked Chicago. It was no accident that during the fifteen years after the completion of the elevated Loop, Chicago's downtown came to be known as the Loop. The four lines of tracks that constitute the rectangle of the elevated structure enclosed and defined the central business district. It was clearly an important structure. Visually, aurally, and physically, the elevated Loop was impossible to ignore.

Names are important. Names signify. Names are not just bestowed but, in certain compelling cases, impose themselves. Once the elevated Loop structure was built, city residents used it as a key reference point in giving directions and in describing the downtown cityscape. Then, over a decade, an evolution took place. The downtown was seen to be so interconnected with the elevated tracks that formed its borders that Chicagoans found themselves using the transportation structure's name for the property it enclosed—eventually calling the central business district the Loop.

No one made a conscious decision to do this. Over the course of a decade and more, Chicagoans unwittingly went through this naming process because, on some subconscious level, it just made sense. The elevated Loop—with its thicket of girders rooted in the street pavements and its mass looming over pedestrians and its rumbles and screeches crowding the open air and penetrating buildings along its border—was a major presence for anyone downtown. And for all the complaints about its ugliness, the elevated Loop made life easier and more comfortable, carrying hundreds of thousands of city residents and visitors into and out of the downtown each day. The Loop train structure was a central fact of Chicago life.

The People Loved It

Not only that, but the elevated Loop formed the outline of what came to be a common ground that all Chicagoans shared. The significance of this cannot be overstated. Chicago has always been a city of sharp divisions. Over its nearly two centuries, it has been a city of battling neighborhoods, of competing churches and parishes, of the very rich and the very poor, of saints such as Jane Addams and sinners such as Al Capone. It has been a city divided even by baseball: You're a Cubs fan or a White Sox fan, and never, it seems, do the twain meet.

Chicago is a three-sided city—West Side, North Side and South Side. At the end of the nineteenth century, each of those three sections had its own house-numbering system completely unrelated to the systems in the other two sections.

And prior to 1897, each had its own elevated railroad terminal, either in service or planned, just outside the downtown area. Upon reaching one of those terminals, riders would have to get out and walk or find a street-level ride into the central business district. The elevated Loop united those lines and gave focus to the downtown as the center of the city. Without it, three central business districts or subdistricts—each concentrated on the ending place of an elevated line—might have developed. Certainly, the downtown core would have been much weaker.

The elevated Loop allowed Chicago to unite. This was a process that had started when cable cars gave Chicagoans a faster way to get downtown from relatively far distances. But the multiplicity of cable car loops didn't give the downtown the cohesiveness that came with the construction of the elevated Loop.

Indeed, when a uniform numbering system was finally imposed on the city in the first decade of the new century, its epicenter was at State and Madison Streets, within the elevated Loop tracks.

Chicago has long been a city of sharply defined neighborhoods. These communities functioned as tightly circumscribed enclaves where residents tended to share ethnicity, economic status, religion, and many other attributes. As a result, a resident felt comfortable in his or her community in a way not possible in other areas of the city.

The one exception was the Loop. Because of the elevated Loop, this clearly defined downtown area belonged to all Chicagoans equally. It felt comfortable to all city residents, no matter their neighborhood. Throughout much of the past 120 years, the Loop was where Chicagoans got their marriage licenses and where they viewed the Marshall Field's store windows at Christmas and where many of them worked and where they went for plays and movies and where they shopped for virtually anything they wanted. And much more.

The people loved it. And they loved riding the elevated trains from their humdrum neighborhoods to the Loop with its glitz of power, entertainment, and plenty spread out before them.

Although he was no fan of the Loop—or Chicago, for that matter—Manhattanite A. J. Liebling recognized the emotional power that the place and the structure had for Chicagoans. His 1952 articles in the *New Yorker* magazine, later collected in a book titled *Chicago: The Second City*, were a caustic critique of what he saw as the city's provincialism, inferiority complex, and bombast. The Loop, he asserted, couldn't hold a candle to Manhattan.

Nonetheless, Liebling mentioned, with a kind of amazement, the great affection that an otherwise canny Chicago friend had for the Loop, loving "that grim rectangle, bounded in its iron crown of elevated-railroad tracks." Indeed, during World War II, "when he was overseas and he thought of Chicago, it was always of the Loop in the rain, with the sound of the low-pitched, bisyllabic police whistles, like sea birds' cries."

Concentrated Wealth

Although both the Brooklyn Bridge and the elevated Loop were created as transportation structures, their impact on their cities has been economically huge in a way that is often overlooked. The bridge and the elevated Loop have each shaped the real estate markets of their cities by the way they benefited—and penalized—properties based on location. Chicago and New York have developed over the past century and more because of the presence of these two transportation structures.

It was not for nothing that early promoters of the bridge saw the structure as a gold mine for property owners in Brooklyn. More than half a century before the bridge was constructed, a promoter argued, "The rise of property [values] in Brooklyn alone would defray the expense of the project."

Trachtenberg argues that Manhattan benefited even more—and the lesson can be read in its skyline. The bridge, he writes, boosted the amount of traffic coming into Manhattan, heightened the concentration of wealth here, and "indirectly promoted the skyscraper."

The story was the same in Chicago. The elevated Loop, more than any other human-made feature of the landscape, defined the city and gave it focus. Its steel and wood, its grit and sound delineated Chicago's most important and expensive property. From the start, real estate dealers recognized that the rectangle of tracks made and broke fortunes. Location, location, location—the elevated Loop was called "the magic circle" and "the golden circle" because land inside its borders was highly precious, more valuable and more profitable than any other property in the city. Outside was second-rate.

Even before the elevated Loop was finished, real estate officials were noticing that the value of land within the boundaries of the elevated tracks was rising, while for the property outside the structure, it was falling. Like the Brooklyn Bridge, the elevated Loop concentrated real estate wealth into a densely packed quarter of a square mile that, as a result, became even more densely packed. Chicago had already had skyscrapers. With the elevated Loop, many more were built—and they went higher and higher.

Over the past 120 years, Chicago's downtown, as defined by the four sides of the elevated Loop, has evolved. Much of upscale shopping moved to the Magnificent Mile on Michigan Avenue after the 1975 opening of Water Tower Place, a combination of shopping mall and high-rise residences. Even so, Macy's, in the former Marshall Field's building, remained as an anchor well into the twenty-first century.

Skyscrapers have sprouted throughout the Near North Side and have clustered outside the four sections of the elevated Loop. Nevertheless, within those tracks is still one of the greatest concentrations of the tallest of the world's buildings.

Even through hard times in the 1970s, the Loop remained home to one of the world's most important financial districts, as well as a one-stop-shopping concentration of city, county, state, and federal government services and courts. And so it remains today, even as it undergoes a renaissance of new residential towers and a boom in college classrooms and student housing, as well as a growing wealth of entertainment and dining opportunities.

After dodging the wrecking ball in 1978, the elevated Loop increasingly has come to be seen as a unique and attractive part of Chicago's character. A tourist draw and a singular Chicago experience. "A fitting symbol of Chicago's nitty-gritty style of life," notes one writer.

Without the elevated Loop, Chicago would have been just another Rust Belt city with a rundown and discarded downtown. With it, Chicago is Chicago.

Extraordinary Characters

Yet much about the elevated Loop and the downtown that took its name has been ignored, misunderstood, undervalued, and distorted. That's not the fault of Bruce Moffat's authoritative history, *The "L": The Development of Chicago's Rapid Transit System, 1888–1932*, and a handful of other books about the city's elevated railroad lines and the elevated Loop. These well-researched books, however, have stressed the transportation aspects of the story, such as routes, fares, ridership, station design, trackage, timetables, power sources, and rolling stock.

Until now, no book has been written about the impact of the elevated Loop on Chicago and on the city's development, on the city as a physical place and as an idea.

That is the subject of this book. *The Loop* is a biography of a structure that has shaped and saved Chicago. It tells how the elevated Loop came to be, how it rooted Chicago's downtown in a way unknown in other cities, how it played an important role in unifying the "schizophrenic" three-sided city, and how it protected Chicago's downtown—and the city itself—from the full effects of the suburbanization of America during the second half of the twentieth century.

This book uniquely combines urban history, biography, engineering, architecture, transportation, culture, politics, and other fields and synthesizes masses of data and theories to develop new and surprising insights into what has made Chicago tick.

It puts the story of the elevated Loop into the context of the evolution of public transportation in the city and in the world. It delves deeply into the history of Chicago's cable car operations, which, in many ways, set the stage for its elevated lines and the elevated Loop. Indeed, as this book explains, the word "loop" began as a technical transportation term to describe the rectangles around a few downtown blocks that were employed by cable trains as turnarounds. This book reports how the elevated Loop nearly wasn't built and how it narrowly avoided mutilation and even demolition after eight decades of service.

Chicago's downtown and the city as a whole are major characters in this book. The opening chapter describes the vibrancy of both Chicago and its central business district on the celebratory night of New Year's Eve 1911. That date was important as a landmark in the renaming of the downtown as Chicago's Loop.

Colorful and significant Chicagoans also make appearances within the pages of this book, among them legendary lawyer Clarence Darrow, poet Edgar Lee Masters, Mayor Carter Harrison II, real estate entrepreneur Levi Z. Leiter, novelist Nelson Algren, Mayor Richard J. Daley, and three saviors of the elevated Loop—*Chicago Tribune* reporter Paul Gapp, architect Harry Weese, and Mayor Jane Byrne—as well as members of the notorious Gray Wolves of the Chicago City Council, including Johnny Powers, John "Bathhouse" Coughlin, and Michael "Hinky Dink" Kenna.

The most singular presence in this story is Charles Tyson Yerkes, a man demonized in the city's history as a corrupt financier who, as the *Chicago*

Tribune asserted in early 1897, "treats Chicago as a milch cow" and "debauches Councils [and] plunders the city." Yet Yerkes was a larger-than-life personality who put his imprint in a major way on not one, but two world cities—Chicago and London. Yes, he was corrupt and greedy, but so were his opponents. Unlike them, he didn't shy away from the limelight.

This book argues that Yerkes was as important to Chicago as Daniel H. Burnham and Richard J. Daley. That he was a visionary urban planner who was the right man at the right moment to create centralized transportation systems—first with the elevated Loop in Chicago, and then with the Tube in London. As a result, more time is spent on his work in London than would be usual in a book about Chicago. What Yerkes did there provides an important context to what he did in Chicago.

While Yerkes has been notorious in Chicago history, the man he hired to design the elevated Loop—John Alexander Low Waddell—is unknown. Waddell was an engineering genius and international bridge builder whose role in bringing the elevated Loop into existence has been overlooked by Chicago historians and even by civil engineers who honor him as a seminal figure in their field. During his sixty-three years as an engineer, Waddell designed more than a thousand bridges and other structures, none more significant than Chicago's elevated Loop. Nonetheless, his role in that design was given no mention in the obituaries in the *New York Times* and the *Chicago Tribune* at the time of his death in 1938. His ostentatious personality has been absent from Chicago history, and this book rectifies that omission.

Finally, an important character and a major source for this book is the *Chicago Tribune*, the only newspaper for which complete daily editions are available for nearly the entire history of the city. The history of the elevated Loop begins in the early 1880s, even before the elevated railroad technology itself, and runs through to the present. The digital archive of the *Tribune* editions for every day during that period, available to me through the Chicago Public Library, has been of untold value.

By delving deeply into those daily stories, I was able to trace the rise and fall of the cable car, the development of the word "loop," the rise of the elevated railroad, the questions about how the elevated trains would serve the city's downtown, the maneuvering of Yerkes to bring the Union Loop into existence, the impact of the Union Loop on Chicago over the past century and a quarter, and the efforts in the 1970s to bring the elevated structure down.

The benefit of having a single institutional voice describing these events as they happened has been incalculable for me, and the tens of thousands of daily *Tribune* stories that were written over those years, combined with reports from other newspapers and publications, as well as books by scholars in a dozen or more fields, have enabled me to develop a textured understanding of the city as it evolved over those decades and of the role the elevated Loop played in that evolution.

"The City's Rusty Heart"

The most significant character, of course, is the elevated Loop itself, which has been the most important structure in the history of Chicago. This is a book about the looming steel-and-wood downtown presence that has been loved by millions of Chicagoans for making the city's central business district easy to get to and worth wanting to get to. A structure that was long hated as an unseemly eyesore by the city's movers and shakers, who failed to understand how it had brought them wealth and was protecting their investments. A structure that's been called the "most distinctive of all man-made Chicago landmarks" and "one of [Chicago's] most distinctive trademarks."

A. J. Liebling may have been bewildered at how the elevated Loop and the downtown it defined could tug at the heartstrings of Chicagoans. But novelist Nelson Algren understood.

In October 1951, eight months before Liebling's caustic send-up of Chicago arrived in bookstores, Algren published his tempestuous paean to his native city, *Chicago: City on the Make*. While Liebling laughed at the pretensions of the city's boosters, Algren exploded them, embracing Chicago in all its ugliness and greed. He writes, "It's every man for himself in this hired air. Yet once you've come to be part of this particular patch, you'll never love another. Like loving a woman with a broken nose, you may well find lovelier lovelies. But never a lovely so real."

As *Chicago: City on the Make* comes to its final page, Algren identifies the core of the city, its "broken nose," as the elevated Loop, faulting the Potawatomi for leaving nothing behind by the muddy river. "While we shall leave, for remembrance, one rusty iron heart. The city's rusty heart, that hold both the hustler and the square. Takes them both and holds them there. For keeps and a single day."

The Loop: The "L" Tracks That Shaped and Saved Chicago is a book about Chicago's "rusty heart" that has beat for more than 120 years and continues to keep the city and its people vital.

← 1. The Loop, New Year's Eve 1911

The stately seven-ton bronze clocks gracing the corners of the Marshall Field & Co. store on State Street are ticking down to midnight, and scores of police horses clomp idly along the main thoroughfare of Chicago's Loop. Their hooves sound sharply off the steel trolley tracks and creosoted wood blocks in the center of the avenue and less loudly on the asphalt pavement along the curbs. Three hundred mounted police have been assigned here to handle an expected crowd of thousands of New Year's Eve revelers welcoming in 1912. But they have little to do. "My, but it's quiet," one of the officers says.

This year, the holiday throng is much smaller than usual. December 31, 1911, is a Sunday, and some Chicagoans feel it's unseemly to taint the Sabbath with raucous festivities.

Just yesterday, the Young People's Civic League sent a telegram to Illinois governor Charles S. Deneen seeking help in toning down the booze-fueled merrymaking. "Chicago officials refuse to endorse the [state's] 1 o'clock saloon closing law prohibiting the sale of liquor Sunday," read the telegram from Edward G. Walter, the league president. He added, "Decent citizens of Chicago protest against the desecration of the Sabbath and nullification of state law by city politicians and call on you to stand back of law enforcement." Mary F. Balcomb, the league secretary, asserted that the National Guard should be called out to enforce the law. Deneen, however, didn't intervene.

Closing saloons has rarely been a smart strategy for a Chicago politician, and Mayor Carter Harrison II, the son of a mayor, is no fool. He's let it be known that not only will city officials ignore the state law banning liquor sales on a Sunday, but they also will permit drinking establishments to keep pouring drinks until three hours into the new year. Even so, it's evident that some potential celebrants have stayed home out of religious feeling or because they are among the unlucky few who have to get up early for work the next morning.

Much more important, though, for keeping the numbers low on State Street in the final minutes of 1911 is that it's just plain cold. Temperatures are hovering around nine degrees above zero Fahrenheit, and only the most diehard fans of this annual outdoor civic ritual in the Loop are here.

The Heart of Chicago

Chicago—a speck of a settlement eighty-two years earlier—is, at this moment, the fourth most populous city on Earth. And one of the richest. When, in 1830, surveyor James Thompson drew the street grid that opened the way for land development, he included much of the future Loop. At the time, the outpost at the mouth of the Chicago River had only about a hundred residents. Today, though, as 1911 pivots into 1912, more than two million people call the city home.

Chicago, described by one Japanese visitor as "almost a baby city," is the capital of Middle America, the link between East and West. A manufacturing goliath, the center of the nation's meat-processing industry. Home of great American writers. Headquarters of Jane Addams and the settlement house movement she invigorated. The railroad nexus of the United States. Chicago is the heart of the nation. And the heart of Chicago is the Loop.

The proper name "Loop"—often not capitalized before 1950—is a complex term of great importance in Chicago with several meanings, all interconnected. "Loop" refers to the set of elevated railroad tracks, officially known as the Union Loop, that form a 2.1-mile-long rectangle around the most important and expensive real estate in the city. These tracks run at the second-story level of buildings, more than twenty feet above Van Buren, Wells, and Lake Streets and Wabash Avenue.

Dubbed "the golden circle" by its promoters, this Loop of tracks has turned out to be all that and more. At this moment, the elevated Loop has been in existence for only fourteen years, but it has already begun to shape Chicago in myriad ways, the most important of which is rooting the city's central business district in a minuscule site that covers roughly a thousandth of the city's landscape. Later, a critic from New York City will scoff at how congested Chicago's downtown is in comparison to Manhattan—how constrained it is by the elevated tracks. But in midcentury, this will be the salvation of the central business district and the city.

During the late nineteenth century, Chicago's downtown moved around— wandered—as the downtowns of American cities are wont to do. It was on South Water Street, then Lake Street, and then State Street. After the Great Fire of 1871, there was consideration of centering it around what is now Madison and Wells Streets, and in the 1890s, there was a possibility that if the Union Loop weren't built, the city would develop three competing downtowns or subdowntowns at terminals of the elevated railroads.

The elevated Loop has focused investment on what has become a densely packed quarter of a square mile of land. Throughout the coming decades, this will continue. Chicago's economic, civic, and political leaders will pour wealth into this tiny spot in the form of ever taller buildings, ever larger businesses, theaters and government offices, restaurants and department stores, as well as local and national headquarters, hotels, and taverns. Indeed, so much fortune will be sunk into the land bounded by the four sides of the elevated Loop that Chicago's downtown—its Loop—won't empty out the way the central business districts of so many other American cities and towns did in the face of suburbanization after World War II.

This area was the center of the city's business for a quarter of a century before the coming of the Union Loop. What that elevated structure has done is to lock in the importance of these thirty-nine blocks. Just a year earlier, the *Tribune* reported that some land on State Street was selling for $40,000 per frontage foot (the equivalent of about $1 million today).

The land encompassed by the elevated Loop has become a unifying force in a city that rejoices in its many Jekyll and Hyde qualities. It has become the place where Chicagoans work and play and shop before going home to their neighborhoods and homes.

More than ever before, Chicago's downtown has become the crossroads of the city because of the elevated Loop. It has become, in a profound new way, the one place where the people of the South, West, and North Sides come together. Where rich and poor come together. Where the Irish and Lithuanians and African Americans and Germans and Poles and Chinese and all the other varieties of nationality and ethnicity of this polyglot city come together, along with the native-born.

Each day, many of the hundreds of thousands head downtown for work, shopping, and recreation—and most take the elevated trains and get off in the Union Loop. Indeed, many of the celebrants tonight—in downtown restaurants and hotels and out on State Street—have arrived by the elevated and will go home the same way. The story of the elevated Loop is the story of Chicago's downtown. And of Chicago itself.

Calling Downtown "the Loop"

A major indication of the significance of the rectangle of elevated tracks is that "Loop" has also come to mean the city's downtown. This is the soul of Chicago—its business district, its financial center, its governmental center, its shopping and entertainment center. The place where Chicago is most Chicago. The property of every Chicagoan.

Since the completion of the Union Loop in 1897, there has been an evolution in the use of the word "loop" in reference to the downtown. And this New Year's Eve is a significant moment in that progression. Since 1886, the *Tribune* has been reporting on the New Year's Eve celebrations in its January 1 editions. During almost all those years, the location of the party was identified as "down-town" or "downtown." More recently, that term was intermingled with the "loop district."

The celebration story for January 1, 1912, however, will be different. For the first time, the central business district will be identified throughout the story as the "loop." The word "downtown" won't be used at all.

This may seem minor. After all, there were earlier stories that referred to the downtown area as "the loop." And in the future, the word "downtown" would continue to be used for the central business district. Nonetheless, it is an indication of how Chicagoans have come to embrace the elevated Loop and to recognize its profound importance to the city and its downtown.

In coming years, the term "Loop" will gain an added meaning. At certain times and in certain contexts, it will be used to describe all the buildings and activities in the area inside and just outside the elevated Loop tracks. In the late 1920s, when the social scientists at the University of Chicago will divide the city into seventy-five "natural" community areas (large versions of neighborhoods) for research purposes, they will include "The Loop" as community area number 32. This area will encompass all the land bordered by Roosevelt Road, Lake Michigan, and the main and south branches of the Chicago River—1.58 square miles.

Nonetheless, on this day and for more than a century into the future, when it comes to talking about the heart of Chicago, the common use of the term "Loop" refers to the area bounded by the elevated tracks. Here, in these final hours of 1911, is the Loop. Here is Chicago.

A Hardy Band of Celebrants

As the Marshall Field clocks, with their swirling ornamentation and green patina, tick down the final minutes of 1911, an estimated twenty thousand well-lubricated revelers are packed into warm, brightly lit downtown hotels and restaurants, but the streets of the Loop are virtually deserted.

The one exception is State Street, where, awaiting the approach of midnight, the hardy band of celebrants, most of them young, congregate along the west side of the thoroughfare, hoping to use the towering office buildings, stores, and hotels looming over Chicago's downtown to block the frigid wind. "Vendors did a poor business in feather ticklers and false mustaches," the

Tribune will report the next morning. "Some of them peddled labeled hat bands, but they were not in favor. . . . No vendors of racket making toys were permitted on the streets."

Over the previous thirty years, the city's businessmen and architects created in the center of Chicago the second greatest concentration of skyscrapers on Earth. At a time when few structures anywhere in the world are as tall as ten stories, the thirty-nine blocks inside the Union Loop tracks are crammed with no fewer than fifty-six towers, ranging from ten to twenty-two stories.

Even as they shiver and huddle together awaiting 1912, the revelers along State Street can look up at ten such behemoths. Scattered among these giants are many older-vintage buildings of five stories or fewer. This is the nature of the rest of the Loop as well—smaller structures, some dating back to just after the Great Chicago Fire of 1871, and much more imposing edifices.

And it is also true for the area just outside the Loop, where modest-size stores and offices are cheek-to-jowl with another thirty-nine structures of ten stories or more, many of them located along Michigan Avenue, giving thousands of office workers and hotel guests a view of Chicago's rough-and-ready lakefront, much of it landfill, and the sweeping grandeur of Lake Michigan.

A Different Sort of Skyscraper

Without question, Chicago, one of the birthplaces of the skyscraper, is a treasure house of some of the tallest buildings in the world. Yet it can't hold a candle to New York City, the undisputed leader. For every one building in Chicago that is ten stories or taller, New York has ten. Not only that, but the skyscrapers that hulk above the mounted police and revelers on State Street in the Loop during the final minutes of 1911 are much different from the skyscrapers that were the setting for New York's celebration in Times Square an hour earlier.

Developers in both cities have to work within a street grid. The blocks in Manhattan, though, are shorter and narrower, and lots are generally 100 feet deep as compared with the 180-foot depth in much of the Loop. In addition, there are no height limitations in New York, so its skyscrapers have shot up as high as 700 feet, tapering to a point and looking like daggers stabbing into the heavens. The taller they are, the greater their fame.

By contrast, the Chicago City Council, fearing the street congestion that accompanied skyscrapers, voted in 1893 to limit how tall a new building could be, and those limits, ranging from 130 to 260 feet depending on various revisions to the original ordinance, will remain in place until the early 1920s. Even so, the Loop, on a weekday, is one of the most congested areas in the world.

Because of the limits, Chicago skyscrapers tend to look boxy. They are tall, flat-roofed rectangles, and—despite various architectural touches to break up the planes of the facade and to give windows a bit of character—they prefigure the starker rectangles to come later in the century from Ludwig Mies van der Rohe and other adherents of the International Style.

In both cities, those designing skyscrapers work from the inside out. They figure out how to create offices that provide workers with what they need to get their jobs done, and then they fit the outer shell around those spaces. Air circulation is a key consideration, but even more important is sunlight. In fact, natural light will remain the decisive element in office design until the widespread use of the fluorescent bulb in the 1940s.

So in Chicago, there are two general types of skyscraper. One version is a solid rectangle, and this is more common south of Van Buren Street. Here the blocks are long and narrow, and developers can take up an entire block with their building. Bordered on all sides by streets, the structures are bathed in sunlight and have a lot in common with the pointy towers of Manhattan—except, of course, they are stumpy.

Farther north, where a new building usually has to share a block with other structures and thus make do with less access to sun and air, the solution is a building with a light court—a cube with a hollow center or shaped in a U. The brawnier a Chicago skyscraper looks, the greater its reputation.

Like a Mountain Range

Chicago's skyscrapers don't just look different from those in Manhattan. They are positioned differently in the cityscape as well. New York's skyline has a spiky quality to it. In Chicago, on the other hand, the collection of bulky skyscrapers has the appearance of a mountain range. "All about you they rise, the mountains of buildings, not in the broken line of New York, but thick together, side by side, one behind the other," wrote George Warrington Steevens, an English journalist, after a visit to Chicago in the summer of 1896.

Three years later, Scottish drama critic William Archer was also struck by the mountainous nature of the high towers inside the Loop, describing them from ground level: "The gorges and canyons of [Chicago's] central district are exceedingly draughty, smoky, and dusty. . . . With your eyes peppered with dust, with your ears full of the clatter of the Elevated Road, and with the prairie breezes playfully buffeting you and waltzing you by turns, as they eddy through the ravines of Madison, Monroe, or Adams Street, you take your life in your hand when you attempt the crossing of State Street with its endless stream of rattling wagons and clanging trolley-cars."

"Chicago Smoke"

While New York far outdistanced Chicago in its number of skyscrapers, it couldn't "compare with Chicago in the roar and bustle and bewilderment of its street life," Archer noted.

Like Steevens, Archer rode an elevator to the top of the Auditorium Building, where, looking out, he found "on the one hand, the blue and laughing lake, on the other, the city belching volumes of smoke from its thousand throats, as though a vaster Sheffield or Wolverhampton [two major English steel-producing cities] had been transported by magic to the shores of the Mediterranean Sea." Initially, American cities had taken pride in the black smoke pouring out of their factories and buildings. These torrents of soot were visible signs of progress and the triumph of civilization. But that changed soon enough.

Smoke has become an intractable problem in all major cities of the world where coal is burned for heating large buildings and fueling locomotives, in addition to driving the machines of every industry. But perhaps because the nearby Lake Michigan looks so pure and clean, the sooty skies seem much worse in Chicago. And have seemed worse for a long time.

In 1884, for instance, approaching the city on a train, the young novelist-to-be Hamlin Garland glimpsed Chicago under "a huge smoke-cloud which embraced the whole eastern horizon." Five years later, Rudyard Kipling, already a British literary star at twenty-four, visited the city and quipped, "Its air is dirt." Japanese poet Yone Noguchi was astonished upon arriving in the city in 1900: "O Lord, what is that overflowing in the sky—that vast, writhing flood of blackness? A Chicagoan said: 'That's merely a smoke.' 'Merely a smoke,' you say? Merely a smoke that divorces the sun from his bride the flower; that shuts out heaven from the sight of men? . . . 'Smoke' means Chicago as 'flower' means Japan."

In an article titled "Chicago Is Enveloped in Smoke: Dirty, Black Clouds from Down-Town Chimneys Hang over the City like a Pall," the *Tribune* reported in 1898, "The lungs of the people [downtown] are filled with the tiny black flakes. The clothing and faces and hands are soiled, and the fabrics on sale in the marts are damaged if not ruined." The Loop chimneys became "volcanic" at 4 a.m. as the office buildings and stores begin preparing for the work day. Then, at 4 p.m. when the generators for electric light revved up, "the stacks pour out masses of soot and gases."

In fact, the smoke-clouded skies are such a routine part of life in Chicago that tailor Samuel Reichman, the president of the Chicago Women's Tailors Association, has used them puckishly as inspiration. Early in 1912, at a runway show at the Congress Hotel on January 9, Reichman will unveil a gown of wool toweling fabric in a color dubbed "Chicago smoke." A *Tribune* reporter will comment, "'Chicago smoke' is a light drab—the kind dispensed by the Illinois Central railroad."

Of course, in the darkness of near-midnight, those out on State Street waiting for the birth of 1912 can't see much smoke at all, if any. Even so, they can see the effects of all that soot and dirt and "tiny black flakes" that belch out of downtown chimneys Monday through Saturday. All they have to do is glance a few feet away at the facades of the buildings they're using as wind breaks.

Throughout the Loop and along its outskirts, every building is lacquered with layer upon layer of grit and grime, discoloring the exterior to a deep dinginess. Last August, in a letter published in the *Tribune*, Charles W. Anderson wrote, "Our average downtown sunset is a saffron smudge. At its worst it is what the impressionist might term a nocturne in lamp-black and mustard."

A Study of Contrasts

Those waiting on State Street to greet 1912 may be cold, but they aren't standing in darkness. For more than half a century, Chicago's downtown has been the first area of the city to get successive new waves of technologies for keeping the darkness at bay—gaslights, arc lights, and now, electric lights. And for more than half a century, it has been a dazzling contrast to the rest of the city.

The fledgling aviation industry is still cautiously experimenting with night flights. But if a Chicago pilot took his or her craft up on this New Year's Eve, the aviator would see the Loop as a bright blossom of radiance with long, thin lines of lesser lights fanning out along the commercial streets and connecting, across the street grid, with others. Streets lined by homes, especially the homes of the working classes, are served only by gaslight and look dingy next to the electrically lit commercial strips.

Window displays at Loop shops remain illuminated well after the stores close. Hotels, restaurants, and theaters are also ablaze. And then there are the billboards, one of which measures 240 by 40 feet and boasts two thousand light bulbs spelling out the name of its sponsor—the electric company—and the company's more prominent new customers.

The bright lights of the Loop are a magnet, not only on this celebratory night but every night. And they are a metaphor for Chicago's important standing as a major world metropolis—and for the city's and the nation's rush into the glow of a dazzling future.

In the final minutes of 1911, the celebrants out on State Street are joyfully huddling together, buffeted by the freezing winds, and the thousands of other partiers—probably older and better-heeled—are crowding together in Loop restaurants and hotels. And just a few blocks to the west, outside the Loop elevated tracks along Wells Street and over on the other side of the Chicago River, some six hundred homeless and jobless men are moving quietly forward in a slow double line for a roll and a cup of hot coffee from a horse-drawn wagon on Jefferson Street.

Chicago's downtown has long been a study of contrasts between rich and poor. A year earlier, in a story titled "Congested Loop Immensely Rich," the *Tribune* labeled the city's downtown "the richest spot on the face of the globe" but didn't ignore those contrasts.

> There are many thousands of unemployed in the loop. One lodging house in Van Buren street alone houses 700 men and frequently turns away as many as 300 seekers of shelter. . . .
>
> A few yards from where a party of wealthy business men are enjoying a "big spread" a vagrant in a cheap rooming house contentedly is split-ting up a dollar bill into several small packages of coin—each package representing a day's spending money. Not a hundred feet from where a financier is trying to negotiate a loan of $150,000 a hard pressed Chica-goan is trying to get 150 cents on a "silverine watch."

The men lined up behind the wagon on Jefferson are in worse financial shape. Some have overcoats to ward off bitter cold of the single-digit tem-peratures, but others, maybe half, are in shirtsleeves. They shuffle forward, get their free coffee and roll, and then, before hurrying away, wish "Happy New Year!" to Malcolm McDowell. This is the fourth year that McDowell, the secretary of the Central Trust Co. and a former newspaperman, has been organizing this service during the winter for the indigent. The "little attempt to do good," he once explained, began as a kind of New Year's resolution.

By 8 o'clock this evening, the 130 beds in the municipal lodging house at 160 North Union Avenue—the city's homeless shelter—were filled. Mattresses were laid out on the floor, and another 425 men were accommodated by 11 p.m. But for most of the men lined up behind McDowell's wagon, the night is just beginning. From now until dawn, they will be "carrying the banner," slang for walking the streets to keep warm.

"A Million Dollar Celebration"

Back to the east, the evening's festivities in Loop theaters, hotels, and cafés are so profitable that the night will be characterized by hoteliers, restaurateurs, and other businessmen as "a million dollar celebration" (the equivalent of about $26 million in the present day). Earlier in the night, the downtown theaters were packed, and the Art Institute, normally closed on Sunday nights, hosted two thousand visitors for free between 7 and 11 p.m. Some of those people may be out on State Street now, in the last minutes of 1911, but the majority of the art lovers and theatergoers are likely to be at one of the many indoor celebrations downtown.

The greatest crowd—1,300 people—is packed into the Congress Hotel, but the Hotel La Salle and the College Inn are nearly as full, each with 1,200 partiers. A dozen other gathering places in the Loop are mobbed with at least 250 merrymakers each. And as the final seconds tick away, the well-dressed roisterers stand at their table and on the dance floor and at the bar and, at the stroke of midnight, raise a glass to toast the new year as orchestras play "Auld Lang Syne." At the Hotel La Salle, the old year is banished by a curly haired boy who, dressed in tights and waving a banner proclaiming 1912, runs through the closely packed dining rooms.

Outside, in the cold, there is, amid all the shivering, a carnival spirit on State Street. When midnight finally arrives, church bells toll and factory whistles blow. The small crowd cheers. Some of the revelers employ horns and other noisemakers, but these are quickly confiscated by the mounted police.

The outdoor civic ritual completed, the celebrants head for somewhere warm. Within half an hour, "the fun spirit," as the *Tribune* will later describe it, is "frozen out." Meanwhile, those in the hotels and restaurants party on. By 3 a.m., the closing time set by Mayor Harrison, absolutely no more booze is being sold—except for champagne.

By 3:30, space has been cleared in the downstairs room of the Boston Oyster House, and two "fair young things" in blue dresses, their cheeks red with exertion and perhaps intoxication, are dancing the Grizzly Bear. In it, they mimic the awkward, heavy, side-to-side movements of a bear. They finish their dance without falling down, to the disappointment of a circle of male admirers.

In these early morning hours of 1912, the area bounded by the four-sided elevated Loop is quieting down. Yet the heart of Chicago never stops beating. Even as the "fair young things" are catching their breath, other Chicagoans are already starting their day, heading to work or already at work. And many are taking an elevated train, headed for the elevated Loop and the land it encircles, Chicago's downtown, its Loop.

Part One →

Lots of Loops

⬅ 2. Academic Fashion

In 1997, Arnold Lewis won high praise from the mainstream news media and his academic colleagues with his publication of *An Early Encounter with Tomorrow: Europeans, Chicago's Loop, and the World's Columbian Exposition.* As the nineteenth century drew to a close, Chicago was the only major world city—it ranked sixth in population—that had not existed a century before. In the vast emptiness of the midcontinent, it had seemingly erupted out of the prairie, an adolescent Hercules. Lewis, focusing mainly on the years 1884 to 1894, tells the story of the awe and alarm with which visitors from Great Britain, France, Germany, and other European nations viewed the upstart city on the Lake Michigan shore, particularly its central business district. As Lewis's title indicates, a trip to Chicago was, for these European visitors, a trip to the future—a crass, mercantile, congested, frenetic future. A trip into an unsettling new world to come.

His subtitle—*Europeans, Chicago's Loop, and the World's Columbian Exposition*—indicates something else as well. Lewis identifies Chicago's central business district as the Loop, noting, for instance, that "foreign visitors were fascinated by the crowds of the Loop."

"Loop" is a term that's much easier to use than the clunky "central business district" or even "downtown," and it is a proper name that Lewis employs hundreds of times in his text. Indeed, it is at the core of the story he tells. Other cities had skyscrapers and huge industrial plants and great masses of humanity, but, Lewis writes, Chicago was unique because of its central business district: "It was exceptional because its transformation was expressed so concisely in space and time. Spatially, the heart of Chicago, the Loop, was named in the 1880s when cable cars and horse cars looped around the business district before commencing their return runs to residential neighborhoods."

In asserting this history of the name, Lewis is going against the commonly held belief of millions of Chicagoans over the past century that the elevated Loop structure, completed in 1897, gave the city's downtown its name as the Loop. He provides no source, although later in his book, he quotes a mid-twentieth-century statement by Swiss architecture historian Sigfried Giedion that "from 1880 to the time of the Columbian Exposition in 1893 the 'Loop' area in Chicago . . . was the center of architectural development not merely for the United States but for the whole world." It is not clear if Giedion is using the term "Loop" retrospectively here for the sake of convenience—since by 1941, when he was writing, it was known internationally as the name of Chicago's downtown—or if he believes it had been in use for more than a decade before the construction of the Union Loop. He provides no source or note.

In preparing *An Early Encounter with Tomorrow*, Lewis consulted the writings of 117 European visitors, and he refers to nearly 100 of them in his text. Yet not one is quoted calling Chicago's central business district the Loop. In addition, Lewis makes extensive use of a *Chicago Tribune* reporter's 1888 account of a typical working day in the city's downtown.

Starting at 6 a.m., the reporter stationed himself at State and Madison Streets and described the unfolding of the day—the arrival of the men and women who worked in light factories on the upper stories of downtown structures, then the wave of office workers, then the wave of shoppers, the lunch rush, and finally, the crescendo of commuters heading home at the end of the afternoon. The fifty-four-hundred-word article was unusual for its length and took up half of the front page of the newspaper's fourth section. But nowhere in the long story did the reporter describe the central business district as the Loop.

Revising History

Fashion is an essential part of human life. People follow fashion to fit in, and they challenge fashion to express their individuality. Clothing is an obvious example, but there are many others—the shape of automobiles and the shape of the ideal man and woman, drinking habits and smoking, teaching style and dance style, music and food, and on and on.

The field of history writing is no exception. Contrary to public perception, a historian doesn't simply lay out facts. That's the role of an almanac or a database. The job of a historian is to interpret facts, and from age to age, there are different approaches—different fashions—to those interpretations.

Among historians, there's even a term for this—"historical revisionism"— which came into use in the twentieth century. Prior to 1900, history writing had been in the hands of elites, and there was a general tendency to accept the status quo, including the way in which a historic event had been described and analyzed. The next hundred years, though, saw class divisions begin to break down, and a much wider segment of society became college educated. That was especially true in the United States after World War II, when tens of thousands of veterans enrolled in higher education under the GI Bill. Women and people of color joined the fraternity of historians, bringing along much different perspectives and concerns.

The result was a greater willingness to reevaluate and reinterpret the past. And often the goal of historians and other writers was to debunk the work of earlier historians, pointing out flaws in their analyses and errors in their research.

Common knowledge or conventional wisdom—what everyone *knew* to be true—was a prime target. For instance, in the hundred years following the Civil War, historians and the American public saw Abraham Lincoln as the Great Emancipator, but for the past quarter of a century or more, scholars have been reevaluating Lincoln's attitudes toward black Americans, some with great nuance and others in a more heavy-handed manner. Perhaps the most extreme reanalysis was by Lerone Bennett Jr., who, in a 652-page book published in 2000, described the sixteenth U.S. president as a racist, a white supremacist, a proponent of ethnic cleansing, and "one of the major supporters of slavery in the United States for at least fifty-four of his fifty-six years." He titled the book *Forced into Glory: Abraham Lincoln's White Dream.*

Common Knowledge

Generations of Chicagoans grew up "knowing" that the city's central business district got the name "Loop" from the rectangle of elevated train tracks. It was common knowledge, something everyone knew. But over the past half century, especially in recent decades, historians and popular writers have told them that they're wrong. Here is a sampling:

- George W. Hilton, *Cable Railways of Chicago* (1954): "It was from these cable car loops that the 'Loop' got its name, not from the Elevated loop built several years later, as is commonly assumed."
- Perry Duis, "The Shaping of Chicago" (1993): "In Chicago most of the public transit systems which included the world's largest cable car system were built to carry passengers into the central business district. This area acquired the nickname the Loop in the early 1880s because it was encircled by the transit tracks."
- Robert G. Spinney, *City of Big Shoulders* (2000): "The initial cable car lines carried passengers from the South Side suburbs into the heart of the city, deposited them near Field's State Street store, and then looped around on an end-of-the-track turnaround to return to the South Side. . . . This is how downtown Chicago came to be known as the Loop, a name derived from the turnaround that appeared fifteen years before elevated streetcar tracks (more commonly referred to then and now as 'the el' or 'the L') encircled the downtown area."

- Gerald A. Danzer, "The Loop" (2004): "The Loop is the popular name for the Chicago business district located south of the main stem of the Chicago River. The name apparently derives from the place where the strands powering cable cars turned around on a pulley in the center of the city. The concept was extended to the ring of elevated rail tracks for rapid transit lines connecting downtown with the neighborhoods."
- Richard Junger, *Becoming the Second City* (2010): "In turn, as growing numbers of shoppers flocked to Chicago's 'Loop,' a term for its central shopping and business district that first appeared in Chicago's papers in 1882, department stores needed the newspapers to support and build their businesses."

Yet neither Hilton nor Duis nor Spinney nor Danzer nor Junger indicates the source for their assertions. Not one of them provides a quote from the period between 1882 and 1897 to show the central business district was then called the Loop. Even though Junger's book is about Chicago's newspapers during this period, he offers no quotations as evidence that the papers called the downtown the Loop and cites no sources in his endnotes.

No source is needed, it seems, because it's seen as common knowledge that the central business district began to be called the Loop because of a cable car loop or multiple cable car loops. At least, common knowledge among the cognoscenti. The fact that writers continue to feel the need to address the issue—to knock down the idea that the name came from the elevated rail Loop—is an indication of persistence of that belief among most Chicagoans.

Yet even when writers offer a source, it's problematic. Consider the one used by Brian J. Cudahy. In 1982, Cudahy published an important history of Chicago's elevated train system, extensively detailed and heavily illustrated, titled *Destination: Loop; The Story of Rapid Transit Railroading in and around Chicago*. In the opening pages of the book, he provides a quick, two-page overview of the city's municipal and transit history, including these sentences: "These [cable car and horse car] surface lines terminated at or in the Loop, which got its name in the '80s because of the cable car routings therein. This explanation of the origin of 'the Loop' is the conclusion of the Chicago Historical Society, searcher out and custodian of Chicago's past in fact and folklore." In other words, Cudahy's source is hearsay, not the sort of proof that would be accepted in court nor, for that matter, in a high school sophomore's research paper.

Sometimes, a writer will make the assertion based on a misreading of a document. For instance, on April 19, 1940, a Chicago newspaper published a story that said, "How did the Loop come by its name? That's what we thought, too. But you're wrong—just as we were. It isn't because the 'L' structure bounds the area between Lake, Wells and Van Buren streets and Wabash avenue. . . . The first 'Loop' district in Chicago was in the section bounded by Madison, Lake and State streets and Wabash avenue, and was enclosed by the tracks of cable cars of the Chicago City Railways—and that was in the '80s."

As the source for this statement, the writer cites a brochure from 1889 titled *Souvenir: A Short Description of the Cable System as Operated by the Chicago City Railway Co.*, written by H. H. Windsor, the company's secretary. And sure enough, the pamphlet has a page titled "The 'Loop.'" But that title doesn't refer to Chicago's downtown. As Windsor explains, it relates to the route of his company's cable cars around a three-block section of the central business district.

A cable car system involved the use of a constantly moving underground cable that ran just below the surface in the center of the tracks. The first car in a cable car train would grip this cable through a slot and be pulled forward. In Chicago's central business district, the system of underground cables formed a rectangle, or loop, around two or more blocks. By going around this loop, the train would be able to return to its starting point without needing to use a turntable or a switchback. Nowhere in his brochure does Windsor state that the business district was called the Loop.

"Synonymous"

In *City of the Century*, one of the most popular books on Chicago history and the basis for a three-part public television series, Donald L. Miller writes, "By Christmas of 1882, the South Side cable lines converged near [Marshall] Field's State Street store to create a loop, or turnabout, that the cars swung about 'on the fly' before heading back to the fringes of the city to pick up more holiday shoppers. The term 'Loop' became synonymous with downtown Chicago fifteen years before the completion of the elevated railway system around the central business district that still remains a defining Chicago landmark." In contrast to most other writers who make that assertion, Miller lists four sources.

One is Cudahy, whose own source, as we've seen, was hearsay. Another is "Rationalizers and Reformers: Chicago Local Transportation in the Nineteenth Century," a PhD dissertation by Robert David Weber. However, this important painstaking account of the transit systems in Chicago in the late 1800s is silent about the origin of the use of the name Loop for the central business district.

Miller's third source is *Chicago: Growth of a Metropolis* by Harold M. Mayer and Richard C. Wade, a magisterial work and one of the foundational books in the study of the city's history. Mayer and Wade note that the establishment, operation, and expansion of the first cable car system in 1882 improved land values, and they add, "It also created an early version of the Loop, for the cable lines all converged to make a loop around the business section before making return runs into the residential areas on the edge of the city."

The phrasing is ambiguous. Mayer and Wade seem to be saying that the cable car loop—actually, there were eventually several loops serving several companies, circling separate sections of Chicago's downtown—was a predecessor of the elevated Loop structure. But perhaps they're saying that the area enclosed by the initial cable car loop was the equivalent of the city's downtown. That seems far-fetched, since that loop enclosed only three city blocks at the northeast corner of the central business district, whereas thirty-nine blocks would be enclosed when the rectangle of elevated tracks was erected in 1897. They certainly never make a direct statement that the central business district was called the Loop before the construction of the elevated Union Loop.

A Baffling Place

Miller's fourth source—"Chicago," an article by Charles Henry White in the April 1909 edition of *Harper's Monthly Magazine*—is confusing, but that's because White is trying to make a point, with exaggerated humor, that Chicago's downtown is a baffling place. Also, most likely because White himself was confused.

As the article opens, White is searching for Chicago's "loop"—but it's not clear whether he is looking for the elevated Loop structure or for Chicago's downtown, which, by 1909, was also known as the "loop district" and occasionally as simply the "loop." He gets on an electric trolley and asks the conductor where he's headed. "The loop," the conductor replies. Where is it? "You're on it." What the conductor means is that the trolley is on its rectangular route—its loop—around several downtown blocks. Once this loop is completed, the trolley will be headed back the way it came.

Maybe White understood this, and maybe he didn't. He certainly doesn't indicate that the loop mentioned by the conductor isn't the equivalent of the elevated Loop or the central business district. It's just one of many trolley loops. For the next several paragraphs, White plays up his confusion, asking three men, in turn, the name of the downtown street where they are standing and getting replies in Italian, German, and French. Finally, he hears the conductor of another trolley car say, "Loop car—all out!" From this, he determines, "To find the loop, look for a panic-stricken group of strangers groping about in a futile effort to find the street name."

A few lines later, White writes, "The Chicagoan is very proud of the loop, and will glow with sunny radiance the moment you approach the subject." As an example, he quotes a policeman: "It is the greatest system on earth. . . . You see, each car, as it comes into the city from the suburbs, goes immediately into the loop when it reaches the business section of the city, and returns along parallel lines to the point it started from. Do I make myself clear? . . . The loop is near enough for any man's place of business. You can always walk."

The policeman is talking about the elevated Loop structure. If he were referring to the multiple trolley loops, he would have talked about "loops" rather than "the loop." He clearly isn't talking about "the loop" as a synonym of downtown, since the loop he describes is a transportation system that goes into "the business section of the city." In this case, too, White may not have understood what the policeman was trying to tell him. If he did, he doesn't make it clear to the reader.

⬅ 3. Silence

Writers who assert that Chicago's downtown was called the Loop well before the construction of the elevated Union Loop have had a hard time finding ways to prove their contention. As a result, either they haven't cited sources or they've gone far afield and trotted out questionable proofs in order to buttress their "common knowledge" belief. That's because contemporary writings—which should be the best documents to tap for such proof—aren't helpful at all. Indeed, they're silent on the subject.

Consider the work of influential American writer Theodore Dreiser, whose fiction and nonfiction described Chicago in the decades just before and just after the turn of the century. Two paragraphs before his assertion that the Loop name predated the Union Loop by fifteen years, Donald L. Miller discusses the creation of the cable car lines. In that discussion, he quotes from Dreiser's memoir of his early life, *Dawn: A History of Myself*: "And all of the principal street car lines, which formerly had been drawn by horses, were now pulled by cables and threaded the downtown thoroughfares in clanking rows." Although Dreiser wrote *Dawn* in 1916, he didn't publish it until 1931, out of concern for the feelings of his family at his frank discussion of his life. In the 619-page book, he describes Chicago in the late 1880s and early 1890s and never uses the word "loop."

By contrast, Dreiser makes good use of the word "downtown," such as in the quote Miller employs, as well as in a reference to his job as a delivery man "in the business heart of Chicago, the great downtown section where traffic was so congested as to spell hours of delay for an unskillful driver, which for all my driving I still really was." Similarly, Dreiser doesn't call Chicago's central business district "the Loop" in the naturalistic novels that made him a major literary figure, even though the city plays an important role in those works: *Sister Carrie* (1900), *An American Tragedy* (1925), and the *Trilogy of Desire* (*The Financier*, 1912; *The Titan*, 1914; *The Stoic*, 1947), his thinly fictionalized life of Charles T. Yerkes, the entrepreneur who brought the elevated Loop into existence.

The first half of *Sister Carrie*, for instance, takes place in and around Chicago's central business district from the summer of 1889 to the summer of 1890. Yet if the term "Loop" was in common use for that area at that time, Dreiser gives no indication. He writes, "They arose and went out into the street. The downtown section was now bare, save for a few whistling strollers, a few owl cars, a few open resorts whose windows were still bright. Out Wabash Avenue they strolled, Drouet still pouring forth his volume of small information." In *Dawn* and in *Sister Carrie,* Dreiser uses the term "downtown section" but never the word "Loop."

"A Restricted Yet Tumultuous Territory"

There's no reference to the downtown area as "the Loop" in a wide array of important nonfiction works, including *If Christ Came to Chicago,* by William T. Stead (1894); *History of Chicago,* edited by John Moses and Joseph Kirkland (1895); *The Plan of Chicago,* by Daniel H. Burnham and Edward H. Bennett (1909); and *Twenty Years at Hull House,* by Jane Addams (1910). It's also missing from such novels as *Sweet Clover,* by Clara Burnham (1894); *Rose of Dutcher's Coolly,* by Hamlin Garland (1895); *The Pit,* by Frank Norris (1903); and *The Jungle,* by Upton Sinclair (1906).

Mr. Dooley, the comic Irish persona created by newspaper columnist Finley Peter Dunne, who wrote in Chicago in the 1890s, never mentions "the Loop" as a term for the central business district (although he does give a passing reference to "th' Union loop"). But he has a lot to say about "downtown," such as this comment on gambling reform: "I wud rigidly rigulate it to th' downtown sthreets, where it wud help th' business interests iv this gr-reat an' growin' city iv ours."

The absence of the proper noun "Loop" is particularly striking in two works that centered on Chicago's skyscrapers—"After the Sky-Scrapers, What?," a column in the *Chicago Record* by George Ade, published between 1893 and 1900, and *The Cliff-Dwellers,* by Henry Blake Fuller (1893). In his essay of about nine hundred words, Ade notes that the new tall buildings have helped create "the condensation of the business activity of the city into that small area bounded on the east by the lake, on the north by the Chicago River, on the west by the south branch and on the south by no fixed line or street." This "small area" he calls "down-town" and the "business region" and "this great business center of Chicago." But not "the Loop."

Fuller's novel focused on the multifaceted life in one of Chicago's new skyscrapers. In his opening sentences, he describes the city's central business district:

> Between the former site of old Fort Dearborn and the present site of our newest Board of Trade there lies a restricted yet tumultuous territory through which, during the course of the last fifty years, the rushing

streams of commerce have worn many a deep and rugged chasm. These great cañons—conduits, in fact, for the leaping volume of an ever-increasing prosperity—cross each other with a sort of systematic regularity, and in deference to the practical directness of local require- ments they are in general called simply—streets. Each of these cañons is closed in by a long frontage of towering cliffs.

But this "restricted yet tumultuous territory" he never calls "the Loop."

"Grand Buildings"

During the late 1880s and throughout the 1890s, newspaper and magazine reporters frequently came to Chicago and returned home to write lengthy profiles of the city, aiming to capture its essence and explain its significance. One such outsider was a correspondent for *The Times* of London who pub- lished a lengthy article in the October 24, 1887, edition of that newspaper, titled "Prominent Characteristics of Chicago." He writes, "An overhanging pall of smoke; streets filled with busy, quick-moving people; a vast aggregation of railways, vessels, and traffic of all kinds; and a paramount devotion to the Almighty Dollar are the prominent characteristics of Chicago. . . . The profits of [the railroad] traffic have piled up grand buildings on the broad-streets in the business section." Despite the writer's interest in Chicago's downtown and its skyscrapers, he makes no reference to that area as "the Loop."

Four years later, the visiting reporter was Captain Charles King, who had served as a Union soldier at the battlefront during the Civil War and was later sent to West Point by President Abraham Lincoln. King's article in the November 1891 issue of *Cosmopolitan* magazine was titled "The City of the World's Fair," referring to the World's Columbian Exposition to be held in Chicago two years later.

Nonetheless, most of his comments had to do with the vibrant multiplicity of activity and people in the city's downtown, a noisy jarring place of crowds, hurry, and collisions. He writes:

> Stand with me here at the corner of State and Madison as the evening clock strikes six. From all the huge retail shops that line the great thor- oughfares swarms of men and women, girls and boys are pouring forth upon the crowded pavement. Along the rows of parallel tracks of the main avenue, far as the eye can see, north and south, a long perspec- tive of cable cars, crowded with passengers; mothers with children two deep upon their laps; men with newspapers oblivious to the dozens of tired-looking shop women who cling desperately to the handing straps;

bevies of men and boys perched on the footboards and hanging on by
the skin of their teeth; probably a hundred human beings on every car,
four cars on every train, four trains in every block, all banging, clanging, whirring and, one loaded stopping for nothing and nobody; all
bristling with people.

King is clearly captivated and more than a bit overawed by Chicago's central business district, and he's very aware of the presence of cable cars in that
area. Yet he never calls that district "the Loop."

"The Main Exhibit"

A year later, in the February 1892 issue of *Harper's New Monthly Magazine*,
Julian Ralph published a ten-thousand-word profile of the city as a curtain-
raiser for the World's Fair. He had spent more than two weeks in the city
and came away so impressed that he titled his article "Chicago: The Main
Exhibit." It began: "Chicago will be the main exhibit at the Columbian Exposition of 1893. No matter what aggregation of wonders there, no matter
what the Eiffel-Tower-like chief exhibit may be, the city itself will make the
most surprising presentation. Those who go to study the world's progress will
find no other result of human force so wonderful, extravagant, and peculiar."

Ralph, a New Yorker, was dazzled by Chicago, amazed and more than a
little appalled by the midcontinent upstart, writing, "I have spoken of the roar
and bustle and energy of Chicago. This is most noticeable in the business
part of the town, where the greater number of the men are crowded together.
It seems there as if the men would run over the horses if the drivers were
not careful. Everybody is in such a hurry and going at such a pace that if a
stranger asks his way, he is apt to have to trot along with his neighbor to gain
the information, for the average Chicagoan cannot stop to talk." He mentions
that "business part of town" several times, calling it "the business district" and
"the bustling business district." But he never calls it "the Loop."

Nine years later, the Local Transportation Committee of the Chicago City
Council produced a map of the cable train routes, including their six loops,
in the city's downtown. This map fills the back cover of *Cable Railways of
Chicago*, by George W. Hilton, the definitive work on the city's cable train
history, published in 1954. On page 2 of that book, Hilton asserts—without
offering proof—that the downtown got its "Loop" nickname because of the
cable car loops. However, the 1902 map of the cable lines doesn't mention
"Loop" in its title. Instead, it's labeled, "Present Tracks of the Chicago City
Railway and Chicago Union Traction in Business District."

"What Is Now 'the Loop'"

In those years early in the twentieth century, two of the most famous Chica-goans—indeed, two of the most famous Americans—were Clarence Darrow and Edgar Lee Masters, who shared a law office from 1903 to 1911. Darrow was the brilliant, radical, unscrupulous, larger-than-life lawyer renowned for representing clients that other attorneys ran from. Such as Nathan Leopold Jr. and Richard Albert Loeb, the two wealthy teenage University of Chicago law students accused of the "thrill killing" of a fourteen-year-old neighbor boy in 1924. And John Scopes, the Tennessee substitute teacher charged in 1925 with violating a state law by teaching the theory of evolution. Although an attorney, Masters made his mark as a poet, essentially with a single book, one that was immediately popular in 1915 and has been a perennial bestseller ever since, *Spoon River Anthology*. This collection, an elegiac meditation on small-town life, is focused on the cemetery hill of the fictional Illinois town of Spoon River, and its 244 poems are the self-spoken epitaphs of the people buried there.

When they came to Chicago—Darrow from Ohio and Masters from cen-tral Illinois—they were just two among millions of obscure hopers and dream-ers who bustled to the city in the 1880s and 1890s, seeking their main chance. One of Darrow's earliest friends and an important mentor was Judge John Peter Altgeld, later famous as the Illinois governor who pardoned three of the men convicted in the Haymarket bombing case. In Darrow's autobiogra-phy, *The Story of My Life*, he devotes a chapter to Altgeld and mentions the Unity Building, which the future governor constructed in November 1891 near Dearborn and Washington Streets in Chicago's central business district. He writes, "During his period of prosperity, Altgeld had erected a building sixteen stories high; one of the most expensive and elaborate of the time. It was one of the first 'sky-scrapers' within what is now 'the Loop' in Chicago."

It would have been simpler for Darrow, who wrote *The Story of My Life* in 1932, to have said the Unity Building was in the Loop. By then, it was a widely used and widely understood term. Indeed, just nine years later, Swiss architecture historian Sigfried Giedion would write that between 1880 and 1893, "the 'Loop' area in Chicago" was the international center of architec-tural innovation. But Giedion, born in 1888, had not been in Chicago in those years. Darrow had. And he goes out of his way to indicate that as of 1891, "the Loop" wasn't a name that was applied to Chicago's downtown.

Masters makes the same point in his own 1936 autobiography, *Across Spoon River*, not once but twice, and more emphatically. Recalling his arrival in

Chicago in July 1892, Masters writes of walking north on Dearborn Street toward the city's downtown—"the city of the Loop district, not then called the Loop." Four pages later, he describes wading through terrible heat during a walk with his Uncle Henry around "the district since called the Loop."

"Down in the Loop"

The completion of the Union Loop elevated tracks in 1897 began a social, cultural, linguistic, and psychological process that eventually resulted in the use of the proper noun "Loop" for Chicago's central business district. In fact, by 1914, if not earlier, Masters was comfortable using the term, even with non-Chicagoans. That was the year that the first of his Spoon River poems began appearing in the St. Louis magazine *Reedy's Mirror* under the pseudonym Webster Ford. Among those impressed was New Hampshire–based poet Witter Bynner, who sent an admiring letter to Ford in care of the magazine. In response, Masters acknowledged to Bynner his authorship: "This is me— Webster Ford of Spoon River, also the Loop."

Spoon River Anthology was published in 1915 and, a year later, was followed by a second edition with thirty-five additional poems. One of those was "English Thornton," a diatribe against "fops" and "parasites" and bribe-takers and "the descendants of those / Who bought land in the loop when it was waste sand." That same year, in the *New Republic* (and later in his book *Songs and Satires*), Masters published a poem of some two hundred lines titled "The Loop." In this work, Masters sees the Loop as the elevated structure and also as the central business district, as these lines demonstrate:

> Down in the loop the blue-gray air enshrouds,
> As with a cyclops' cape, the man-made hills
> And towers where the city crowds. . . .
> Around the loop the elevated crawls . . .
> Slop underfoot, we pass beneath the loop.
> . . . And a man with jaw
> Set like a tiger's, with a dirty beard,
> Skulks toward the loop . . .

← 4. Lots of Loops

In late 1880, just nine years after the Great Fire, Chicago, always boast-ful, was feeling its oats. Having risen like a phoenix from the ashes of that tragic conflagration, it was on its way, its boosters were certain, toward becoming the greatest city in the world. A *Chicago Tribune* reporter tapped into that euphoria but added a note of chastisement when he wrote that Chicago was, "in some respects, the most enterprising city on the continent today." That qualification—"in some respects"—was unusual. Rarely did those champion-ing Chicago modulate their bombast. In this case, though, the reporter was making a point. Despite the city's usual get-up-and-go, Chicago had, "strangely enough, allowed herself to be outstripped in the matter of street-car travel by her two great rivals—New York at the East and San Francisco at the West."

New York had the elevated train. San Francisco had the cable car. But the best that public transportation had to offer in Chicago was the ploddingly slow horsecar, which moved no faster than a man or woman could walk. Now, though, in December 1880, the Chicago City Railway Company was looking to change that. It was planning to replace many of its horsecars with cable car trains, which had been operating successfully in San Francisco for the past seven years.

And the *Tribune* was all for it, arguing in an editorial that the cable tech-nology was proven: "Under this arrangement the cars will not be crowded, for, with such a powerful motor, the Company can put on any number of cars. . . . Their motion is very easy, and they can be stopped and started with perfect ease, and they are absolutely safe. There will also be a decided gain in time. At present, including stops, our cars make about four miles an hour, while under the new system they will make six, and can, whenever the emergency requires it, make eight." All in all, the editorial determined, "as to the success of the new plan there hardly seems to be a doubt." And this transportation breakthrough "promises to work a complete revolution in the system of street travel in this city."

The cable car did eventually revolutionize mass transportation in Chicago. In fact, the city's cable car system soon became the busiest and the most ex-tensive in the world. At its peak, the system provided rides to more than eighty million passengers annually, and over its quarter century in operation, more than a billion fares were collected. In its early years, the city's cable service was so popular that it even had a cigar named for it. "Chicago Cable Havana 5c Cigar Is Equal to the average 10c Cigar," an 1885 ad in the *Tribune* read.

Yet despite the *Tribune*'s rosy expectations, Chicagoans would learn that the cable cars were far from perfect. They could—and often did—become very crowded indeed. Breakdowns were not uncommon. And as for safety, a defect in the basic technology of the cable system meant that on occasion, riders would suddenly find themselves on a runaway train, rumbling along the rails toward the rear of another train farther up the tracks. All that was in the future, though.

In 1880, Chicago had 503,185 residents and was the fourth most populous city in the nation, behind New York, Philadelphia, and Brooklyn. Endless miles of flat land north, west, and south were available for development, but those couldn't be fully exploited because most Chicagoans had to walk wherever they wanted to go. The city, with great visions of its manifest destiny as the major world metropolis, was yearning for a better, more modern way of getting around the town.

"Mud, Rubbish, and Confusion"

Mass transportation in the United States began in New York City in 1827, when hackney operator Abraham Brower put into service a horse-drawn, open-air, four-wheel carriage, called an omnibus. The name, later shortened to bus, comes from the Latin word for "all" because, unlike a taxicab, the omnibus—which looked like a bit like an elongated version of the stagecoach in use out on the western plains—was available for anyone to board as long as he or she paid the fare and could find room. The first modern omnibus service had gone into operation in France a few years earlier.

At the time Brower introduced his omnibus service on Broadway, serving New York's 200,000 residents, Chicago was still a frontier settlement with no need to consider public transit. It was home to only about 100 people in 1830, when surveyor James Thompson plotted the site, making possible the buying and selling of real estate. But within three years, the population had grown modestly to 350, and the community was organized as a town. "The interior of the village was one chaos of mud, rubbish, and confusion. Frame and clapboard houses were springing up daily under the active axes and hammers of the speculators, and piles of lumber announced the preparation for yet other edifices of an equally light character," wrote an English visitor.

By 1837, when Chicago was incorporated as a city, the number of residents had ballooned by more than 1,000 percent to 4,170. Compared with New

York, that was still minuscule, but it was a harbinger of things to come. By 1850, Chicago's population had grown sixfold to 29,963. And ten years later, it had more than tripled to 109,206.

Getting from one place to another in Chicago grew progressively more difficult as new homes, stores, factories, warehouses, and shipping facilities were built. So in the late 1840s, omnibuses started serving the city's residents. They held sway until 1859, when the Illinois legislature incorporated three Chicago companies (one each for the North, West, and South Sides) to operate a new version of public transit that was part omnibus and part railroad—the horsecar.

Picture an omnibus—but much larger—rolling on rails down the middle of a street and providing a much smoother, roomier ride. While an omnibus had seating for twelve passengers, a horsecar easily accommodated twenty—and during peak travel times, it could hold as many as ninety, although that must have been a tight fit. Rather than rattling over cobblestones or getting mired in mud, a horsecar was able to move fluidly—and more quietly—along the tracks. Also, the rails made it possible for one or two horses to pull heavier loads. Most empty Chicago horsecars weighed about two tons. During heavy travel periods, however, the horse or horses would have to pull along the rails a total weight of more than fourteen thousand pounds.

The "Organic City"

Chicago, at this time, like every other city, town, and village in the United States, was what historian Ted Steinberg has called an "organic city"—that is, "a place swarming with pigs and horses" where life "was dirty, but it also had a certain social and environmental logic." For instance, the poor were able to raise pigs for food. The animals essentially cared for themselves, feeding on garbage and manure, and to some extent, they provided a street-cleaning function.

For residents and visitors, Chicago was awash with smells: From the sewage-filled Chicago River. From the coal smoke spewing from the surging flood of locomotives in and out of the city and the forest of stacks atop buildings and factories. From the bodies of people of all classes, especially manual laborers and the poor, and from the bodies of animals, such as the horses pulling the horsecars. Describing what it was like to ride a horsecar, writer Frank Rowsome Jr. notes, "In the passenger compartment, there was a special horsecar smell, blending the odors of smoky coal-oil lamps, sweating horses, and the pungency that came when the straw on the floor was dampened with many a dollop of tobacco juice. . . . Up front the driver squirted his tobacco forward, some of it landing on the dash, some of it on the horses' rumps, and the rest of it atomizing in the breeze to float back over the car."

And then there was the manure and the urine. In the 1880s, Chicago's street railways had about sixty-six hundred horses in operation. According to one estimate, a working horse, during the course of an eight-hour day, would deposit a half gallon of urine and 20 pounds of feces onto the roadway. For sixty-six hundred horses, that came to 3,300 gallons of urine and 132,000 pounds of manure. Each day. "Such sights and smells," writes historian Carolyn Merchant, "contributed to characterizations of urban areas as wilderness."

This was a reality that Chicagoans couldn't just walk around, but one they lived with in a very elemental way, as much as the air they breathed. Actually, as Ted Steinberg notes, it was the air they breathed: "Worse still, the stinking piles bred countless numbers of flies, which harbored disease, including typhoid fever. Then there was the dust to contend with. Horse turds dried up in the heat, only to be pulverized by the creatures themselves as their hoofs made contact with the pavement. Ground horse excrement was the nineteenth century equivalent of auto pollution—and was just as irritating to people's respiratory systems."

Installing a cable car system wouldn't eliminate the problem. For one thing, it wouldn't replace all the horsecars. For another, horses were used for many other purposes, such as pulling delivery wagons. Still, it was an important selling point. As that *Tribune* reporter delicately put it in the first story about the proposed new service: "Being freed from the disagreeable accompaniments of the ordinary horsecar, they are considered desirable and are placed upon the choicest residence street of [San Francisco]." Later, a cable company official described those "disagreeable accompaniments" more bluntly: "The value of removing from a street the voidings of two or three thousand horses is a matter not to be lightly estimated in point of health."

"A Solution"

Promoters glowingly described how the cable car would be yet another step in Chicago's rise to grandeur, an assertion the *Tribune* fully endorsed, publishing stories every month or so about the wonders of the new technology and updates on the construction of the "system destined to furnish a solution to the rapid-transit problem." Even so, it wasn't a sure thing. The cable car was still viewed by transportation experts as an experimental method, and no one could be sure how it would operate in a city with such extreme temperature swings, from subzero readings in winter to scorching, humid summers. Nonetheless, on December 27, 1880, an ordinance to allow the cable service was introduced in the City Council and approved three weeks later with little substantive debate.

Work, however, was delayed until State Street between Twelfth Street (Roosevelt Road today) and Twenty-Second Street (Cermak Road) could be widened by moving all the buildings along the east side back from the roadway. Once that was done, the Chicago City Railway Company had the responsibility under the enabling ordinance to bring State Street to an even grade. This required lowering the portion of the street south of Twelfth Street by a foot and a half and raising the northern section by three feet, a task of almost Sisyphean difficulty given Chicago's boggy soil. "Day after day saw load after load [of stone] cast into these seemingly insatiable sink-holes, until the workmen declared an evil genie below removed the material as fast as it was thrown in," reported the Chicago City Railway Co. Meanwhile, the city was putting in granite curbstones and twenty-five-foot-wide plank sidewalks on both sides of State.

But State Street property owners were soon in an uproar. In the early 1880s, State Street south of downtown, as well as the area around it, particularly to the east near the shore of Lake Michigan, was the most fashionable section in the city. Chicago's power brokers, including Marshall Field and George Pullman, lived in the district of Second Empire mansions along Prairie Avenue between Sixteenth and Twenty-Second Streets. As the decade went on and the cable line became an amenity to the community, the imposing homes, including many simple and elegant Queen Annes and bulky, muscular Romanesques, filled both sides of Prairie down to Thirtieth Street.

At the moment, however, few residents of the area saw the future cable line as an amenity. The condition of the roadway between Polk Street and Twenty-Second was "utterly demoralized" and "hopelessly torn up and obstructed," the *Tribune* reported. The street looked as though a "cyclone had demolished iron-foundries, sewer-pipe factories and lumber-yards and scattered the debris all along the street."

After holding "an indignation meeting," a group of property owners went to the Council to air their grievances. There was a lot of back and forth among the aldermen, but no one from the delegation was permitted to speak. And no action was taken. Nonetheless, perhaps spurred by the protest, the pace of construction accelerated, and within a week, the workers were completing as much as a block a day. Efforts to have the street repairs finished and the cable cars running by the fall, though, were hampered by bad weather, including a small flood, and an explosion at the engine house. Then, finally, after all the delays, the great day came.

"Her Power"

"I have seen Chicago in her infancy. I see her now in her power." The speaker was William Bross. It was January 28, 1882, and tens of thousands of Chicagoans were celebrating the inaugural run of the city's first cable car line along State Street.

A former Illinois lieutenant governor, Bross was something of an unofficial booster in chief for Chicago. Six years earlier, he had published his *History of Chicago*, which was less an objective look at the city's past than it was a paean to its future. The centerpiece of that 126-page book was an account of the Great Fire of 1871 and of Bross's efforts in the immediate aftermath to reassure the eastern money men that Chicago would rise again.

On October 13, five days after the fire, he was in New York, giving a lengthy interview to the *New York Tribune*, in which he asserted, "That indomitable perseverance and genuine 'grit' which made Chicago in the past will in a very few years raise up the Chicago of the future." As the ashes of the fire were still cooling back home, Bross addressed the relief committee of the New York Chamber of Commerce, insisting with real chutzpah that Chicago wasn't a ruin but an opportunity: "There has not been, for the last twenty years, so good a time for men of capital to start business in Chicago as now. . . . With few exceptions, all can now start even, in the race for fame and fortune. The fire has leveled nearly all distinctions. . . . Now, therefore, is the time to strike."

Bross was key to what became an essential element of the city's self-concept—that the fire, while a disaster, had been *good* for Chicago. He was the first to frame the conflagration in this way, and his account, according to historian Ross Miller, was "repeated, embroidered, and improved upon, but not essentially changed." Chicago, in this view, was a unique city in its ability to turn even a catastrophe into an advantage.

At the cable car celebration, the sixty-eight-year-old Bross compared the occasion to the 1848 opening of the Illinois & Michigan Canal, which linked Lake Michigan and the Chicago River to the tributaries of the Mississippi River and was a pivotal event in the creation of Chicago as the midcontinent crossroads and market of the nation. Bross told the assembled dignitaries that the Chicago City Railway cable line on the South Side, eventually to be joined by similar operations on the West and North Sides, would permit even greater development, even greater growth, even greater progress in the future. As someone who had witnessed Chicago's emergence over the past half century, Bross asserted that "there is no limit to what we have a right to expect in the way of its growth and advancement in everything that can promote the welfare, and prosperity, and comfort of our people."

"Like Flies"

The celebration started at the corner of State and Madison Streets where the pavement and sidewalks "were fairly black with people," despite a temperature just above freezing. According to one estimate, at least fifty thousand Chicagoans were jammed there and along the length of cable route. Just before 2 p.m., seven linked, flag-bedecked cars, known as trailers, were pulled along the rails to the intersection by a team of eight horses. The trailers were coupled to a red grip car on the southbound track. As its name suggests, a grip car used a mechanism to take hold of the constantly moving cable. The cable then pulled the car and its attached trailers down the tracks until the grip was loosened.

Boarding this grip car was a contingent of reporters, twenty of the city's aldermen, and Charles B. Holmes, the Chicago City Railway president. Many of the spectators made a dash to get a seat on one of the trailers, but police cleared them out to make room for more than five hundred invited guests. About half a block ahead of the train was another grip car, packed with Mayor Carter Harrison and other city officials, as well as the band sponsored by the downtown music instrument store Lyon & Healy and headed by a "gorgeous drum-major."

By 2:14 p.m., everything was ready, and the lead grip car took hold of the 3.8-mile-long cable and headed quietly down the rails while, about two hundred feet behind, the second grip car and its trailers followed suit. The task of the lead car was to keep the tracks clear, an effort assisted by two mounted policemen who shooed small boys out of the way. Without great success. "The small boys were not to be put down in this way . . . ," the *Tribune* reported, "and they covered the cars like flies."

The heavily burdened train made its way slowly down the tracks, stopping often, while the crowds that lined the route sent up cheer after cheer. Indeed, the joyous reception led the *Tribune* reporter to suggest that residents and property owners along State Street "had recovered from the indignation they expressed when the street was torn up." The reporter noted that horses on the street gave no notice to "the mysteriously-moving cars," putting to rest the fears of some that the new technology would frighten the animals. He also wrote, "The cars moved along beautifully, and there was no jarring, such as is experienced on the horsecars."

The smooth operation of the grip cars led to a bit of levity as the train neared Harrison Street midway through its journey south. A horse-drawn wagon was crossing the track, and the lead grip car stopped to let it go past. Passengers on the second grip car were shocked to see their train barreling down the tracks at great speed toward the rear of the lead car. Fearing a collision, three or four aldermen jumped to the sidewalk, and Tom Currier, the corpulent chief of detectives, tried to escape as well. "He succeeded in making very quick time through a small hole just as the train was brought to a standstill with ease by the engineer," the *Tribune* reported, "and the brave occupants of the car gave him a laugh." Then, the reporter noted, "four of them appropriated the seat that he had occupied."

The train arrived at its destination at Twenty-First Street just after 2:30 p.m., and those with invitations filed into the engine house there, while gawkers crowded the windows to peer in. After the guests had toured the machinery, Holmes rapped for order and introduced a series of speakers, including William Bross, Mayor Harrison, and former Illinois Supreme Court justice John D. Caton. Using the occasion to take a swipe at those who had criticized him for backing the venture, the mayor said, "Then you remember the howls that were made about the obstructions on State Street. I was abused for having allowed it to go by." Now, he said, anyone could see that the new cable service, built at a cost of $2 million (or the equivalent of about $50 million today), was "a bigger thing than any other Mayor has witnessed heretofore."

Following the short ceremony, the return was a quick run, and the train with all the dignitaries arrived back at Madison Street around 4 p.m. Each grip car then headed back south with some trailers attached, giving those in the huge crowd who hadn't had invitations to the inaugural event a chance, finally, to experience a cable ride for themselves. Anyone who paid a nickel.

A Loop

Although regular cable service began the next day, it wasn't full service. At least, not at the downtown end of the line. For that first month, when a cable train reached Madison Street, the Chicago City Railway had to engage in a cumbersome process to reorient the grip car and its trailers so they could head back south. This probably involved the use of crossovers between the two parallel tracks. (Reversing direction wasn't such a difficult proposition for horsecars. At the end of the tracks, the horse or horses would be unhitched from one end of the car and walked around to the other end.)

The solution in the hilly city of San Francisco was the turntable. When a cable car came to the end of the line, it rode onto the turntable; the mechanism then rotated until the car was pointed in its new direction. But a turntable could handle, at most, only a grip car and one trailer. Unlike San Francisco, Chicago was flat, and cable officials realized that the company could make more money and provide many more rides by attaching several trailers to a grip car. As it turned out over the quarter century of cable service in Chicago, the typical cable train was a grip and two trailers. To make that possible, the Chicago City Railway had to find another method of sending a cable train back the way it came. That method was a loop.

In several *Tribune* stories published in the two months leading up to the inauguration ceremony, including one on the day itself, this loop was called the "downtown belt." Although expected to be ready within a week of that celebration, it didn't go into service until February 23. The next day, the *Tribune* reported, "The Grip-Cars Successfully Worked on the Loop Cable." This appears to be the first time the *Tribune* referred to the "downtown belt" as the "loop cable." Quickly, "loop" became the predominant and soon the only term for this sort of cable.

Given the importance that the word "loop" came to have in Chicago's transportation lexicon and in the city's history, what might have happened if "belt" hadn't been replaced? Would Chicagoans take rapid transit trains to the center of the city, where they would ride around the Belt elevated structure? Would the city's central business district be known as the Belt?

This 4,386-foot-long downtown "loop cable" ran continuously in a counter-clockwise direction to form a rectangle around three city blocks. A Chicago City Railway train would be pulled along State Street toward downtown by the north-south cable. At Madison Street, the gripman would let go of that cable and permit his car to glide a short distance into a turn in the tracks, where he would grip the other cable, the "downtown belt." This would pull the train east along Madison to Wabash Avenue, north to Lake Street, west to State, and then back to the north-south cable.

George W. Hilton, the preeminent American historian of the cable car, as well as other small and esoteric aspects of transportation, writes that this downtown loop was the "most spectacular engineering feature" of the Chicago cable service. Even so, over the next decade, the cable car company found that this handoff from one long cable to a second, shorter one led to endless malfunctions and chronic congestion. In 1892, a new system was installed in which a series of horizontal pulleys guided the cable into and around the loop.

The idea for a transportation loop wasn't without precedent. In Chicago, one horsecar company, the North Chicago City Railway Company, had been operating a loop route along Center Street (now Armitage Avenue), Lincoln

Avenue, Webster Avenue, and Racine Avenue since 1878. This early horsecar loop on the North Side wasn't to avoid switching horses but to provide access to a greater portion of the affluent homes in the area.

In addition, railroads, on occasion, had turned trains around by building a balloon loop. As its name suggests, the tracks of this loop had the appearance of a balloon when seen from above. To reverse direction, a train would leave the terminal station and follow the tracks initially to the right, then around a half circle, and then back left to the station, ready to make an outbound journey. While there were advantages to this method of reorienting a train, the biggest drawback was that it required a great deal of land and left a large area in the middle that was generally unusable.

The Chicago City Railway Company solved this problem by setting up its loop around three city blocks. Not only did that eliminate the need for a large land purchase, but it also provided the cable car riders with an added bonus—access to businesses on three other key downtown streets, Madison, Wabash, and Lake. Chicago's loop innovation was adopted by many other cities that established cable systems over the next decade, including Cincinnati, Cleveland, Kansas City, New York, Oakland, Philadelphia, Pittsburgh, Seattle, Tacoma, and Washington, D.C. Although the cable car companies in San Francisco generally employed turntables, two began using loops after the Great Earthquake and Fire of 1906.

Indeed, Chicago played a key role in the spread of cable systems throughout the United States and Europe, according to British engineer J. Bucknall Smith. In 1887, he wrote the most extensive book on cable car operations to be published during the heyday of the transportation technology, *A Treatise upon Cable or Rope Traction, as Applied to the Working of Street and Other Railways*. The system in Chicago, he wrote, "was decidedly a most bold undertaking" because it showed that cable cars could work in places with extreme variations in temperature, from ninety-degree days in the summer to deep snowfalls in the winter. As a result, he said, "the introduction of the cable systems into New York and Europe appears mainly due to the crucial tests it has undergone in Chicago."

Enlarging the City

The cable service inaugurated in 1882 by the Chicago City Railway Company and the many later lines changed the nature of life in Chicago, as Chicago cable car historian Greg Borzo points out: "Transit cars not only carried people to their desired destinations; they also brought people together—physically and even socially—in a public space, similar to the way a plaza or park brings people together, where different kinds of people gather together and experience or even engage each other. Being much larger and more popular than horsecars, cable cars enlarged and expanded upon this shared public space. . . . Thus, riding in a cable car had a humanizing and democratizing effect on the populace."

In replacing horsecars, the cable system also literally enlarged the metropolitan area. Most nineteenth-century Americans, writes Chicago transportation historian Robert David Weber, were willing to commute only about an hour to work, so "the horse car imposed a limit on the outward expansion of the city of about three or four miles from the center."

Suddenly, with the inauguration of cable cars, Chicagoans found that they could live much farther from work and still keep their commuting time to sixty minutes or less. Consequently, the city and its suburbs could spread out—or sprawl, to use the term that has been employed, mostly with negative connotations, to describe the same phenomenon in the late twentieth and early twenty-first centuries. In the 1880s, however, there was nothing negative about this growth.

Chicago's location was uncluttered by natural obstacles, except for Lake Michigan to the east and the three branches of the relatively narrow Chicago River. There were virtually no hills, ravines, swamps, or forests to block real estate development in any direction. The area then, as it is today and has been for thousands of years, was as flat as the surface of a pool table. This wealth of land and ease of development meant that many single-family homes were built on lots with a front yard, a back yard, and sometimes even a side yard. In contrast to Chicago's downtown, homeowners in most city neighborhoods had elbow room—a lot of elbow room.

The cable tracks became magnets for subdivisions. Less than two years after the inaugural cable ride, a *Tribune* reporter noted that "the increase in value of real estate on the line of the cable roads" was more than double what the cable company had spent to build the twenty-five miles of tracks then in operation. Indeed, real estate ads quickly began to include proximity to cable lines as an enticement to home buyers, and cable company officials, such as Henry H. Windsor of the Chicago City Railway Co., bragged about the boost they gave property values:

> Within six months after the conversion of this company's lines from horse to cable power, property along those lines rose in value from 30 to 100 per cent, and on adjoining and contiguous streets in amount proportionate to its distance from the cable line.

So well established is this fact that the mere announcement that
this Company was considering the construction of a cable line on any
street in this city, would be sufficient to put values up at once. One
of Chicago's earliest, most successful and best-known financiers has
said,—"Only let me know six weeks in advance where the City Railway
intend building a cable line, and I will make an independent fortune
every time."

But it wasn't just that the cable cars made it possible for Chicago to spread
out. They also were an important factor in efforts to weave the city and suburbs
into a single metropolitan community—and improve the lives of all residents,
particularly the poor. Weber notes, "Improved transportation offered not
only the prospect of holding cities together as unified communities despite
their growth, but also a 'moral influence' which would permit even the poor
to live in uncongested, clean and healthy housing away from the center of
the city." The hope among social reformers, Weber writes, was that better
public transportation would act as a "safety valve" to ease the overcrowding
in slum neighborhoods.

A year after the inauguration of cable service on State Street, the Chicago
City Railway Co. began operating a second line along Cottage Grove and
Wabash Avenues and employing the same loop in the downtown area. But
while South Siders reaped the transit, housing, and financial benefits of the
new cable technology, the rest of the city was forced to put up with horsecars
as the only mass-transit option for much longer.

It wasn't until March 1888, six years after the South Siders began riding
cable cars, that the North Chicago Street Railroad started running cable
cars north of the Chicago River. And people living west and southwest of the
central business district had to wait even longer, until June 1890, when West
Chicago Street Railroad brought cable to Milwaukee Avenue.

Eventually, seventeen of Chicago's major streets had cable service: Blue
Island Avenue, Clark Street, Clybourn Avenue, Cottage Grove Avenue, Des-
plaines Street, Division Street, Halsted Street, LaSalle Street, Lincoln Avenue,
Madison Street, Milwaukee Avenue, State Street, Van Buren Street, Wabash
Avenue, Washington Street, Fifth Avenue (now Wells Street), and Fifty-Fifth
Street. Not included on that list are other streets in the central business district
that were served for short distances by cable loops.

And there were a lot of cable car loops. By the end of 1890, each of the three
cable companies had its own downtown loop. Four years later, the central

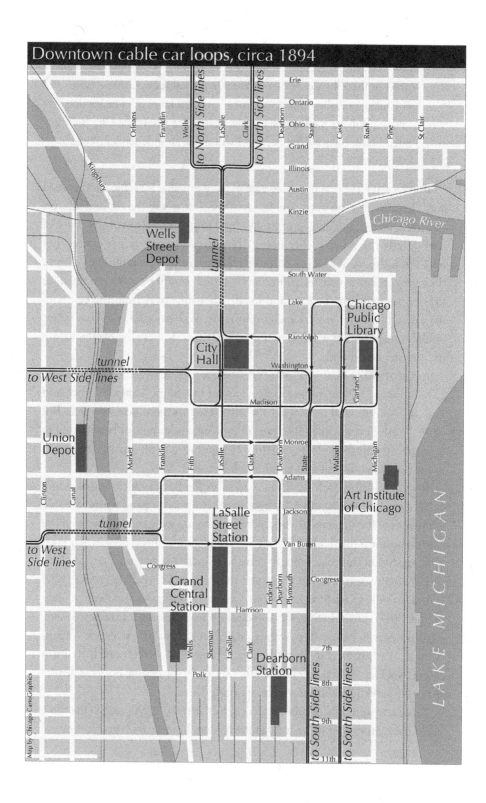

Downtown cable car loops, circa 1894

Erie
Ontario
Ohio
Grand
Illinois
Austin
Kinzie

Orleans
Franklin
Wells
LaSalle
Clark
Dearborn
State
Cass
Rush
Pine
St Clair

to North Side lines
to North Side lines

Kingsbury

Chicago River

Wells Street Depot

tunnel

South Water

Lake

Chicago Public Library

Randolph

City Hall

Washington

Garland

tunnel
to West Side lines

Madison

Union Depot

Market
Franklin
Fifth
LaSalle
Clark
Dearborn
State
Wabash
Michigan

Monroe

Adams

Clinton
Canal

tunnel

LaSalle Street Station

Jackson

Art Institute of Chicago

Van Buren

to West Side lines

Congress

Congress

Grand Central Station

Federal
Dearborn
Plymouth

Harrison

Wells
Sherman
LaSalle
Clark

7th

Dearborn Station

to South Side lines
to South Side lines

8th

Polk

9th

11th

LAKE MICHIGAN

Map by Chicago CartoGraphics

business district had six loops—two for South Side trains, one for North Side trains, and three for those from the West and Southwest Sides.

Each downtown loop was significant for riders from certain sections of the city and suburbs, and each enclosed a different section of central business district real estate. No loop was seen as more important than the others. And no one section of real estate enclosed within a loop was viewed as more important than the others. Chicagoans knew that all those loops and all those rectangles of real estate were simply part of the downtown, the central business district.

⬅ 5. The Word "Loop"

In the final decades of the nineteenth century, the word "loop" entered deeply into the way Chicagoans talked about transportation and the way they thought about it. And it had a crucial impact on the city's development. In some ways, it was a flexible term with several meanings.

Occasionally, the word was employed to refer to the full extent of a cable company's operation. For instance, in 1893, *Rand, McNally & Co.'s Bird's-Eye Views and Guide to Chicago* called the cable service operated by the North Chicago Street Railroad the "North Side loop." It also described the West Chicago Street Railroad service as a "loop." But this seems to have been fairly rare. It doesn't appear that the *Tribune* in its hundreds of stories about cable cars and loops ever used the word in this manner.

At times, "loop" was used as a synonym for the cable that drew the train along, generally six strands of reinforced steel wire woven around a thick hemp rope. This cable formed a constantly running loop, or belt, just below the street surface. Generally, the cable was 1-1/8 to 1-1/4 inches thick, but it could be thinner or thicker. A mile of cable weighed eight tons, which came to three pounds per foot. In Chicago, the longest cable was 27,770 feet long, or 5.3 miles, and it was in use on the Chicago City Railway's Cottage Grove line.

An example of "loop" as a synonym for the cable was the headline on a *Tribune* story in March 1888: "Jack Frost Grips the Cable—The South Side Loop of the North Side Line Frozen Thicker Than a Wedge." According to the story, workers had spent two weeks making repairs to the cable equipment inside the tunnel under the Chicago River at LaSalle Street. In a final test at 2 a.m., a southbound grip car went through the tunnel easily, only to come to an abrupt stop as it neared downtown. "It was quickly found," the newspaper reported, "that the cable was frozen fast in the channel under several inches of mud for nearly its entire length." The problem was that the cable—the "Loop" of the headline—had sat idle for all those days during a warm spell when repairs were being done in the tunnel. As a result, thousands of gallons of mud-thick melted snow poured into the grip slot of the cable mechanism and hardened around the cable when the weather again turned cold.

In most other stories, to avoid confusion, the *Tribune* called the steel-encircled rope a "loop cable" rather than simply a "loop." That's because, in the public mind and in the transportation lexicon of the day, the word "loop" had come to mean something very specific—one of the rectangular routes that cable cars took when they reached downtown.

Eventually, there were six of these downtown loops, each around a different rectangle of real estate, and the *Tribune* was filled with stories about them. For instance, in the late spring of 1883, the Chicago City Railway Co. stopped using its downtown loop for several weeks, unloading passengers at Madison Street instead. The result was "An Energetic Protest against the Disregard of the Loop," according to a *Tribune* story. "It is understood that one reason why the running around the loop was discontinued was that the cable which is used for that purpose often got out of order, which of course entailed considerable delay and much vexation in the people." But the people and downtown store owners were even more vexed by the absence of the loop run, even though it had been in operation for only a year. The *Tribune* noted that "the traveling public . . . greatly preferred the old system." So did those storekeepers whose customers were no longer arriving at their front doors. The loop, it appears, was back in operation in less than a month.

Four years later, the *Tribune* was writing that certain members of the City Council, whom they called "boodle Aldermen," were licking their chops in anticipation of bribes they could squeeze from the North Chicago Street Railroad. Simply put, the cable line needed an ordinance to permit it to operate a downtown loop. "With simply the present right of way on LaSalle street," the newspaper said, "the company would be terribly hampered in running its cars, and loops are absolutely essential to the success of the cable line. The boodle Aldermen appreciate this."

The cable car riders knew how important the loops were for getting around the crowded central business district with ease. They knew the route of the loop used by the line they usually rode. And they certainly had a general idea of the other loop routes. So they understood—and were interested in—all things having to do with the cable service and the loops, even such a short esoteric news item as the one headlined "For the State Street Loop" and published by the *Tribune* in August 1891. It read, in its entirety, "The new power house on Desplaines street, between Washington and Randolph, for which the West Chicago Street Railway company broke ground Friday, will be used to operate the new State street loop when that is finished, and the old power house at Jefferson and Washington streets will be used to run cars on the La Salle street loop. This change has been necessitated by heavy traffic."

For Chicagoans in the final two decades of the nineteenth century, a "loop" was a cable car route. It was one of several in the city. All but one of these loops were downtown. No one used the word "loop" as a synonym for "downtown." That wouldn't happen until the early twentieth century.

Transportation Language

Chicagoans liked the loops. Although not perfect, the cable car loops worked so well that the concept of a loop was readily proposed for or implemented in a wide variety of transit forms in Chicago—movable sidewalks, long-distance railroads, trolleys, subways, and ultimately, the elevated railways. To loop or not to loop was even one of the few controversies in the construction of the site of the World's Columbian Exposition of 1893. Loops just seemed to make sense.

Indeed, a year and a half after the institution of first cable loop in Chicago, the *Tribune* reported that someone had the bright idea of setting up horsecar loops in the central business district. Under this proposal, the City Council would insist that the horsecar companies arrange "their terminal systems in the centre of the city [so] that each line, by means of a loop similar to the one used on the cable lines, could do without switching, which is at present the cause of interminable delays in starting the cars for the outward run."

Loops were also important elements of Chicago's electric trolley lines. Although there apparently wasn't a loop in the first trolley line, which went into service in late 1890 on the South Side, some of those that followed had one or more. For instance, in April 1892, a new kind of trolley service, employing a wire just below the pavement surface instead of the troublesome and fear-inducing overhead lines, went into service on the North Side. And its route was a loop, running on Fullerton Avenue west to Racine Avenue, south on Racine to Webster Avenue, east on Webster to Halsted Street, and north on Halsted to Fullerton.

If loops were good enough for cable cars, horse cars, and trolleys, they were good enough for railroads. Three years after the start of Chicago's cable service, a visionary *Tribune* reader, signing himself "An Old Citizen," wrote to the newspaper with his own bright idea. The Illinois Central Railroad, he proposed, should construct a suburban line serving thirty-one towns, including South Park, Pullman, Burnside, Riverdale, Hegewisch, South Chicago, Kensington, South Shore, Hyde Park, and Kenwood. The tracks, he said, should be laid out in such a way that they would form "three loops and [enable] everybody to swing around either of the circles." That system of loops was never built, but a proposed railroad loop for the 1893 World's Fair nearly was, and it resulted in Daniel H. Burnham very uncharacteristically banging heads with a colleague.

Burnham, the charismatic architect and organizer, was hired as construction chief for the exposition in October 1890, and one of his top aides was Abram Gottlieb, the chief engineer, whom the *Tribune*, for an unknown reason, always identified as Abraham Gottlieb. Known as "Uncle Dan" to his fellow architects and planners, Burnham was someone who, through force of personality and a huge well of optimism, inspired confidence in clients, employees, and coworkers. Kristen Schaffer, one of his biographers, writes, "Burnham had a natural ability to lead. Those who knew him said he "had a huge-hearted belief in men which impelled them to live up to it, which enabled him to get the best work out of people—a power which achieved great results . . . at the World's Fair."

The original layout of the fair buildings called for Illinois Central (IC) trains to roll directly onto the grounds, drop off passengers, and following a loop of tracks, return the way they'd come. In February 1891, Gottlieb developed a detailed plan for this loop, and four months later, he revised it. Then all hell broke loose. Property owners and real estate speculators along Stony Island Avenue and Jackson Park were up in arms because Gottlieb's new loop plan called for northbound IC trains to enter the fair at Sixtieth Street instead of Sixty-Seventh.

"As a result of this," the *Tribune* reported, "six and eventually eight tracks, with long trains and snorting locomotives, will run along the east side of Stony Island Avenue from the Midway plaisance to Sixty-seventh street. . . . To the east, in addition, there will be a high board fence and the view from the contemplated hotels, boarding-houses, restaurants, etc., along Stony Island avenue will be cut off to a large extent." In other words, the huge profits expected from development of property right across the street from the fair were seriously threatened.

Initially, Burnham told reporters that this loop plan was "fixed"—that is, solid and unchangeable. But then he changed his mind. "A few weeks ago Mr. Burnham conceived that a series of parallel stub tracks would be better than the loop." That's what the *Tribune* reported in an August 12 story about Gottlieb's abrupt decision to resign. A disagreement over the loop was a key issue that led to the chief engineer's resignation. Burnham, according to the newspaper, "argued with the Chief Engineer, but the latter stuck to his plan, and the controversy was carried before the Committee on Grounds and Buildings. There was a wrangle there for several weeks, and Mr. Gottlieb invited the opinions of representative railroad men with the result that the Chief Engineer knocked out the Chief of Construction, and the Committee on Grounds and Building decided to stand by the loop."

Gottlieb won the battle but lost the war. Not only was he driven from the World's Fair staff by Burnham, but also, less than two weeks later, the *Tribune* carried the headline "No Loop on the Fair Grounds." Burnham may have been "huge-hearted," but he knew how to play hardball when he was crossed.

Loops on the Brain

Throughout the 1890s, there was talk of an elevated railroad loop in Chicago's downtown. But some people, discomfited by the idea of massive trains roaring along twenty feet overhead, proposed as an alternative a subway system under the central business district—employing one or more loops. This seemed like a dicey proposition to the *Tribune*: "At the first glance it would seem as if there must be some risk involved in running tunnels between the skyscrapers of this city and having trains using them constantly. But if the engineers say there is no danger that settles it."

Another alternative to an elevated railroad loop was a version of the movable sidewalk that had been used at the 1893 World's Fair. At the cost of a nickel, passengers from steamers that docked at the end of Casino Pier rode a twenty-five-hundred-foot-long moving sidewalk—either standing or sitting in chairs provided—to the edge of the fairgrounds at the shoreline. Although service didn't start until several months after the opening of the fair, just under one million people were carried by this sidewalk. For downtown, the idea was that instead of thundering into the central business district, elevated trains would halt on its outskirts. Commuters, shoppers, and visitors would leave the trains and step onto a moving walkway that would loop them around to or near to their destination.

In the spirit of "if you can't beat 'em . . . ," a proposal surfaced to have a motorized sidewalk on the platforms of an elevated railroad loop. More ambitious was a suggestion by a young Swede named D. A. Engstrom: a wooden bike path that would be constructed as a roof over the entire length of an elevated loop. This "aerial bicycle highway," wrote a *Tribune* reporter, would be well lighted and securely walled. And it would provide a place where "scorchers [a term for fast bicyclists] will have rapid transit trains to set them a pace and where they will meet none of the earthly incidents which vex patience and puncture tires." Except for the elevated railroad loop, none of these ideas got very far. Nonetheless, they're indications of how much late-nineteenth-century Chicagoans had "loops" on the brain.

⬅ 6. The Last Cable Car

Colonel Stephen Henry Clement was a colorful, thick-bodied man in his late sixties who cultivated an extravagant gray mustache, jutting down four inches below his chin. And his speech was just as vivid. So it wasn't surprising that in December 1891, during a special meeting of the Taxpayers' Association about a host of transit woes, including Chicago's downtown cable loops, Clement was called upon to speak.

He immediately laid into the "dubs, demagogues and pagans" who, he said, made up the majority of the Chicago City Council. And despite an attempt by the meeting chairman to call him to order, he went on: "Where we want loops most is around the necks of these scoundrels—they need it, and by the eternal, they'll get it." The crowd of some three hundred Chicagoans at Farwell Hall that afternoon responded with laughter. So did the *Tribune*, which, the next morning, reported that Clement had failed to make clear "whether he wanted them all executed at once or wished sixty-eight separate hangings."

Clement wasn't the only speaker at the meeting to facetiously threaten violence. William Halley, the publisher of several weekly neighborhood and suburban newspapers (all called the *Vindicator*) and a former union leader, bemoaned the unreliability of the city's cable car service. And he aimed his sarcasm at the man known as the czar of Chicago's cable cars, Charles Tyson Yerkes, whose lines served the North, West, and Southwest Sides: "This morning, I went to see several West Siders at their [downtown] offices. They were not at their desks. Why? Cable broke. I had to go west afterwards myself. The conductor said: 'Fare, sir.' I said: 'Will you guarantee that I will get to my destination on this particular occasion?' He laughed. We went a quarter of a mile—the cable broke again. That's the daily history of West Side transportation—cable broken in the morning, at noon, and at night. Yerkes' neck ought to be broken!"

Halley was interrupted by a voice in the crowd: "Let's have some recommendations. We've known all about that for years." "The only accommodation I know," Halley said, "is to walk."

"A Kaleidoscopic Devil's Dance"

Despite all the humor, however, getting around Chicago and its suburbs was a serious problem and a constant source of irritation for tens of thousands of commuters. Chicago's love affair with its cable cars and cable loops had soured badly. And the bickering would go on for the next decade and a half, as the number of downtown loops increased from three to six.

In the winter, the cable cars were unheated. In the summer, when open cars were used, there was little protection from the rain. Throughout the year, riders complained that they were frequently jerked backward when a gripman grabbed the cable, making for a jolting trip. On top of that, Chicago's cable cars were often so crowded that many riders couldn't find a seat. In response, speakers at the Taxpayers' Association meeting wanted the aldermen to pass a "no-seat, no-fare" ordinance, ensuring a free ride for anyone who had to stand. Especially infuriating was the multiplicity of cable car tracks that clogged downtown streets, competing for space with carriages, horsecars, delivery wagons, and thousands of pedestrians—as well as the multiplicity of cable car trains on those tracks. "Since trains could not pass each other, they tended to bunch together, adding to overall street congestion," writes Chicago cable car historian Greg Borzo.

At peak travel times, in an era before stop-and-go lights, the streets in the central business district were a chaos of vehicles often clotted together in barely moving logjams, while swirling around and through were streams of shoppers, office workers, laborers, tourists, shop girls, pickpockets, business executives, store clerks, and beggars. The one constant in that confusion was the cable car, following its tracks down the center of many downtown streets. And increasingly, those cars on their fixed routes were identified as the culprits causing the congestion. In March 1904, the *Tribune* editorialized, "Ever since the surface loops were installed, the street car map of downtown Chicago has looked like the Gordian knot in convulsions. And evidently it takes more than seventy aldermen to make one Alexander. Chicago is the only city in the world which brings its cars from all directions to one central district, and there puts them through a kaleidoscopic devil's dance from which escape is as tedious for the performers as it is dangerous for the spectators."

Cutting and weaving across a street amid all the animals, vehicles, and humans without getting hit by a cable train could be a risky business, and riding on one could also be hazardous. Borzo writes that cable train accidents were far from commonplace and rarely fatal. Still, the sorts of safety protections that present-day Americans take for granted weren't in place as the nineteenth century drew to a close. In 1888, the *Hyde Park Herald* provided a terse report about what Borzo describes as a typical accident: "Mrs. Thos. Otis was thrown from the cable car last Saturday by the sudden starting of the car and very severely bruised. She will be confined to the house for several weeks."

The *Tribune* gave big play to major service disruptions on the cable lines, such as an 1888 article headlined "Thousands Have to Walk—The North Side Loop Cable Breaks at the Worst Time." The page-one story explained that twenty-five thousand commuters were stranded when a North Chicago City Railway train "slipped a cog, or a pawl, or an eccentric or something or other and the cable broke." The front-page headlines were even more sensational when cable problems resulted in collisions and accidents:

- "Thrown from a Cable Train—Four Men Injured in Accident on a Down-Town Loop" (1893).
- "Cable Wreck Hurts Nine—Misplaced Switch Causes Collision in State Street" (1900).
- "Car Crash Hurts Women—Four Injured When Crowded Trains Collide Down-Town" (1901).

Each cable car was a couple tons of metal and wood rumbling down the tracks, and Chicagoans grew adept at getting onto and off the cars, moving from one car to another, and as pedestrians, maneuvering around moving cable trains. Still, everyone knew that one slip or a moment of inattention could be deadly. For instance, in June 1888, William Burtrass, a South Side machinist, attempted to step from one car of a Chicago City Railway to another. He stumbled, fell under the wheels, and was fatally injured.

Fifteen years later, on the evening of March 9, 1903, Maria Stanton wanted to cross Clark Street at Goethe Street, on the edge of Chicago's Gold Coast neighborhood, the enclave of many of the city's richest families. A household servant in her early thirties, she was dressed plainly in a heavy brown blouse and skirt of rough material and a dark blue jacket. Her only jewelry was a pair of plain gold crescent earrings. In her pocketbook, she carried $1.50, the equivalent of about $25 today.

Stepping off the western curb, she started across the pavement, only to look up and see a crowded cable train bearing down on her. "Bystanders said the victim started to cross Clark street toward the east, immediately behind a south bound train," reported the *Tribune*. "As she stepped on the other tracks she found herself a few feet from a north bound Lincoln avenue train. She paused, looked back, and saw another car approaching from the north, shutting off retreat. The gripman rang the gong and the passengers shouted, but the dazed woman still stood motionless on the tracks while the north bound Lincoln avenue train struck her and knocked her down. She fell forward and the fender passed over her body." The newspaper reported that "many people were drawn to the corner by the cries of the woman."

This was a period in Chicago and in the United States when the threat of sudden violent accidental death in factories, on construction sites, in tunnels, amid giant machines, and on city streets was a routine, albeit regrettable, part of daily existence. Laws and government agencies aimed at protecting workers and others were, for the most part, many decades in the future.

Yet even when laws were enacted, they weren't always followed. One egregious example was the railroads, which rumbled through every neighborhood of the city at grade level. Since there were few gates or signalmen to block cross traffic, an unwary pedestrian or wagon driver courted injury or death.

"If the stranger's first impression of Chicago is that of the barbarous gridironed streets, his second is that of the multitude of mutilated people whom he meets on crutches. . . . The railroads which cross the city at the level in every direction, although limited by statute and ordinance as to speed, constantly mow down unoffending citizens at the crossings, and those legless, armless men and women whom you meet on the streets are merely the mangled remnant of the massacre that is constantly going on year in and year out." Thus thundered William T. Stead, a pioneering English investigative journalist, in his 1894 book, *If Christ Came to Chicago*, an exposé of the city's political corruption and black market.

Madame Leon Grandin, a Parisian woman who lived in Chicago for a year in the early 1890s, wrote of arriving in the city by train: "Every now and then, the train cut through a street filled with carriages and pedestrians. With no barriers to protect them, they all simply moved back as the train approached; the railroad tracks are as unprotected as those of the streetcars and the locomotive's bell is the only warning that alerts people to get out of the way."

The difference, though, was speed. The fastest a cable car could go was fourteen miles an hour (and, by ordinance, half that in the central business district). By ordinance, the railroad trains were supposed to observe a ten-mile-an-hour speed limit. But to stay on time, some trains had to travel more than triple that rate. "Railroad companies not only disregarded this speed limit, they announced their guilt ahead of time by publishing schedules requiring faster speeds," writes historian Arnold Lewis. An 1887 investigation found that most trains had to travel at least 20 miles an hour—and, on at least one regular run, 35 miles an hour—between stops to stay on schedule. According to Stead, there were an annual average of 340 people—nearly one a day—killed by trains on Chicago streets during a five-year period, rising from 257 killed in 1889 to 431 in 1893.

The railroads were able to get away with such carnage, in part, because they were so important to Chicago's economy. In addition, these deaths occurred in the context of a city and an American urban culture that was riding the crest of a wave of constant radical change. Arnold Lewis summed up the attitude of the era: "The intricate cogs of the city must turn; let the user beware."

"Mad Ride"

Life was moving and changing so fast for Chicagoans that they learned to put up with dangers that would shock later generations. The railroad carnage, of course, is a prime example. Another was a design flaw in the cable car technology that, at any moment, could send cable train passengers on a tumultuous and hair-raising journey. One such incident was described in a *Tribune* story in April 1893, under the headline "Mad Ride on a Grip—A Lincoln Avenue Train Runs Wild around the Loop." At about 2:30 on a Friday afternoon, a Lincoln Avenue cable train crossed under the Chicago River and came out of the tunnel onto the downtown loop of the North Chicago City Railway Company.

The grip car and its two trailers, filled with passengers, were heading south on LaSalle Street when, suddenly, at Washington Street, gripman William Elliott realized that he was unable to stop the train. He began ringing the grip car bell and, together with conductor J. Hickey, did everything he could to alert people on the street. The train was traveling at only about seven miles an hour, which to twenty-first-century readers may seem like a crawl. But cable trains were the fastest vehicles on downtown streets, and this runaway six-ton train had enough momentum to turn it into a battering ram.

Some male passengers leaped from the cars, but the conductors wouldn't let the women or children leave their seats. Hickey jumped off near Monroe Street to pull an alarm to alert the powerhouse to stop the cable. But that didn't do any good. As the *Tribune* reported:

> There was a Clybourn avenue train in front. It learned of the trouble.
> Then the race became exciting. By the time Dearborn street corner was
> passed, the scenes in the loaded cars became desperate. The Kinsley
> café wagon wheels and trucks were thrown from the track and the sides
> of the grip platform smashed. . . .
>   A howling crowd of several hundred men and boys followed the
> runaway train. . . . At Madison street the way was crowded with wagons
> and cars and people, but the Clybourn avenue train crossed safely.
> Then a Northwestern depot and State street horse car attempted to go
> west. The car escaped with its rear platform smashed by the runaway. A
> heavy truck wagon was thrown half way around and its horses injured.

Windows were smashed in the wild train and women and children begged for help.

A policeman identified simply as Officer Schlichter reported, "When the 'crazy' train came up Dearborn street I did not know what to make of it at first. Hundreds of men yelling and police and conductors running was unexplainable to me." Eventually, the crowd running alongside the out-of-control train grew to a thousand. In an age before radio, television, or any mass entertainment medium, people found most of their entertainment on the street.

That "wild train" closed the distance and smashed into the rear of the fleeing Clybourn Avenue train. The impact sent some women with babies in their arms to the pavement. Three large policemen reached up to pull to safety other women "dazed with fright" off the car platforms or through windows. Meanwhile, the Lincoln Avenue train, now pushing the Clybourn train ahead of it, kept rumbling around its loop, knocking wagons and horses out of its path. At the sharp turn on Randolph to leave the loop and head back north, the cars started to derail, and the unstoppable train finally came to a halt in the middle of the LaSalle Street tunnel. An estimated thirty-three people were injured, none seriously. And although the *Tribune* devoted a fourteen-hundred-word front-page story to the electrifying incident, its reporter pointed out that a similar incident had happened ten days earlier, and another wild accident five months earlier.

The cause of the hazardous rides? The cable apparatus itself. The method that a gripman used to stop his train was to release the grip mechanism from the constantly moving cable. In other words, to let go. The train was then coasting, and he could apply his brakes to bring it to a halt. However, after long use, a cable would begin to fray, and strands of steel wire would loosen. If one of those strands became entangled with the grip mechanism, it could tie the mechanism onto the cable, and the gripman wouldn't be able to release it.

That's what happened on the "mad ride." The gripman tried applying his brakes, but they weren't enough to counter the forward movement of the cable. "The only way to bring a runaway train to a halt," writes cable historian Greg Borzo, "was to stop the cable and untangle the broken strand from the grip. Some lines in Chicago installed trackside alarm boxes so the conductor could signal the powerhouse when a cable strand became entangled." Conductor Hickey had tried to do that, but apparently the powerhouse didn't get the alarm. In such cases, the train went on its wild way until it derailed or, finally, the cable was stopped.

"The Deadly Trolley Wires"

When it came to cable cars, George W. Hilton, the preeminent historian of small and esoteric aspects of American transportation, was a romantic. In his history of the cable system in Chicago, he writes that no one, except "a thorough-going Sancho Panza," is immune to the fascinating story of the cable car and waxes eloquent about the "vastness of the power houses—the immensity of the stationary engines—the artistry of the gripmen—the agility of the conductors." Yet Hilton was also a realist, and he adds that only a Don Quixote, blinded by love, would refuse to recognize that "if the electric [trolley] car had been developed a dozen years earlier, none of the three Chicago companies would have laid a cable."

In 1873, San Francisco became the first American city with a successful cable system (although an attempt had been made in New York six years earlier that failed as a result of mechanical and financial problems). Chicago followed nine years later, and over the next decade, cable cars were running in many American cities, large and small. By the mid-1890s, U.S. cable ridership rose to a peak of about four hundred million a year—nearly six rides for every man, woman, and child in the country. But even as the cable car era was getting underway, a parallel transportation revolution was beginning to take shape.

In 1879, Werner von Siemens unveiled the first electric railway at the Berlin Trade Fair, and nine years later, the world's first successful large-scale electric trolley system began regular service in Richmond, Virginia. It took the new technology only a short time to reach Chicago, where on October 4, 1890, the Calumet Electric Street Railway began operating in the South Chicago neighborhood.

Despite their investment of an estimated $25 million (the present-day equivalent of about $650 million) in equipment, machinery, and routes, Chicago's three cable companies quickly sought permission to replace their horse-cars and cable cars with trolleys. The same thing was happening across the United States as trolley lines were rapidly supplanting cable car systems in cities with relatively flat terrain. (The cable cars continued to have the advantage in hilly locations.) For one thing, the trolley equipment, which supplied power through overhead lines, was simpler, more reliable, faster, and less prone to breakdowns. For another, it was cheaper to operate.

However, despite the many complaints about Chicago's cable operations, the city lagged behind in shifting to trolleys. And the reason was fear. "The word 'trolley' rarely appeared in print in Chicago without the preceding adjective 'deadly,' " writes transportation historian Robert David Weber. "Yet the exact nature of the supposed deadliness usually remained unclear."

The widespread use of electricity as a source of power was still fairly new, and among the general public, including newspaper reporters and editors, it was little understood. A selection of *Tribune* headlines from a six-month period in 1895 show the level of hysteria that the idea of electricity evoked:

- "Insurance Affairs: Menace Is Seen in Overhead Trolley Wires"
- "Death in the Wire: Why Firemen Oppose the Electric Trolley System"
- "Death in the Air: Wires Break and Cross the Live Trolley Feeders"
- "Where Trolley Wire Danger Is: Experts Make Signed Statements on the Terrors of Monday Night"
- "Remove the Deadly Trolley Wires"

That last headline was from a *Tribune* editorial, which asserted that during the previous eighteen months, the list of trolley casualties in Chicago "includes 40 killed and 336 others seriously injured by trolley wires." It went on: "The trolley wire is charged with a current of some 500 volts of intensity, sufficient to instantly kill a man or a horse in spite of the assertion by some selfish, cold-blooded persons that the shock from such a current is not necessarily fatal."

"Volts of intensity" is a phrase that gives a sense of the heightened emotions (and lack of scientific knowledge) that the editorial writer brought to his task. Where he found his numbers isn't at all clear. Certainly, the pages of the *Tribune* over the previous year and a half didn't record such a swath of deaths and injuries.

As far as can be determined, the *Tribune*, during those eighteen months, never reported on a single Chicagoan who was killed by a live trolley wire, although the newspaper was quick to recount such deaths in Brooklyn and Philadelphia. And in November 1895, it gave a page-one headline to a short story about the death of a horse on the South Side. In fact, Weber writes that the current was dangerous but not often lethal, even to someone in contact with the rail and both overhead wires. The first recorded electrocution death apparently didn't occur until five years after trolley operations began in the United States, and it involved a small boy who appears to have done everything he could to give himself a shock.

The Last Cable Car

Quickly, Chicago's three cable companies won permission to run trolleys everywhere in the city except downtown. In addition to the fear of electrocution from "the deadly trolley wires," there were concerns that the wires would hinder firefighting efforts at tall buildings and mar the look of the central business district. As late as October 1904, a *Tribune* editorial writer was asserting, "It is also impossible that [one of the cable companies] should be allowed to string trolley wires all over the downtown district. The appearance and the safety of that district have to be considered." And an August 1905 editorial stated, "The public has shown itself averse to the extension of the overhead trolley in the business district. It does not wish to see Madison, State, and Washington streets disfigured."

Nonetheless, within four months, the newspaper had changed its tune. Public anger and protest over the flaws of the city's cable operations were coming to a head, just as the three companies were pressuring the city for permission to "trolleyize" their cable lines. Suddenly, apprehensions about the overhead trolley lines downtown no longer seemed so worrisome. "State street should carry many more passengers, but it will not so long as it is in servitude to the cable," a December 1905 *Tribune* editorial contended. "If the steel rope, with its slow pace and liability to breakage, could be got rid of, there would be an immediate change for the better. The public has much confidence in electric power and little in cable power." In less than a year, the cable cars were gone.

In late spring 1906, after months of negotiations, the City Council approved two ordinances to permit the three companies to replace their cable cars with trolleys, and the *Tribune* crowed, "The people of Chicago were as much pleased to see the cables come as they are to see them go."

The first to cease operation was the Chicago City Railway Co. At 1:35 a.m. on July 22, an aged State Street grip car and trailer began the final run as a great crowd watched. As with the inauguration of cable service twenty-four years earlier, the end of each of the cable car lines was free entertainment, even though they occurred in the wee hours of the morning. And the crowd had its fun. By the end, the grip car and trailer were "splintered and smashed by 'relic hunters.'" Fifty-five-year-old F. L. Goddard, the train's conductor, was asked if he felt a pang of regret at the passing of the cable cars. "Pang, nothing!" he responded. "I'm progressive. This is an age of electricity."

The scene was even more rambunctious at 12:45 a.m. on August 19, when "a riotous crowd of hoodlums tore to pieces and turned over" what they thought was the last West Chicago Street Railroad Co. cable train. They were wrong. The grip car and trailer were jammed full as they left the barn at Fortieth Street (now Pulaski Road) and traveled east along Madison Street. Several times on the route, the train was blocked by youthful mobs, and pieces of the cars were ripped off. Finally, at Sheldon Street (now Loomis Street), someone yelled, "Let's wreck her!" And after the gripman and conductor were dragged away, the shout went up, "Heave ho!" Within moments, the cars were on their side and were being looted for souvenirs.

The actual last North Side train drew up to Sheldon moments later, but even though it was guarded by a contingent of police during its trip around the company's downtown loop and during its return trip, it arrived at the barns with its seats torn out and its curtains in tatters.

A similar crowd gathered just after midnight on October 21 to wreak similar havoc on the last train of the North Chicago City Railway Co., the *Tribune* reported, but they were duped. "Several thousand persons who had assembled on street corners and along the curbs in the downtown district, waiting with enthusiasm and exuberance to overrun the 'last' cable train and chop it into fragments, had their trouble for nothing."

A Lincoln Avenue cable train went by, but a Clark Street cable train, scheduled to leave the barns at 12:30 a.m., never came. Instead, the first trolley, pulling one of the old trailers, headed south toward the central business district. As it passed a large crowd of young men at Chicago Avenue, someone yelled, "There's the first electric. They've fooled us."

But a short time later, the boisterousness ended tragically. Souvenir hunters mistook another early trolley with an aged cable trailer for the "last" grip train and attacked it. Twenty-eight-year-old John O'Brien was attempting to climb aboard when he slipped and fell in front of a northbound train. He suffered a fractured right arm, as well as head and back injuries, but survived. Ten-year-old Fred Peters wasn't as lucky. Attempting to remove a sign from the train, he fell, fracturing his skull. He died at Alexian Brothers Hospital. Meanwhile, Chicago's last cable train—running on the Chicago City Railway Co.'s Cottage Grove line—left downtown at 1:28 a.m., packed with noisy, horn-tooting passengers. A half hour later, apparently without incident, the grip car and two trailers arrived at the Thirty-Ninth Street barn, and the cable car era in Chicago was over.

A Sign of the Times

The cable car left a lasting mark on Chicago. It played a key role in extending real estate development well beyond previous limits and in knitting together the city and its fast-growing suburbs, particularly in the south. Indeed, it made the great annexations of the late nineteenth century not only possible but also logical and inevitable.

The cable car gave to Chicago—and the rest of the nation—the word "loop" and the idea of using a transportation loop to reorient a train to return to its starting point. The loops that took cable trains around portions of the city's downtown worked so well, at least initially, that Chicagoans began proposing loops for everything from subways to movable sidewalks to trolleys.

Even so, during the first eight years of cable operations in Chicago, the word "loop" rarely made it into a headline or a subhead in the *Tribune*. The loops were important, but not all that important. On average, the word "loop" appeared in a headline or subhead only once each year during that period, with one exception. That was 1888, when it showed up ten times in stories dealing with problems on the loops of the North Chicago Street Railway and the Chicago City Railway Co. One article was headed "Thousands Have to Walk—The North Side Loop Cable Breaks at the Worst Time." Another dealt with the crash of two cable trains serving the South Side: "A Cable Road Collision: One of Mr. Yerkes' Trains Crashes into Another—A Strand of the Loop Cable Became Twisted about the Grip . . ."

Although the newspaper didn't use the word "loop" in any headlines the next year, it mentioned cable loops twenty times in headlines in 1890 and twenty-seven in 1891, the most ever during Chicago's cable car era. Again, trouble on the cable lines and loops was either the direct or indirect subject of the stories, such as this one from November 29, 1891: "Many Had to Walk: Worst Day in the History of the Yerkes Cable—Two Systems Blockaded . . . Trains Cover Down-Town Loops." It dealt with "one long series of delays" throughout the previous day, affecting fifty thousand people heading into or away from the city's downtown.

The Taxpayers' Association meeting in Farwell Hall—where Colonel Stephen Henry Clement railed against the "dubs, demagogues and pagans" in the City Council and William Halley joked about hanging Yerkes—was held a week later. Alderman Julius Goldzier, an Austrian-born Jewish lawyer and soon-to-be U.S. representative from Illinois, couldn't attend the gathering but sent a letter that was read to the audience of three hundred. An independent in the City Council, Goldzier weighed in on various transportation issues before stating, "Our streets are so crowded that anything even distantly approaching rapid transit is impossible on the surface. . . . I think that the elevated road offers, after all, the greatest advantages. . . . I would suggest that your organization try to impress the people with the necessity and the advantages of elevated roads." It was a sign of the times.

Over the next six years, the use of the word "loop" in a *Tribune* headline had less and less to do with the cable operations. Indeed, from 1894 through 1896, only three of these headlines dealt with cable loops. By contrast, *Tribune* headlines increasingly were about the elevated railroads and the efforts of backers to establish an elevated loop in the central business district. In the same three-year period, more than two hundred stories with "loop" in the headline were about this elevated loop, which came to be called the Union Loop. In 1895 alone, the newspaper published eighty-six such stories. That was only one fewer than the eighty-seven *Tribune* stories with cable-related "loop" headlines that were published during a seven-year period, as the table shows.

This table was based on an analysis of 382 articles over the decade and a half that used the term "loop" in a headline or subhead, or both (not including uses unrelated to transportation). What it shows is that years before the Union Loop became a reality, the idea of one was already looming over the central business district and the city itself. Over time, the cable car loops came to be irritants to the daily lives of Chicagoans. But the elevated loop was shaping up to be something much different.

Use of the Word "Loop" in *Chicago Tribune* Headlines, 1882–96

Year	Cable loops	Elevated loops	Other transit loops	Total
1882	1	0	0	1
1883	2	0	0	2
1884	0	0	0	0
1885	0	0	0	0
1886	3	0	0	3
1887	1	0	0	1
1888	10	0	0	10
1889	0	0	0	0
8-year total, 1882–89	17	0	0	17
1890	21	2	0	23
1891	27	4	13	44
1892	20	7	0	27
1893	16	13	1	30
1894	0	49	2	51
1895	3	86	11	100
1896	0	69	3	72
7-year total, 1890–96	87	230	30	347
15-year total, 1882–96	104	230	30	364

Chicago's elevated Loop—the single most important structure in the history of Chicago—is a stumpy 2.1-mile-long rectangle of railroad tracks twenty feet or so above four downtown streets that is woven deeply into the physical fabric of Chicago's central business district. Photo by Steve Kagan.

Above, By the end of 1894, Chicago's downtown had six small cable car loops, each of which enclosed a different small section of the central business district. Photo from the collection of Greg Borzo.

Left, Charles T. Yerkes was a larger-than-life personality who put his imprint in a major way on not one but two world cities: Chicago, through the elevated Loop, and London, through his championing of the Tube. Photo from the collection of Bruce G. Moffat.

Although demonized as a corrupt power broker, Yerkes was one of the
premier American art collectors in the final decade of the nineteenth
century, owning such works as Auguste Rodin's marble sculpture
Orpheus and Eurydice, now in New York's Metropolitan Museum of
Art. Author's photo.

Calls to tear down the elevated Loop began even before it went into operation, as is shown in this illustration from the *Tribune*, published in September 1897 with a story headlined "Chicago's Great Down-Town Nuisance—The Union Loop." *Chicago Tribune* photo.

John Alexander Low Waddell, the man who designed the four sections of the Union Loop, was an engineering genius whose role in bringing the elevated Loop into existence has been overlooked by Chicago historians and even by civil engineers who honor him as a seminal figure in their field. Waddell, *Economics*, frontispiece.

Once elevated trains were running along the Union Loop, the land in the thirty-nine city blocks encompassed by the track structure—the area to the west, or left, in this photo of the Wabash section, looking north—skyrocketed in value because businesses were desperate to take advantage of the compact location. Photo from the collection of Bruce G. Moffat.

The new Union Loop was "the clearing point for all elevated trains in the city," linking the North, West, and South Sides. Quotation and image from Lake Shore & Michigan Southern Railway, *The Union Elevated Loop in Chicago*, courtesy of LeRoy Blommaert.

Once the elevated Loop structure was built, city residents used it as a key reference point in giving directions, eventually calling the central business district "the Loop," as this 1913 advertisement shows. Photo from the collection of Bruce G. Moffat.

The public gave New York's Flatiron Building its name, even though its builders wanted to call it the Fuller Building. The same process took place when the public decided that Rodin's *Paolo and Francesca* should be called *The Kiss* and when, in the first decade of the twentieth century, Chicagoans bestowed the name "Loop" on the city's downtown. Author's photo.

In his 1917 valedictory to his hometown Chicago—which included many evocative illustrations from Lester G. Hornby, such as this one of the Randolph Street elevated station—Hobart Chatfield-Taylor wrote that "the Loop is literally, as well as metaphorically, the heart of the city." Chatfield-Taylor, *Chicago*, 78.

Part Two →
The Union Loop

← 7. Dreaming of a "Union Loop"

In London during the summer of 1835, demonstration trains began giving free rides along a newly completed section of the London and Greenwich Railway, the first railway of any sort in the city, as well as the very first *elevated* railroad in the world. In addition to testing the track and viaduct, these trial runs, reports rail historian R. H. G. Thomas, were aimed at boosting public awareness of the new technology and were so successful that taking a trip on the trains became the fashionable thing to do: "For a few weeks in the summer ladies made up parties to ride in the [train] carriages. . . . Groups of foreign visitors, members of the Society of Friends and parties of Cambridge scientists all found their way there, as did several MPs [Members of Parliament], the Swedish ambassador and the Prince of Orange [the future King William II of the Netherlands] and suite." The line was constructed on a viaduct of 878 brick arches. Once fully operational, it extended from near London Bridge about four miles southeast to the London neighborhood of Greenwich, the home of the Royal Observatory, which served as the defining point for the Greenwich Meridian (0° longitude) and for Greenwich Mean Time.

London was an old city, originally settled around 50 A.D. As the capital of the expanding British Empire, it had grown by this time to some 1.7 million residents and had pushed past Beijing to become the most populous city on the planet. It had also evolved into the world's most powerful and most influential metropolis.

Because London was so densely crammed with warehouses, factories, churches, and houses, construction of the London and Greenwich Railway required the sort of massive urban demolition that would become routine in cities around the world over the next two centuries. Landowners were forced by law to sell their property, hundreds of buildings were razed, and thousands of angry people had to find new homes to make way for the elevated railway.

Portions of London's vast slums, deep abysses of poverty and disease, were often targeted for demolition. Indeed, George Walter, a financial backer of the railway, complained of having to drive the rail line "through the most horrible and disgusting part of the metropolis, and during the period when the cholera was raging in that particular neighborhood." Nonetheless, the people didn't want to leave their homes, and company officials were threatened with violence on several occasions. This same take-no-prisoners approach to remaking the urban landscape was employed twenty years later by Baron Georges-Eugène Haussmann in slashing fifty miles of new boulevards through Paris. In the twentieth century, the strategy was similar for Robert Moses as he crisscrossed the boroughs of New York City with highways, bridges, and housing complexes.

During the same summer of 1835, some four thousand miles to the west, a remaking of a different sort was taking place on the sparsely settled banks of the Chicago River in a new city, still being formed—a remaking not of the structures on the landscape, but of the people who lived on that landscape.

As some of the first demonstration elevated trains were speeding down their viaduct over the dense fabric of London, eight hundred Potawatomi warriors proceeded through the streets of frontier Chicago in a violently sorrowful and cacophonous requiem dance to mark the tribe's eviction from the last of their land along Lake Michigan. They were part of a group of five thousand tribe members who had gathered along the lakefront on the north side of the Chicago River's main branch to complete the formalities of the Treaty of Chicago, agreed upon two years earlier. "They appreciated," wrote John D. Caton, an eyewitness, "that [the dance] was the last on their native soil—that it was a sort of funeral ceremony of old associations and memories."

The Potawatomi, who had sided with the British in the War of 1812 and had won the bloody Battle of Fort Dearborn, were ceding the last of their lands in Illinois and Wisconsin in return for land west of the Mississippi and annual cash payments, known as annuities. The agreement, one of more than a dozen over a twenty-six-year period, was yet another recognition of the tribe's inability to block the ever-growing flood of American settlers and its deepening dependence on American trade goods.

On a day at or near the end of August 1835, with the treaty ceremonies completed, the eight hundred Potawatomi men assembled at a spot on the north bank across the river from the new Fort Dearborn. They wore nothing but loincloths, and their bodies were painted in bright colors, with their "foreheads, cheeks and noses . . . covered with curved stripes of red or vermillion which were edged with black points," Caton recalled.

A twenty-three-year-old immigrant from Monroe, New York, Caton was a go-getter just at the start of his legal career. Although a new arrival to Chicago, he had already been elected a justice of the peace for the insignificant, unincorporated hamlet of 3,265 souls. As he recounted in a lecture more than three decades later, the procession of warriors, brandishing tomahawks and war clubs, moved slowly up Carroll Street along the north bank, crossed the river's North Branch on a bridge, advanced along West Water Street to the Lake Street bridge, and danced along that structure over the river's South Branch. Throughout the march, they "uttered the most frightful yells in every imaginable key and note, though generally the highest and shrillest possible," augmented "by a rapid clapping of the mouth with the palm of the hand."

It was a hot day, and the dancers were sweating profusely. Their arm and leg muscles glistened and stood out like "great, hard knots. . . . The dance, which was ever continued, consisted of leaps and spasmodic steps, now forward and now back or sideways, with the whole body distorted into every imaginable unnatural position, most generally stooping forward, with the head and face thrown up, the back arched down, first one foot thrown far forward and then withdrawn, and the other similarly thrown out, frequently squatting quite to the ground, and all with a movement almost as quick as lightning."

After crossing the South Branch, the grieving dancers moved along Market Street (the north-south section of present-day Wacker Drive) past the Sauga-nash Hotel, named for a mixed-blood Potawatomi chief, also known as Billy Caldwell. Caton, who was watching the march from a parlor on the second floor of the rough-hewn hotel with other settlers, remembered the sight as fearsome, even for those who were used to seeing individual or small groups of Potawatomi dancing. Here, though, was a small army of warriors. "What if they should, in their maddened frenzy, turn this sham warfare into a real attack? How easy it would be for them to massacre us all, and leave not a living soul to tell the story." Yet for all their ferocity, the warriors continued on their way, past the hotel and down Lake Street, where fewer than half of the lots had buildings on them, and on farther east to Fort Dearborn, where the procession came to a peaceful end.

Within a month, the first group of about seven hundred Potawatomi, under the leadership of Billy Caldwell, left Chicago for Iowa with an army escort. They were followed by later groups until September 1837, when the last of the Potawatomi headed west. Nearly half a century later, Caton, by then a retired chief justice of the Illinois Supreme Court, was one of the dignitaries who took the inaugural ride along State Street on Chicago's first cable car line. This new cable transportation technology, Caton said in a speech during the dedication ceremonies, was "the culmination of city locomotion."

It was also, for many Chicagoans, an excellent alternative to the loud, smoky, steam-powered elevated trains that had been rumbling through Man-hattan since 1868. The *Tribune* praised the cable car system for removing "all necessity for any elevated railroad scheme in this city." The editorial went on to say, "The cable line will furnish the public with just as much accommodation as could be obtained from an elevated railway, minus the noise, smoke and other conditions of elevated railways which render the streets uninhabitable where they are erected. . . . The locomotive will be safer and more comfortable since it will be on the street-level, and over a roadway as solid as a rock." Elevated trains may have had bad press in 1882. Nonetheless, for more than a decade already, they'd been a tempting transportation possibility for Chicagoans.

"Run on a Loop"

In early 1869, eight months after elevated trains began operating in New York, a bill was introduced in the Illinois General Assembly to create the Chicago Elevated Railway. The railway's backers had an ambitious plan to run trains over tracks on each side of a street and to establish elevated lines throughout Chicago. But the state legislature wasn't interested, and the idea never came up for consideration, perhaps because the state and Chicago governments had long been at odds over who should have control of public transportation on the city's streets.

Nonetheless, just months after the Great Chicago Fire, the Chicago West Division Elevated Railway was incorporated as the first elevated company for Chicago. Over the next eighteen years, it was followed by more than seventy other companies, most of which, like the Chicago West Division, never laid any track. Real estate developers were often significant supporters of these schemes, expecting that the train lines would make their properties more attractive to buyers. Behind some companies were aldermen and other politicians, hoping to cash in on their positions by catering to the need for public transit or simply by blackmailing the owners of rival lines to buy them out or cut them in.

From the start, a key focus for the elevated train proposals was Chicago's downtown—and the myriad workers, shoppers, and visitors who traveled to and from there every day. One plan proposed in the mid-1870s called for construction of a line on the lakefront from Randolph Street to Park Row, the elegant street of mansions along the southern border of Lake Park (later expanded and renamed as Grant Park). Another, from J. M. Hannahs, an inventor and an early Chicago resident, envisioned an elevated railway on State Street from Lake Street to Twenty-Second Street (Cermak Road today).

In 1875, an exasperated J. Esaias Warren complained that "tens of thousands who live in the suburbs demand some more effectual and rapid mode of transit" than the horsecar lines then in operation on Chicago's streets. A wealthy society leader and a frequent writer of letters to the editor, Warren asserted that the solution was "construction of elevated railways from the heart of the city, like the spokes of a wheel, in different points of the circumference."

Initially, as the *Tribune* noted, cable cars seemed a much more convenient and safer way of getting around Chicago, and the cable companies were already using that "spokes of a wheel" approach to serve all parts of the city. On top of that, they weren't as scary as elevated trains or as threatening to businesses. Describing the elevated trains operating in New York, the newspaper wrote, "The constant jarring and the inclement and infernal noise of the trains have seriously damaged business, and created such a nuisance as to drive people away. There is no privacy, for the trains run along at an elevation which enables the passengers to look in second-story windows, into bed-chambers and living rooms at night as well as day. The stores cannot be rented at anything like their proper value, because business is practically excluded from the street. The elevated railroad is death to the sick, and unceasing misery to the well people."

Nevertheless, after a decade of overcrowded cable cars and delays caused by broken cables, Chicagoans were fed up. In addition, the World's Columbian Exposition was set to open in 1893 in Jackson Park, and some better method of transporting the expected millions of fairgoers to and from the event had to be found. That method was the first of the city's elevated lines, which sent trains thundering through the South Side in the spring of 1892.

As the nineteenth century drew to an end, Chicago had three elevated lines in operation:

- The Chicago and South Side Rapid Transit Railroad Company, also called the Alley "L," with trains running north-south along alleys east of State Street and Indiana Avenue as far south as Thirty-Ninth Street before turning east and heading south through alleys to Sixty-Third Street (in service in May 1892)
- The Lake Street Elevated Railroad Company, with trains running east-west over Lake Street through the city's West Side and western suburbs (in service in November, 1893)
- The Metropolitan West Side Elevated Railroad Company, also called the Met or the Polly "L," operating through neighborhoods west, southwest, and northwest of the central business district (in service, initially to Robey Street, now Damen Avenue, in June 1895 and eventually into the western suburbs)

But as with the long-distance railroads, elevated train companies weren't permitted to enter the city's downtown. Under their city franchises, each of these three lines had to dead-end on the fringes of the central business district (as long-distance railroads had been doing since 1848), with a terminus that was about a half mile from State and Madison Streets. The Alley "L" ended at Congress Parkway and State Street; the Lake "L," at Madison and Market Streets; and the Metropolitan "L," at Franklin Street between Jackson Boulevard and Van Buren Street. (The future Northwestern line, which would have a test run on December 30, 1899, also was to end in a stub terminal.) This meant that riders had to walk several blocks to get to stores, offices, hotels, theaters, and government offices. And for that reason, many commuters continued to take the cable trains, even though these were slower and subject to greater technical problems.

Surprisingly, it was a man who was deeply invested in streetcars who suggested the solution in 1888, more than four years before the first elevated train ran in Chicago—Charles Tyson Yerkes, the Cable Car Czar. Yerkes was a major political and business player in the city, as the owner of two cable operations serving the North, West, and Southwest Sides, as well as the horsecar lines affiliated with them. Even so, he proposed a new transit project that, on the face of it, would compete with his street-level system—an elevated railroad connecting the West Side to the central business district.

And the elevated service suggested by Yerkes wouldn't stop at the edge of downtown. Instead, as the *Tribune* reported, "There is to be no terminus, the cars [are] to run on a loop that shall go up one street and return on a parallel one." Nothing came of the proposal—which, given the devious mind of Yerkes, might have been the idea.

A Union Loop

In late nineteenth-century Chicago, there was a tendency to want to adopt the loop technique for many forms of transportation because of the success of the cable car loops as a means of turning trains around. But that was also the problem.

The central business district in the mid-1890s was overlaid with six loops of cable car tracks, each enclosing a different section of downtown real estate although, in some cases, overlapping. And the cable trains running on those tracks—two lines serving the South Side, one for the North Side, and three for the West and Southwest Sides—competed for space with carriages, horsecars, delivery wagons, and tens of thousands of pedestrians. The thought of tightening and thickening those same streets even more with the girders of multiple elevated train loops was crazy-making, conjuring up visions of an exquisitely urban hell.

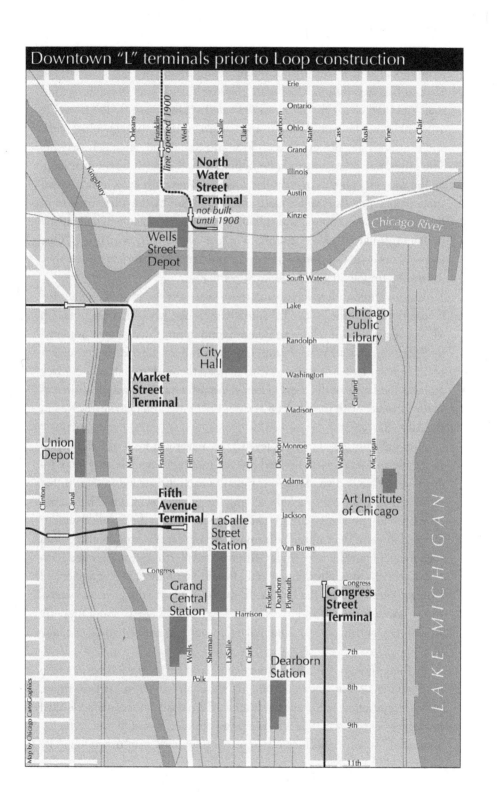

Downtown "L" terminals prior to Loop construction

Yet at the time, clotting the central business district with several elevated loops appeared to be a distinct possibility. For instance, in February 1893, the Central Elevated Railroad Company, backed by such heavyweights as Marshall Field and Cyrus H. McCormick, floated a plan for two "L" loops serving different lines. One would be long and narrow, running through alleys north and south of Lake Street between Franklin Street and Michigan Avenue. The other, much larger, would be bounded on the north by the first loop, on the west by Franklin or a similar street, on the south by an unidentified street (apparently Harrison Street), and on the east by the alley just east of State Street. That proposal was still alive nearly a year later, when company president William E. Hale, a prominent real estate owner, explained, "One loop will not do it. One loop would be insufficient to accommodate the Alley 'L,' the Metropolitan and the Lake Street roads."

Also under consideration during these years was the idea of an elevated loop serving only the Alley "L." Initially proposed when that line was still under construction, this loop would have gone around the city block bordered by State, Van Buren, Wabash, and Congress Streets. Levi Z. Leiter, owner of the Second Leiter Building, which took up the western half of that block and was the home of the Siegel Cooper department store, was described as "fully satisfied" with the idea. Of course, Leiter was also heavily invested in the Alley "L."

Although this loop for the Alley "L" was never was built, the discussion raised the specter of each elevated line attempting to erect its own loop. Indeed, in mid-1894, two elevated companies each threatened to do just that rather than participate in a loop serving the entire downtown. That would have been just fine for Charles D. Mosher, who, in early 1895, called for four elevated loops in the central business district, one for each of the three lines then in operation plus a fourth for the proposed Northwestern Elevated Railroad Company line. These loops, said Mosher, a prominent photographer and Chicago resident since the Civil War, would run over "the principal streets in the business district and . . . increase the value of every foot of property where [they] would pass . . . and make Chicago a greater city than the one-loop plan."

By then, though, Chicago's power elite had reached a decision. A single loop serving all four lines was the only reasonable solution. As Leiter said, shortly before sailing to Europe for vacation, "I am not in favor of many elevated road tracks downtown. The streets are too crowded now and the traffic too congested." Initially, this loop was called a "joint loop" or a "union loop." By the fall of 1894, "union loop" was the preferred term. Not only did it describe the function of the rectangular elevated track that would be used in common by the four companies, but it also called to mind the still vibrant memories of the Civil War.

From the start of that fratricidal conflict, the aim of the Northern states had been to save the Union, and the national army was called the Union army. In the aftermath of the war, the Grand Army of the Republic (GAR), a fraternal organization of Northern veterans, founded in 1866 in Decatur, Illinois, was a major force in American politics, representing a voting bloc of nearly half a million men by the end of the century. In 1892, the GAR donated land along Michigan Avenue between Randolph and Washington Streets for a dual-purpose structure to serve as the Chicago Public Library and the fraternal organization's local meeting hall. During the five years this building was under construction, proponents of a downtown elevated loop were using every strategy at their disposal to garner support, including the evocative term "union."

Even so, many obstacles stood in the way of a union loop, and it might never have been built. Indeed, according to one later analysis, the creation of a union loop "was deemed nearly impossible within the political and fiscal constraints in Chicago during this period." Without a union loop, Chicago's downtown might have developed in a fragmented fashion, with much of the downtown shopping, offices, theaters, and services clustered around each of the three or four elevated terminals. In this more diffuse central business district, subdowntowns might have developed—one for the South Side, one or two for the West Side, and one for the North Side. This would have heightened the regional divisions within the city and lessened the sense of a single urban community. It would have also made it more difficult for the city to withstand the many forces of social change, such as suburbanization and the rise of the automobile during the second half of the twentieth century. Even if that didn't happen, the downtown would have been much less cohesive.

As it was, in the mid-1890s, a union loop may have made transportation sense, but downtown merchants and property owners weren't in agreement on whether it made business sense. Some, such as James H. Walker, the owner of a major dry goods store on Wabash Avenue at Adams Street, liked the idea of bringing customers to his doorstep: "So far as I am concerned the Alley 'L' can occupy Wabash Avenue and go past the front of my store. In my opinion it would be a great benefit to property-owners to have it there." Others, though, feared the noise and traffic jams that such a structure would bring to downtown streets. They opposed the idea completely or would accept it only if the loop ran through downtown alleys. "I object to building an elevated road in any of the streets," said John B. Drake, co-owner of the Grand Pacific Hotel on Clark Street between Quincy Street and Jackson Boulevard. "They are congested enough now. But I do not object to going through the alleys."

The idea of an alley route through the central business district was extremely daunting, however. Seven key downtown blocks were covered completely by large buildings constructed over alleys. Also, some alleys were oriented north-south and others east-west, and the result was a crazy quilt pattern. The only downtown alley that could have served as a leg of an alley loop was the one that ran east-west between Lake and Randolph Streets. To create the other legs along alleys would have required razing buildings or driving tunnel-like passages for the "L" tracks through the second floors of buildings. The costs would have been gargantuan.

Another difficulty was the lack of unanimity among the elevated railroads. There were three elevated companies already in service and a fourth on the drawing board, each of them a separate entity competing for riders with the cable car, trolley car, and horsecar lines operating in the city. Moreover, the Metropolitan and Lake Street lines were competing with each other in the same area of the city. For a union loop to be built, those elevated companies had to find a way to cooperate.

They also had to find a way to raise money to build it, no mean feat at a time when the nation was reeling from the Bank Panic of 1893 and enduring the four-year depression it caused. Stock prices declined, some fifteen thousand businesses failed nationwide, and nearly five hundred banks (or one of every twenty in the country) closed. Unemployment in the United States rose to 18 percent, and investigative journalist William T. Stead reported that Chicago had a "floating population . . . [of] about 30,000 single men, who are living at this present moment in lodging houses which are too often foul [and] verminous." And that didn't include men, women, and children who couldn't afford the dime to sleep in such rattraps.

Money was needed not only for the actual work of constructing the elevated loop—but also for other "expenses." Members of the notoriously corrupt City Council, dominated by the Gray Wolves, including John "Bathhouse" Coughlin and Michael "Hinky Dink" Kenna of the First Ward and Johnny Powers of the Nineteenth, were lining up, as usual, for their share of the lucre in exchange for city approval. But even bigger payoffs would have to be made if a union loop were to become a reality.

A Black Market in Signatures

The most significant expense of all—estimated later to have been greater than the cost of actually erecting the loop structure—was the money needed to make payoffs to the owners of property along the route for what were called "frontage consents." The Illinois Supreme Court ruled that such payments were illegal, but no one paid attention. Like the boodle handed out to politicians, these payments were a widely known, widely accepted cost of doing business for an elevated railroad in Chicago.

It all had to do with state legislation known as the Adams Law. Its sponsor was the New Hampshire-born George E. Adams, a graduate of Harvard Law School and a municipal reformer in Chicago. From 1880 through March 1883, Adams represented the city in the Illinois Senate before being elected to the first of four terms in the U.S. Congress. In fact, he had already moved on to Congress when the Adams Law was enacted and signed on June 12, 1883. The law required anyone wanting to build an elevated railroad line along city streets to obtain signatures from the majority of the property owners along each mile of the route—approval for the line to pass the front of the home or business. It came in response to the way that, earlier, developers of horsecar and cable car lines had run roughshod over residents and property owners.

Under Chicago's 1872 city charter, any transportation operator who wanted to put tracks on city streets had to get the approval of the majority of owners along the entire route. That, however, turned out to be an empty protection, as even if opposition developed in heavily settled sections, it could be more than counterbalanced by the signatures of those who owned property in the rural areas and saw the new transportation line as a boon to their real estate values. Such a strategy, though, wouldn't work under the Adams Law, since approval had to be won for each mile of the route.

One of the main consequences of this law was the decision by the Chicago & South Side Rapid Transit Railroad Co. (which was taken over by the South Side Elevated Railroad in 1897) to build its tracks along the alleys east of State Street and Indiana Street, a unique solution in the elevated railroad field and one adopted by two of the other Chicago companies. This approach required the operators to purchase the right-of-way over a strip of land next to or alongside the alley, a relatively simple real estate deal not covered by the Adams Law. That was cheaper and more straightforward than the other major consequence of the Adams Law—the creation of a black market in signatures to approve (or oppose) an elevated line above a Chicago street. For instance,

Victor Lawson, the publisher of the *Chicago Daily News*, gave his consent for the Fifth Avenue (now Wells Street) section of the union loop to be built in front of the newspaper's offices in return for $1,250 (the equivalent of about $35,000 in present-day money).

Using the Adams Law as a club (and apparently looking to Chicago's corrupt politicians as models), property owners quickly began refusing to sign consent forms for an elevated structure on their street unless they were paid for their signatures. Citizen groups, writes transportation historian Brian J. Cudahy, "were formed to insure that all property owners were kept informed of the going rates for approval signatures. In addition to straight payments *for* approvals, the reverse was not uncommon; the competitors of a proposed new route would offer payments to abutters provided they *refused* to sign an approval petition."

Chicago's cable car titan Charles Yerkes employed the Adams Law in a different way—harassing elevated companies by taking them to court to challenge the signatures on consent forms for which the firms had paid good money. Anything to distract and discombobulate these firms competing with his cable car, horsecar, and trolley car lines.

It was, in fact, just one of the myriad strategies he employed to block or hinder his business foes. Consider his suggestion of a downtown elevated loop that he threw out back in 1888. He never pushed the idea, and it became clear in retrospect that Yerkes hadn't really wanted an elevated loop. Instead, his proposal had all the earmarks of what would later be known in football as a misdirection play. It was an effort by Yerkes to distract and confuse competitors, politicians and the public regarding his real goals, among which was to make it difficult for anyone to get an elevated train service even started.

In fact, a few years later, Yerkes wrote a long public letter to a joint committee of politicians and city residents arguing that elevated train service on the North and West Sides would be a waste of money for any investor. In May 1893, he told a newspaper reporter, "The city is not ready for elevated roads. The city is gridironed with cable roads, which are always fatal to the success of elevated traffic. If there was anything in the elevated road business I would have been in it long ago."

That's what he said then. Just a few months later, however, Yerkes's hostility to elevated railroads had evaporated. He had a new strategy to pursue.

⮐ 8. Willing the Union Loop into Existence

In building the Union Loop, Charles Tyson Yerkes deceived, deluded, and outsmarted his opposition. He played his foes off against each other. He played on their greed. He gambled and blustered and employed elaborately complicated financial manipulations that no one's ever been able to figure out completely. The Union Loop wasn't built as a single structure. Instead, for political, economic, and business reasons, Yerkes constructed it in four stages—in four sections. He used two of his elevated companies and created two others to build each section: the Northwestern Elevated for the western section, the Lake Street Elevated for the northern section, the Union Elevated Railroad for the eastern section, and the Union Consolidated Elevated Railway for the southern section. Yerkes willed the Union Loop into existence, reaping huge profits and, even more important, bestowing onto Chicago a steel-and-wood structure that has been a civic anchor for more than a century.

He began secretly. In October 1893, Yerkes dropped his opposition to elevated train operations and jumped into the business himself by incorporating the Northwestern Elevated Railroad Company, ostensibly under the control of others. But it was Yerkes, working behind the scenes, hidden from the public, who was the real power in the enterprise. His conversion to a belief in elevated rail lines was an acknowledgment that this form of public transportation had become a threatening competitor to his cable car and horsecar operations. As a major player in all three types of public transit, he would be able to wield a greater influence over transportation policy and decisions in the city—and be in a position to make greater profits.

Despite his low profile, Yerkes's involvement in the Northwestern Company didn't stay secret very long. Within weeks, he was widely rumored to be pulling the corporate strings there. All Yerkes would say, after a succession of newspaper stories, was that he was considering an investment in the elevated railroad "in his individual capacity only." It was big news that Yerkes was entering the elevated railroad field. In more than a decade in Chicago, he had become, far and away, the titan of the city's transportation system, trusted and distrusted simultaneously, respected and denounced. He had access to moneymen not only in Chicago but back east as well and was an almost talismanic figure at the Chicago Stock Exchange, where speculators were "inclined to put a great deal of blind faith in [his] financial shrewdness," expecting to follow his lead to greater profits.

He was politically savvy and preternaturally well connected in city and state government; his agent on the City Council was the ruthless alderman Johnny Powers. In fact, for the *Tribune*, Yerkes was a talismanic figure of corruption, a man "who debauches Councils, plunders the city . . . [and] has accumulated his enormous wealth in many devious ways." Yerkes was a hands-on executive who closely oversaw operations, installing innovative techniques and equipment and profiting hugely from the services he provided. He relished his stature as a larger-than-life figure who, though an outcast of polite society, was a major economic force in the city.

So much so that, more than any other figure in Chicago during the last decade of the nineteenth century, Yerkes was a celebrity in the most modern sense of the word. For instance, the *Tribune* breathlessly reported that Yerkes had a gymnasium on the upper floors of his Michigan Avenue mansion, equipped like an athletic club. His rotund figure may have suggested that his was a sedentary life, but the newspaper, in a fawning story that would have fit well in the pages of present-day *People* magazine, described him as "an athlete and a lover of manly sport, whether it be boxing, gymnastics, baseball or football." Indeed, he spent an hour each day working out in the gymnasium. "Dumbbells were his workout tools of choice until 1895, when he became a self-confessed 'bicycle crank,'" writes his biographer John Franch.

Unlike other power brokers in the city, he didn't shy away from publicity. He courted it and used it to his advantage. His name stood equally for scandal and success. In a city of buttoned-down businessmen, Yerkes was a constant fascination to Chicagoans. Investors in the new Northwestern elevated line included such Chicago movers and shakers as Marshall Field, Levi Leiter, and Philip Armour. But no one believed the fiction that Yerkes would be simply a private investor in the railroad. In all his time in Chicago, he had never taken a back seat to anyone in a business deal.

A City Shaper on a Grand Scale

Chicago is a city that puts up plaques at the drop of a hat to commemorate people, events, and buildings important in its history. But it's a city that has ignored Charles Yerkes. No monument recognizes his contributions to the vitality of Chicago's downtown. No bronze memorial recounts his significant role in the city's economic vibrancy in the face of massive social, economic, demographic, and cultural shifts.

Yerkes was a city shaper on a grand scale. His impact on Chicago and its people was as significant as that of Daniel H. Burnham or Mayor Richard J. Daley. He brought Chicago's elevated railroad Loop into existence, the Union Loop, knitting together the city and the region for more than a century. Yet Chicago history has enshrined Yerkes as a bogeyman caricature of a corrupt Gilded Age tycoon.

No question, Yerkes *was* a tycoon, and he *was* corrupt. He was one of the many sharks feeding in the waters of American capitalism as the nineteenth century drew to a close and the twentieth dawned. He was out to make money. He had a brilliant mind for finance and financial schemes, a rather flexible moral code, and a willingness to use every means he could—including payoffs and blackmail—to come out on top.

What's overlooked is that amid all his moneymaking, he was also a visionary urban planner. His profit-making efforts to expand, improve, and centralize the transportation systems in Chicago and later in London had a sweeping impact on both cities. He created integrated public transit networks that opened vast new areas for development and permitted hundreds of thousands to move away from dense, overcrowded city centers to new homes just a streetcar, elevated car, or subway car ride away from jobs and shopping.

In Chicago, Yerkes has been dismissed as "a corpulent plunderer" and "a five-star, aged-in-oak, 100-proof bastard." Yet in London, he is recognized as the man who "brought the 20th century to London" transportation. Yerkes built the foundation of that city's fabled Tube network. Indeed, his role was so crucial that, if he hadn't arrived on the scene in the first years of the twentieth century, the Tube system might never have been built.

In addition, in his private life, Yerkes was one of the premier American art collectors in the final decade of the nineteenth century, owning the most extensive collection of paintings, sculptures, and other art objects in Chicago. He was the first to bring the sculptures of Auguste Rodin to the United States, the first to bring a signed history painting by Rembrandt van Rijn into the country, and the first, in 1893, to publish a catalog of his collection with images and information about each of the artworks. His collection of Asian rugs, often called oriental rugs, was better than that of the shah of Persia and won praise from the eminent (and famously hard to please) art connoisseur Bernard Berenson. His artworks—which included J. M. W. Turner's *Rockets and Blue Lights (Close at Hand) to Warn Steamboats of Shoal Water*, Rembrandt's *Portrait of Joris de Caullery*, and Auguste Rodin's marble sculpture *Orpheus and Eurydice*, as well as paintings by Francesco Guardi and Frans Hals—are now in the collections of art museums from Malibu to Boston to Washington, D.C.

Yerkes's drive to acquire art was fueled by several wellsprings, one of which was an ultimately futile hope of finding acceptance by high society. Born in Philadelphia in 1837, Yerkes, a Quaker and the son of a bank president, was well on his way to a brilliant career as a dealer in municipal securities when the Great Chicago Fire of 1871 caused a panic on his hometown stock exchange. He was caught short, unable to get his hands on the cash he needed when officials demanded that he produce the money he had received as the city's municipal bond agent.

Convicted of embezzlement, Yerkes was sentenced to two years and nine months in prison, but he served only seven months before being freed by Governor John W. Geary on September 27, 1872. This was seen by some as an acknowledgment that his conviction was a miscarriage of justice and by others as an indication that he had used bribery or blackmail to buy his freedom. In fact, Yerkes biographer John Franch writes that his release was the result of a political directive from President Ulysses S. Grant. The president wanted to protect John Hartranft, the Republican Party's candidate for Pennsylvania governor, from being tainted by the same financial scandal that had put Yerkes in prison. Grant feared that unless Yerkes were freed and did his part in keeping the scandal under wraps, Hartranft would lose in October—and that would doom Grant's chances a month later of winning Pennsylvania's twenty-nine electoral votes, essential for his reelection. The newly freed financier cleared Hartranft's name, and both candidates went on to win their races.

Back in business, Yerkes quickly recouped his losses, paid off his creditors, including the city, and announced that he was again a millionaire. Business leaders accepted Yerkes back into the fold, but the wives of the upper crust of Philadelphia society wanted nothing to do with him. Not only was he a convicted criminal, but also his 1859 marriage to Susanna Guttridge Gamble—which produced six children, two of whom survived infancy—was turning sour, and gossip put him in the arms of the daughter of a wealthy Philadelphia chemist, Mary Adelaide Moore, called Mara. Facing ostracism, he left town, divorced Susanna, and in late 1881, married the twenty-three-year-old Mara, settling with her in Chicago.

But social acceptance continued to elude Yerkes and his wife, as Wesley Towner writes in his history of American art collecting: "Mara's bright robes and illumined face failed to captivate the butchers' wives of Chicago. Her fish-scale sequins and lime-colored velvet togas, her strident sensuality, her trailing plumes and outrageous feathers were intriguing to their golden husbands, but the social climbers of the Middle West were themselves too insecure to accept a bird of paradise within their midst."

It would be no different after Yerkes and his wife moved to New York City. The storied Four Hundred of high society, led by the Astors and Vanderbilts, turned their backs on the couple—although they did come out in force for the 1910 auction following Yerkes's death to pick through the his art holdings in search of bargains. Towner described it as "the sacking of the Yerkes palace."

In Chicago, none of Yerkes's art mattered. His contemporaries called him an ex-con and a freebooter, a conquistador, a Caesar, a "seizer," a "master of the arts of political bribery and legislative manipulation," and Public Enemy Number One. Novelist Ernest Poole sneered that the transportation magnate was a "Goliath of graft, the greatest and crookedest of all Chicago's buccaneers." Harold L. Ickes, interior secretary for Franklin D. Roosevelt, went so far as to liken Yerkes to a trio of World War II enemy leaders: Benito Mussolini, Japanese emperor Hirohito, and Adolf Hitler.

Mr. Dooley, the fictional Irish saloonkeeper created by Finley Peter Dunne, compared Yerkes to pestilence and the Great Chicago Fire of 1871. Commenting in his rich Irish brogue on a planned celebration of the anniversary of the fire, Mr. Dooley said, "An' why shud I cillybrate th' fire? . . . D'ye hear iv people cillybratin' th' famine iv forty-eight or th' panic iv sivinty-three or th' firin' on Fort Sumter? We've had many other misfortunes an' they're not cillybrated. Why don't we have a band out an' illuminated street ca-ars f'r to commemorate the day that Yerkes come to Chicago? An' there's cholera."

A Wild Card

Yerkes's sudden emergence in 1893 as an elevated railroad magnate threw into question the future of a union loop. The three "L" firms already in operation had been moving toward a consensus that they would join together to build this structure. But Yerkes was a wild card. At times during the first half of 1894, it appeared the three might go ahead without including the Northwestern. At others, it seemed that Yerkes might be able to scuttle their efforts at a common loop.

"Yerkes Has the Key" was the headline of a *Tribune* story in late May about his plan to run a loop for the Northwestern's own use through downtown alleys by "boring through the second stories of buildings in the way." An official at one of the other three elevated companies said, "If a way is not found to stop it, the Northwestern 'L' will balk the building of any down-town loop, except on its own terms." That was particularly gloomy news for the elevated railroads that desperately needed better access to the downtown to turn a profit. The finances for all three were shaky, at best. Indeed, the South Side elevated would eventually be forced into receivership. Meanwhile, the Metropolitan was still a year away from running any trains at all, so money was pouring out with nothing coming in.

Then the Lake Street Elevated came up with a brazen, in-your-face way to stop Yerkes. In addition to its efforts on behalf of a union loop, Lake Street had an alternate plan, already approved by the City Council, to gain access to the northern part of downtown by constructing a small loop of its own using the alleys north and south of Lake Street. This loop wouldn't be needed if the union loop were constructed, but for the moment, it became a weapon against the Northwestern.

At 7 p.m. on June 7, some one hundred laborers, toting picks and shovels, boarded an eastbound Lake Street train at Rockwell Street and sped downtown. At the alley between LaSalle Street and Fifth Street (the present-day Wells Street), just south of Lake Street, the workmen found wagons loaded with girders, beams, and other construction materials. The job: to build a block-long section of an elevated structure through the alley, ostensibly for the planned alley loop, but in reality to obstruct the route that the Northwestern was planning to use to get to the central business district.

The next morning, the *Tribune* reported that the makeshift structure resulting from the previous night's work was enough "to fill the souls of the Northwestern 'L' officials with dismay" and "signaled a bitter fight between the two companies." In the *Chicago Herald*, a reporter wrote, "Trains on the proposed Northwestern Elevated Railroad will need wings or long experience as hurdle racers when they leave the north side, the river, and South Water street behind and start on their across-lots-and-through-blocks run to Madison Street." In fact, by this point, neither Lake Street's alley loop nor the Northwestern "across-lots-and-through-blocks" loop was a serious proposition. Instead, they were ammunition in a corporate battle for transportation dominance.

Then Yerkes rolled out his ultimate weapon: He bought the Lake Street line. As with the Northwestern, Yerkes sought initially to keep hidden his involvement in the purchase of the Lake Street Elevated, which took place less than a month after that company's audacious move to block his Northwestern line from entering downtown. This time, though, the secret lasted only a few hours. The next morning, the *Tribune*'s stock market reporter asserted, "The purchasers of the Lake Street Elevated are Mr. Yerkes and his associates, and include Marshall Field and others largely interested in the Northwestern Elevated and the North Side and West Side surface companies." The magnate moved quickly to capitalize on his new purchase. Before the end of the month, Yerkes won an important concession from the City Council in that body's final meeting before a two-month vacation. An ordinance spearheaded by his man in the council, Johnny Powers, was approved, giving the Lake Street Elevated the right to extend its tracks from Market Street a half mile east to Wabash Avenue.

This vote, like many others by the council on Yerkes's behalf, evoked charges of corruption. A *Tribune* editorial was headlined "Where Reform Is Necessary—Boodle Work Going On in the Council—Sale of More Franchises." The newspaper noted that the ordinance was pushed through without first being considered by a committee where its merits could have been debated. "Some steps should be taken," the editorial asserted, "to put a stop to the Aldermanic ring railroading valuable franchises through the Council." In a second editorial, the *Tribune* noted, "There is always something suspicious about haste and secrecy." And, the paper might well have added, there was always something suspicious for reformers and good government advocates about anything Yerkes touched.

Quickly, John Alexander Low Waddell, the internationally respected bridge engineer hired by Yerkes earlier in the year, set to work designing sections of the hoped-for union loop. Based in Kansas City, Missouri, Waddell was well known in Chicago as the architect of the unique vertical lift bridge over the South Branch of the Chicago River at Halsted Street, which had opened a few months earlier. However, work to extend the Lake Street tracks to Wabash Avenue wouldn't be carried out for nearly a year. First there was a delay, waiting for the City Council to return from vacation at the end of September. The extension ordinance had been drafted and approved so hastily that amendments and corrections were needed. Then, after the city permit was issued on October 5, financial challenges and court battles delayed the beginning of the work until the next June.

Nevertheless, with disconcerting abruptness, Chicago's transit companies found Yerkes at the center of the union loop discussions. Not only did he control two of the city's four elevated railroads, but also, as his top aide told a reporter, Yerkes saw the Lake Street extension as "the first step toward getting a downtown loop." The first of what could be the union loop's four sections had been approved, and it belonged to Yerkes.

← 9. The Birth of the Union Loop

On November 22, 1894, less than two months after the city permit was issued for the Lake Street extension, the swashbuckling Charles T. Yerkes, backed by a crowd of ready investors, incorporated the Union Elevated Railroad Company to erect a union loop that the four elevated companies had agreed to lease. And the *Tribune* was overjoyed, announcing in a front-page story, "The Gordian knot has been cut. The question of an elevated railroad terminal is settled. There is to be one terminal loop and that will be used by all the companies." The story's headline was "Sure of an L Loop," and one of the subheads praised Yerkes: "His Master Hand Brings Together Various Interests."

The writer noted, "There may be some show of a fight along those lines, but as a matter of fact the controlling interests of both the Alley Elevated and Metropolitan Elevated companies are satisfied with the Union Elevated railroad scheme, and will go into that heartily." That scheme, as the *Tribune* understood it, called for a loop with a northern section along Lake Street, an eastern section along Wabash Avenue, a southern section along Harrison Street, and a western section along either Franklin Street or Market Street.

Another of the subheads in the article—"Chicago Elevated Terminal Question Solved at Last"—indicates how excited Chicagoans were that elevated service downtown had moved a major step closer to reality. And for the next month, they waited on pins and needles for the agreement among the four companies to be finalized, as a series of *Tribune* stories showed:

- "Loop Is Now Assured": "The last serious obstacle in the way of the immediate construction of the Union Terminal railroad was removed yesterday."
- "Hitch in Loop Plan": "The agreement to use the union loop was not signed . . . by the elevated companies yesterday."
- "Loop Will Be Built": "That the Union Terminal road will be built is as sure as a thing can be without being an absolute certainty. . . . The four Chicago elevated roads, existing and projected, will use the down-town loop in common, thus giving people in the heart of the city a chance to get home without walking a long distance to get a good start."

Finally, in its December 19 edition, under the headline "L's Agree on a Loop," the *Tribune* reported, "The loop agreement has been signed at last." Much more needed to be done, however. It would take a year and a half—and many devious maneuvers—before Yerkes would have the route of his loop settled. During that time, Chicago began to get used to the idea of this new elevated structure. In news coverage, the name of Yerkes's Union Elevated Railroad Company was routinely shortened to "the Union Loop Company." Its plans were often called "the Union Loop scheme." For most of 1895, however, the structure itself was known by a variety of terms, all lowercase: the "downtown loop," the "elevated loop," the "union loop," and simply the "loop."

There was also an odd effort, dating back a few years, to call the structure a "parallelogram." For instance, in discussing the location of the projected union loop, Levi Z. Leiter noted, "There are serious engineering difficulties in the way in Congress street, which has been proposed as one side of the parallelogram." An October 1895 story in the *Tribune* reported, "The loop company's plan contemplates the construction of the Wabash avenue, Fifth avenue, and Harrison street sides of the parallelogram. It will purchase the Lake Street extension." One editorial writer even referred to the union loop as a "quadrilateral."

Both terms were technically correct, but neither was a good fit. A quadrilateral is any four-sided figure, even one with four sides of different lengths. A parallelogram, a kind of quadrilateral, is a four-sided figure with two pairs of parallel sides, often with no right-angle corners. The most apt geometric figure for the right-angled, four-sided loop as planned by Yerkes was a rectangle, which is a kind of parallelogram, but strangely, this was one term never applied to the proposed loop, at least, not by the *Tribune*. Indeed, it wasn't until 1913 that the newspaper called the loop a "rectangle," and for more than a century since then, it has rarely used the term. By November 1895, as the loop was beginning to take shape and loom over downtown streets, the lowercase names for it were superseded, and in common parlance, at least, it was finally being called by what became its proper name: the Union Loop.

A War on Three Fronts

By then, Yerkes had already spent a year waging a war on three fronts to make the Union Loop a reality, and it would be another year before the issue was settled. The first front was on Fifth Avenue, three blocks east of the South Branch of the Chicago River.

The "Gordian knot" story in the *Tribune* had identified Franklin Street or Market Street, both close to the river, as a possible western edge of the union loop. But a short time later, the newspaper published an article about "a scramble of property-owners to secure the loop for their street," including those on Wabash Avenue, Clark Street, Franklin, and Fifth. "They begin to recognize that a loop upon which something like 400,000 passengers a day will ultimately be carried will add greatly to the value of their property."

Given the vocal opposition that arose on every street where the Union Loop was built, this article has all the earmarks of having been planted or, at least, inspired by Yerkes or one of his lieutenants. Indeed, along with providing a drawing of a section of the proposed union loop, the reporter wrote, "The structure will be the lightest elevated structure ever erected and will, it is claimed, interfere with the light in the stores little if at all."

As of the first week of 1895, Yerkes had set his sights on Fifth Avenue, not just as the western edge of the union loop, but also as the extension of his as-yet-unbuilt Northwestern Elevated Railroad into the central business district. This double-barreled approach had one other benefit: it was a clever way of undercutting opposition.

North of the river, Fifth Avenue was called Wells Street, the name the entire road has today. Yerkes's proposal was to start the Northwestern extension at Michigan Street (the present-day Hubbard Street), three blocks north of the river, and following the line of Wells Street–Fifth Avenue, continue for a mile south to Harrison Street. This made it much easier for him to gain consent signatures from property owners, since the area north of the river was filled with factories and warehouses. The owners of those businesses, as well as similar businesses around Harrison Street, didn't have to worry about presenting an attractive appearance to draw in customers, and the Union Loop promised an easy way for their employees to get to work. On top of that, the property owners, whether retailers or wholesalers, were paid $50 per foot of frontage in return for their approval. Nonetheless, some retailers who did have to worry about aesthetics banded together to fight Yerkes, taking their case to a City Council committee meeting without success. On June 24, the council gave its approval, and work to erect the Fifth Avenue section began a month later.

As the battles on that front were winding down, a second front on Wabash Avenue was heating up. In late September, the Lake Street line began running trains on its eastern extension to State Street and had extended its structure all the way to Wabash. And the partially constructed loop was immediately a hit. "Public acceptance of the downtown extension," writes transportation historian Bruce G. Moffat, "was immediate. Not only was the service faster than that offered by the Madison Street cable cars, to say nothing of the horse-drawn cars that plied the other near-by thoroughfares, but the extension brought most of downtown area within a short walk of a station."

It also brought Wabash Avenue to center stage. Going south, Wabash was a direct link to the northern end of the Alley "L" and was an essential part of the union loop as envisioned by Yerkes. The Wabash property owners—who included such Chicago powerhouses as Potter Palmer, Levi Z. Leiter, Marshall Field, Cyrus H. McCormick Jr., and John Quincy Adams, a Chicago businessman who was a distant relative of the Adams family that produced two U.S. presidents—knew how essential Wabash was to Yerkes. They took advantage of their leverage by crowing loud and long their opposition, while at the same time negotiating for the greatest profit possible in return for ultimately providing their consent. Their leader was Zephaniah S. Holbrook, president of the Wabash Avenue Property-Owners' Protective Association, who insisted that his group's members were solid "in their determination to prevent a crowd of unconscionable speculators from using one of the finest avenues in Chicago for the purposes of private gain" and that "Mr. Yerkes will never get his loop on Wabash avenue."

The squeeze was on, and Yerkes was squawking publicly, even though he'd known what he was getting into when he set out to build the Union Loop. "The property-owners along the proposed route want to bleed the company . . . ," he said at one point. "One or two of the leaders remind me of wolves who follow a caravan and grab what they can." Months later, he was still complaining:

> You may talk about sandbagging Aldermen and other sandbaggers at the City Hall, but they are not to be compared with some of the gentry who frequent the best parlors and drawing-rooms in the city. That is the place to look for the more accomplished "hold-up" with a nice silken sandbag concealed under the tails of his clawhammer coat. . . .
>
> We sometimes have occasion to call upon men of the supposed better class to speak to some friends for the purpose of influencing them to our behalf. Almost invariably the first question is: "How much is there in it for me?"

Nonetheless, after all the back and forth, property owners along the thoroughfare began to see the writing on the wall and started trading their signatures on consent forms for cash, giving Yerkes the necessary majority. In mid-October, the City Council approved the Wabash Avenue section. Even so, later that month, there were well-to-do holdouts, threatening to go to court to obtain injunctions against any work on Wabash. For them, Yerkes had a trick up his sleeve.

Two days before the Monday when the injunction requests were to be filed, a crew of 150 men and thirty teams of horses suddenly descended upon Wabash and proceeded to tear up the street. Starting at 6 p.m. and working through the night, they heaped mounds of dirt on the east side of the street and mounds of broken paving stones on the west side, and they dug huge trenches in preparation for the foundations of the Loop structure from Lake Street as far south as Washington Street. These trenches were ten feet square and ten feet deep and were set forty feet apart. And some were in front of the property of the men who still opposed Yerkes. The plan, a foreman told a *Tribune* reporter, was to get as far as Adams Street and begin filling in the trenches with concrete. What about any injunctions? "They can't get them before Monday, and one-half the concrete will be dry before that time."

On Monday, two property owners won their injunction, but it wasn't much of a victory. Judge Oliver H. Horton's order required only that Yerkes stop work on the Union Loop in front of two buildings that belonged to the protesting owners. So while work continued everywhere else on Wabash, it stopped in front of those buildings—leaving the giant holes in the roadway. "We are not bothered a bit," said one of the engineers overseeing the work, "as we were stopped only in front of two buildings. We were about ready to fill in these holes, but we won't now. They made us move our tools and material off the property and we don't intend to fill up the excavations for them." Two weeks later, the injunctions were thrown out by the Illinois Appellate Court, and work on the entire length of the street could go forward.

The payments Yerkes made to the Wabash property owners ranged from $25 to $100 per frontage foot but probably averaged about $80, according to Chicago transit historian Robert David Weber. There were eighty-two hundred feet of frontage along the street, and to obtain the required majority, Yerkes needed signatures to cover at least half of that. Which meant he had to spend at least $330,000 (the equivalent of about $9 million in present-day dollars) to get the needed signatures—just on Wabash. No wonder, writes Weber, that Yerkes had to overcapitalize his corporations and faced accusations of watering his stocks.

The newspapers of the time and later writers often accused Yerkes of artificially inflating the value of his holdings to increase his profit margin. In this case, though, Weber argues, the entrepreneur needed to raise more money than what, on the surface, was needed to build the union loop. He needed to cover the huge payoffs for property owner consents, as well as the normal costs of doing business with the Chicago City Council. In fact, Weber estimates that while it may have cost Yerkes less than $1 million to build the Union Loop, he would have spent an even higher amount to obtain the property owner consents and an unknown amount to aldermen for the needed legislation.

One of the big winners among the Wabash Avenue property owners was none other than Zephaniah S. Holbrook, who, as the vocal leader of the antiloop group of Wabash Avenue property owners, had railed against Yerkes and his "crowd of unconscionable speculators." The price for his signature? Eight thousand dollars, the equivalent of more than $220,000 today.

Yerkes versus Leiter

Yerkes now had approvals for three sections of what was starting to be called the Union Loop. The Lake Street section was already in operation, work had started on the Fifth Avenue section, and Yerkes was ready to go ahead with the Wabash Avenue section. But his greatest challenge was ahead of him—winning approval for the southern section of the loop. To triumph on this front, he was going to have to go head-to-head with one of the most powerful men in Chicago, Levi Z. Leiter. And Leiter was hopping mad.

For several years now, the general expectation had been that for whatever union loop might be built, the southern section would be along Harrison Street. In the *Tribune*'s "Gordian knot" article, Harrison was listed as the loop's southern line. But rumors began to circulate that Harrison wouldn't be the choice. Instead, it would be Van Buren Street, a long block farther north.

In late October 1895, Leiter and another major downtown businessman, Lucius B. Otis, sent a terse letter to all Van Buren Street property owners: "We wish to call your attend to the fact that the Union Loop Elevated railroad company has just decided to force the south line of the loop east on Van Buren street (instead of Harrison street) from Market street to Wabash avenue by an organized effort. We are strongly opposed to this measure and believe it will be very injurious to the property on the street."

Two days later, the *Tribune* featured a shocked headline: "Take Off the Mask—Union Loop Promoters Reveal Their Real Plans," and reported, "The Union Loop company will not use Harrison street for the southern side of the elevated parallelogram—if it can secure a street further north. Yesterday all disguise was thrown off and an active campaign began among Van Buren street property-owners for their consents to the structure." Explaining the shift, a company official said Harrison Street was "too far from the heart of town where most of the persons who ride on the roads do business."

Behind the scenes, Metropolitan Elevated executives had complained to Yerkes that Harrison Street would mean that its riders would have to make a detour before getting to the retail areas along both State Street and Wabash

Avenue. In addition, using Van Buren Street would reduce the costs of construction and operation. "Loops," Yerkes told a reporter, "should always be as a small as possible." Then he tossed out a red herring to confuse his opponents: "The south side of the elevated loop should be on Madison street. Then it would be exactly in the heart of the business center. We would prefer to have it there and will build it as far north as possible for that reason."

Yerkes's switch to Van Buren was discovered while Leiter was on a two-month trip to Europe, and that probably increased the mogul's anger. Leiter, though, had more than enough business reasons for wanting the loop on Harrison Street, and as the holder of an immense downtown real estate empire, he was used to getting his way.

Born in Maryland, Leiter wasn't yet twenty when he came to Chicago and began working in 1854 as a bookkeeper at the first of a series of dry goods stores. Near the end of the Civil War, he and Marshall Field went into partnership with Potter Palmer, although soon after, Palmer sold his share to the two men. The firm, called Field, Leiter & Co., survived the Great Chicago Fire and prospered. A decade after the fire, Leiter sold out to Field, and the store became Marshall Field and Company. Leiter, who had shrewdly gobbled up downtown property in the aftermath of the fire, continued to develop his real estate holdings. By the end of the nineteenth century, he was still active in Chicago affairs but, in addition to his frequent trips to Europe, maintained a mansion adjacent to Dupont Circle in Washington, D.C.

Stocky and bearded, Leiter had been a Yerkes ally in the fight over the Fifth Avenue and Wabash Avenue sections, but he was dead set against having the loop structure run along Van Buren Street. For one thing, he feared that it would detract from the value of the jewel of his holdings, the Siegel-Cooper Building, also known as the Second Leiter Building. Like other property owners on Van Buren, he said he didn't want trains roaring overhead. More important, though, Leiter, like many others, believed that the central business district would expand down to whatever was established as the southern line of the loop, thereby bringing business to an area that had been off the beaten path and benefiting his son Joseph, who owned property near Harrison Street.

Quickly, the dispute became a clash of titans. Leiter, finally back from Europe, dismissed the idea of using Van Buren as "the height of folly." Yerkes responded, "There is no question about the fact the Van Buren street people who oppose our plan do so from selfish motives." Then, in a reference to Leiter and his son, the financier added, "Two of these men have confessed to me quite recently their [reason] for opposing the Van Buren street route was not because they objected to the road on that street but because they want it on

Harrison street, where they own property which would be much benefited if it had better transportation facilities."

Leiter told a reporter that Yerkes's charge was "a falsehood," and Yerkes replied with a bitter letter, released to reporters—the *Tribune* headline read, "Yerkes Writes in Gall"—asserting that Joseph Leiter "distinctly informed me his reason for forcing the line to Harrison street was the fact he owned property there." He accused the elder Leiter of being "very unjust" by making what Yerkes said were unfounded charges of fraud against the Union Loop company. Leiter countered, "I do not own property on Harrison street, nor within a block of Harrison street. The record will show neither I nor my son owns one foot of property in Harrison street. And, further, we do not contemplate purchasing any. Therefore, the public can judge where the falsehood is."

Meanwhile, the dispute grew so hot that one of Leiter's allies described DeLancey Louderback, Yerkes's top aide, as acting like the Prince of Darkness in criticizing the Leiter crowd: "So Louderback has assumed the position of Satan, has he, of rebuking the sinful frontage owners against protecting their rights?" And so it went, on and off, back and forth, for a year as Leiter spearheaded the opposition as the chairman of the Van Buren Street Defense Committee and Yerkes fought with all his force and cunning to bring the Union Loop into being.

"A Novel Weapon"

Throughout the effort, Yerkes sought, through guile, misdirection, and bravado, to keep his opponents off-balance and constantly guessing at his true intentions. For instance, only a little more than a month after Yerkes acknowledged that he was seeking Van Buren as the southern section of the Union Loop, Chicago's newspapers reported that, well, no, it wouldn't be Van Buren after all. It would be Jackson Street a block to the north.

"The Union Loop company wants Jackson street," the *Tribune* wrote. "Yesterday concealment was abandoned and the loop company's agents were sent out among the property-owners." Joseph Leiter and other opponents told the newspaper that agents for Yerkes had gone along Jackson, seeking consents from owners for two Yerkes projects, a trolley line and an elevated line. Then, a few days later, it was Congress Street—extended west from Wabash through the city blocks between Van Buren and Fifth—that, according to rumors, would be the southern route. Questioned by a reporter, an unnamed official with the Union Loop company laughed at the idea of Congress and denied that any efforts were being made on Jackson Street to secure approvals for an elevated line there. "There has been no change in the route of the loop," he said. "We desire the southern connecting link to be built on Van Buren street."

Like Yerkes's mention of Madison Street as a southern route, the purpose of this contretemps clearly was to befuddle the opposition on Van Buren Street and garner support for Van Buren from merchants and real estate owners elsewhere downtown who didn't want the elevated structure on their streets. It also may have been a tacit admission that Yerkes knew he was losing the war.

For weeks, Leiter and his supporters had been crowing that they had blocked the Van Buren plan. A list published in early November showed that the anti-Yerkes forces had enlisted the owners or agents of more than thirty-five hundred feet of frontage between Wabash and Fifth Avenues. That represented 83 percent of the total frontage of forty-two hundred feet. In the face of such a united front, Union Loop representatives were said to be offering $100 a foot for a consent signature (well above the estimated loop average of $80) but were failing to make inroads. "Van Buren street, it may be said positively," said Lucius B. Otis, "is safe from the encroachment of the loop."

Yet Yerkes had a trump card up his sleeve. And four months later, the *Tribune* announced, "The south line of the elevated union loop will be built in Van Buren street. Mr. Yerkes has found a way to circumvent the opposition of Levi Z. Leiter and the other property-owners in East Van Buren street."

In a nimble tour de force, Yerkes had changed the rules of the game. Borrowing from his Fifth Avenue playbook, he had enlarged the playing field, guaranteeing his victory. Here's how.

His Union Elevated Railroad had been established to build and operate the Union Loop, but so far, it was set only to construct the eastern section. Yerkes had already employed his Northwestern Elevated to erect the western section and his Lake Street Elevated to build the northern section, both of which were then transferred to the Union Elevated.

So it seemed like just another of his obscure financial machinations when, in March, Yerkes established the Union Consolidated Elevated Railway. Unlike the Union Elevated, which had city permission to build in the downtown area, the Union Consolidated got the OK to carry out construction not only in the central business district but also across the river. Ostensibly, the Union Consolidated needed the greater flexibility because, in addition to building the southern section of the Union Loop, it was going to build a link from the loop to the Metropolitan line at Halsted Street.

In fact, Yerkes never planned to build this link. But for the purpose of winning frontage consents, he joined the two into a single project—an elevated

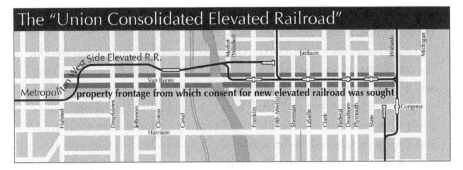

The "Union Consolidated Elevated Railroad"

line from Wabash Avenue to Halsted Street, a distance of a little over a mile. And at a single stroke, Yerkes was suddenly in control.

Leiter and his disciples might have locked up most of Van Buren east of Fifth Avenue, but that only covered a little less than half a mile of front-age. The stretch of Van Buren west of Fifth Avenue to Halsted Street was 50 percent larger, just under seven-tenths of a mile, and it was filled with warehouses, railroads, and factories whose owners would be happy to have the Union Loop nearby and to pocket whatever payoff Yerkes was willing to make for a consent signature.

Yerkes had ambushed his foes. The *Tribune* said the magnate was employing "a novel weapon." Yet he had used a similar tactic on Fifth Avenue to enlarge the consent area to enable him to overcome his opponents. The difference there, of course, was that Yerkes eventually did construct an elevated structure along nearly the full length of the consent area. Not so on Van Buren.

In mid-March, when Yerkes's bombshell hit, a Union Consolidated com-pany official said—prematurely, it turned out—that a majority of the property owners on Van Buren had already given their signatures, and a franchise would be quickly obtained. "The first thing the company will do," reported the *Tribune*, "will be to put in foundations for the superstructure in front of the property of L. Z. Leiter." It didn't happen quite that fast, however.

"Such a Public Demand"

Yerkes submitted his request for a franchise in mid-April, but it wasn't until July 6 that he won the go-ahead from the city. The reason: a city demand for greater compensation for the use of the loop. Yerkes wouldn't hear of it, and he dug in his heels. He had his top aide, DeLancey Louderback, issue a statement that read in part, "As everyone knows, we have been 'held up' by nearly every one of the property-owners along the line of this proposed loop. . . . And if we are now to be loaded down with compensation clauses that are not warranted and which the business will not sustain we shall never build the south side of the loop."

Later, Yerkes went so far as to threaten to operate the Union Loop without any southern section: "I am no soothsayer. I cannot tell when the Union Loop will be able to construct its southern connecting link across Van Buren street. . . . But, with or without the Van Buren street link, the Union Loop will be ready for service within a month. . . . Excepting a natural inconvenience to the loop company and to the public, the loop can be operated with three sides as well as with four. And it will be."

Whether Yerkes actually gave serious consideration to operating a three-legged system, there's no way to be sure. Even without a southern section, the three nonloop sections would bring riders much closer to the central business district than ever before. So it might have been possible, and profitable. What is certain is that this threat was another of his salvos on the battlefield of public opinion.

Eventually, on June 29, the City Council passed the Van Buren ordinance, and following a week of negotiations that resulted in a supplementary compensation agreement, Mayor George Swift signed the bill into law. Although he gave in, Yerkes was bargaining from a position of strength. As a *Tribune* editorial noted, "There is such a public demand for the completion of the loop that the Mayor could not afford to exact too much and thus incur the risk of preventing altogether, or delaying, something which may be called with justice a necessary improvement."

While praising Swift, the editorial criticized the City Council, where "a two-thirds majority of the Aldermen had ceded the use of the street without compensation." Of course, the writer went on mordantly, "most of them were boodlers, who would sell their wives or mothers for bribes."

The editorial was headlined "The Loop Question at Last Settled." But it wasn't. Leiter and his supporters quickly sued to block construction. Three months later, however, on October 16, the Illinois Supreme Court swept aside Leiter's legal arguments and gave Yerkes the go-ahead to build the Union Loop. He wanted to move quickly, but various snags, including a strike by construction workers and the Metropolitan Elevated's bankruptcy, delayed the start of service for nearly a year.

Finally, at 7 a.m. on Sunday, October 3, 1897, a handful of passengers rode the first train, belonging to the Lake Street Elevated, to make the circuit down Lake Street, along Wabash Avenue, west down Van Buren Street, and then north along Fifth Avenue back to Lake Street. The Union Loop was born.

"Hang 'Em! Hang 'Em!"

Although nineteenth-century Chicago loved parades, fireworks, and speeches, no celebration greeted the inauguration of the Union Loop. Chicagoans weren't in a mood to celebrate Charles T. Yerkes. Instead, they wanted to lynch him.

Ten months earlier, after Yerkes had cleared the way to complete the elevated structure, he took aim at a new challenge—to vastly improve the value of his streetcar lines through franchise agreements extending as long as ninety-nine years, dubbed by opponents "an eternal monopoly." He'd been able to win most such battles in the past, but this time, he found himself up against an increasingly organized coalition of reformers who, to their own surprise, were working hand-in-glove with some of the same corrupt politicians formerly in the financier's pocket. Indeed, Yerkes was the target of an unprecedented campaign in which he was routinely and publicly threatened with violence.

In April 1897, for instance, Alderman John Harlan, a tall, brawny reformer who was a former Princeton football center, an amateur boxer, and "all bone and muscle," stood before a crowd of thirty-five thousand with a warning for the transit czar: "That proud and haughty bandit, that great highwayman . . . arrogant Charles T. Yerkes," he proclaimed, was in danger of "decorating a lamp post."

For two years, a violent hysteria gripped officeholders, protesters, and Chicago's newspapers. Even as they sought to cleanse the city's politics of corruption and bring good government to Chicago, Harlan, Mayor Carter Harrison II, and other reformers were playing with fire. Indeed, the talk of lynching, while seemingly not a serious proposition for the reformers, stirred angry crowds to the edge of mob havoc. "Hang 'em! Hang 'em!" thousands of voices shouted at mass meetings, and it wouldn't have been difficult, even inadvertently, to push the hordes over that edge.

During the height of the anti-Yerkes uproar, the central business district was filled with men sporting on their lapels a "noose badge" made of black satin and featuring an image of a gallows with a noose. The *Chicago Chronicle* even published this advertisement: "WANTED: 10,000 Strong-limbed and fearless men. Apply at the council chamber, with ropes, the night the aldermen attempt to pass the fifty-year franchise robbery. Come prepared to do business."

Certainly, Yerkes was corrupt, but so were many of the city's most prominent politicians and business leaders. It was just that he was so much better at it. As Harrison wrote, "Trained in the public utility school [of Philadelphia financiers] he saw a roseate future ahead for the first man who would apply eastern methods of official corruption to the crude half-way measures so far practiced by the novices in Chicago's best financial circles."

All this maneuvering came to a head at two City Council meetings in December 1898, during which tough-looking men seated themselves along the front rows of the galleries, each dangling a noose over the railings, a threat not only to Yerkes but to any alderman who did his bidding. Yerkes, who had spent a fortune in bribes in the Illinois legislature and the City Council, thought he was in the driver's seat, but his council leader, Alderman Johnny Powers, got hoodwinked by Harrison and the mayor's unusual supporters, Gray Wolves aldermen John "Bathhouse" Coughlin and Michael "Hinky Dink" Kenna. The Yerkes forces lost a key vote by a single ballot, and the entrepreneur's hopes for a huge payday were dashed.

Even so, when he divested himself of his Chicago holdings over the next two years, Yerkes didn't do poorly. For $9.36 million, the man who had been the czar of Chicago transit sold seven of his eight streetcar lines in May 1899 to Peter A. B. Widener and William L. Elkins—the Philadelphia "Traction Twins," his occasional business allies and art competitors—as well as a third businessman. Eleven months later, he unloaded his seven suburban street car operations on his partners for $4.5 million. Then, in February 1901, he got $5 million for his elevated railroads and the Union Loop. In return for his Chicago holdings, Yerkes garnered a windfall of just under $19 million—or about $565 million in present-day dollars.

As Yerkes left Chicago, those who had brought about his downfall bade him good riddance. Nonetheless, even his opponents found reason to admire him. Harrison, who had fought him tooth and nail for years, described the magnate in his autobiography as "a fighter, with the heart of a lion, the craft of a fox, the viciousness of a leopard, the watchfulness of a timber wolf guarding her young. . . . He was really a gallant though perverted soul that looked danger in the face unflinchingly. He was of the stuff great war heroes are made of; with the right moral fiber his would have been a truly superb character."

Eight decades after the entrepreneur died, historian Kenneth T. Jackson praised him: "In a purely technological sense, Yerkes gave Chicago a superb transportation system. He replaced horsecars with cable or electric traction, increased surface lines by five hundred miles, and built the renowned downtown Loop, consisting of elevated lines around the central business district. By 1895, Chicago had more miles of track, more routes, and a longer average ride than any other city on earth."

That expanded and centralized system remains in use today, although much adjusted. Remaining, too, is the Union Loop, now called simply the Loop. The four-sided steel-and-wood Loop structure, so important to the strength and stability of the city, is Yerkes's greatest Chicago legacy. Yet in the few years left him, the exiled Chicago businessman had time enough to create a second legacy—the London subway system.

"Five Miles of People"

Modern-day London has its origins in a five-mile hansom cab ride that took place on a Friday in early August 1900. The horse-drawn carriage left Charing Cross at the center of the city, heading northwest in a pounding rainstorm. More than an hour later, the sun was shining as the vehicle reached its destination of Hampstead Heath, one of the highest points in the region. Henry C. Davis, a representative of the punchless Charing Cross, Euston and Hampstead Railway, had a lot riding on the journey. For the past year, he had been working to interest Yerkes in investing in the subway line that had all its government approvals in order but no money. This was a make-or-break moment for that effort.

While the taxi maneuvered through the clotted London traffic amid densely packed buildings, the magnate was quiet and pensive, staring out the window at manure-spotted streets filled with bicycles, omnibuses, and other horse-drawn vehicles, some of them piled with merchandise that loomed ten feet or more above the pavement. And everywhere, there were people walking along the sidewalks and in the streets, any place they could find a gap to give them a chance to get where they were going a little faster: boys in short jackets and knickers; women in bonnets and long skirts that swished along the pavement; and men, some loaded down with huge bundles carried on a shoulder, many, even the laborers, in suits of one sort or another, all wearing a hat (bowlers, caps, fedoras, top hats, even wide-brimmed panamas) and almost all displaying a mustache that was usually flamboyantly idiosyncratic. Amid this mass of human beings, each following an individual route, "one might hear," a historian notes, "the twanging inflections of Australians, New Zealanders, Canadians, and the 'goldbugs' of South Africa, the rounded intonations of the Irish, the unfamiliar enunciations of Asians and Africans." And of course, the accent of an occasional American.

Chicago was this congested, but only downtown. Here, in London, there was no break in the teeming mass of humanity as the carriage wove its way along the subway's proposed route. Yerkes told Davis that "he had never ridden through five miles of people before in his life." Such crowds and such congestion meant potentially huge profits for the proposed subway.

The carriage came to a halt near the pub called Jack Straw's Castle at one of the highest points on Hampstead Heath, a rise of more than four hundred feet overlooking central London. Gazing south, Yerkes could see in the distance the towers and church spires of the tightly packed city, home to more than 6.4 million people, the greatest concentration of population the world had ever seen. (By contrast, Chicago, the fifth most populous city in the world, had just 1.7 million residents.) To the north, "a panorama of pastoral landscape, with here and there bits of forest and clustering villages," was laid out before the American entrepreneur.

From his experience in Chicago, Yerkes knew that the Charing Cross line, once built, would serve hundreds of thousands of Londoners living and working along its path. In addition, the subway would spark housing development across those meadows and turnip fields to the north, attracting even more future riders. "This settles it," the magnate said, and he began negotiations later that day to round up investors to buy the railway.

Nearly four decades earlier, in January 1863, the world's first underground railroad of any sort, the Metropolitan Railway, had been launched in London, featuring steam engines and wooden carriages operating between Paddington and Farrington. This was a type of subway called a cut-and-cover line, which, as the name suggests, involved cutting a trench about thirty feet deep through the cityscape, laying tracks, building a brick tunnel around the tracks, and then filling the remaining hole above the tunnel with dirt. This approach, also called subsurface, obviously caused a lot of problems in any developed areas filled with homes, churches, businesses, and other structures.

The four routes of this type that were in operation after the turn of the century formed a circuit around London, connecting the outer edges of the city and suburbs. However, although they came near the city center, none traveled through. It was just too costly and disruptive to try to push this sort of route across an area that had been occupied and built upon for more than eighteen hundred years.

The solution was another sort of subway, much deeper, anywhere from 45 to 250 feet below the surface, carved out of the London clay, well below the level of drains, sewers, and utilities. The world's first deep-level subway of this sort was built by the City and South London Railway in 1890. Serving electric trains, the tunnels were circular in shape, and riders quickly nicknamed the railway the Tube, although the company frowned on that word. The term was later applied to all of London's deep-tunnel subways, and today it is used interchangeably with Underground in reference to the entire London rapid transit system.

In the nineteen months following his visit to Hampstead Heath, Yerkes on behalf of various groups of moneymen purchased or gained control of five railways, four of them for deep-tunnel lines that had been approved but not built. Even though London had been a pioneer in subways, development of its deeper-level Underground had been at a standstill for lack of money and political will. Now, Yerkes, the brash American, stepped in and laid the groundwork for the construction of the speedy public transit system that is one of the present-day jewels of the British capital.

Without him, plans for the subways most likely would have withered away ten years later with the rise of a seemingly less expensive solution: the motor bus and automobile. The result, though, would have left central London today impossibly jammed with traffic—or, like many American cities, crisscrossed by superhighways. By 1902, Yerkes, with his usual and at times morally questionable maneuvering, had bested fellow American J. P. Morgan for control of the future Tube lines and was dubbed "the Moleonaire" by the British humor magazine *Punch* and "Dictator of London Transit" by the *New York World*.

But his time was growing short. He was suffering from severe nephritis, an inflammation of the kidneys, then called Bright's disease. Laid up in June 1905, he was able to bounce back and return to business. By November, however, the disease had again flared up, and the fatally ill entrepreneur took a ship back to New York. On December 29, at the Waldorf-Astoria hotel, Yerkes died.

At the time of his death, Yerkes's ambitious plans for London were already in motion and would come to fruition within a year and a half:

- The Bakerloo line opened March 10, 1906, less than three months after his death.
- The Great Northern Piccadilly and Brompton line (now part of the modern-day Piccadilly line) opened December 15, 1906.
- The Charing Cross, Euston and Hampstead Railway (now part of the modern-day Northern line) opened June 27, 1907.

Railway historian Christian Wolmar calls the Underground a "magnificent organism living permanently under [Londoners'] feet" and credits Yerkes as the indispensable factor in its success: "Most fundamentally, the Underground allows Londoners to traverse the city in a way which would be impossible by any form of surface transport. . . . In central London, the Underground is the way to get around town, as demonstrated by the fact that it is used both by besuited City gents and their cleaning ladies."

In obituaries, British newspapers lionized Yerkes. "We owe much to the man who revolutionized our old-fashioned methods of going to and from," said the *Westminster Gazette*. And modern writers about London's Tube system agree. One describes Yerkes as "a fresh and virile influence" on the stagnated British transportation field. Another says he was "one of the most rugged of all the rugged individuals who have guided London's destiny." According to a third, he "brought the 20th century to London."

In Chicago, though, later writers have disparaged Yerkes as a devil, "a financial adventurer," a carpetbagger, "an irrepressible predator," a pirate, "the prototype of the money-grabbing tycoon," and even "the precursor of the gangsters" of Chicago's organized crime. The title of John Franch's 2006 biography of Yerkes is *Robber Baron*. Yerkes left his imprint on two major world cities. Even so, at the time of his death, the *Tribune* wrote that he had been "the most unpopular man" in Chicago.

Part Three →

The Loop

⬅ 10. The Rectangular Bridge and the Bridge Builder

A pamphlet, published in 1898 for the riders of the Lake Shore & Michigan Southern Railway, gave a detailed description of Chicago's new Union Loop, noting it was "the clearing point for all elevated trains in the city." And that was certainly true. Every day, more than a thousand trains of the three (later four) elevated railroad companies, carrying an average of some 180,000 passengers, entered the downtown and then, after making the Union Loop circuit, headed out to the city's neighborhoods again. Yet the recently completed structure wasn't just a means for smoothly and efficiently turning trains around.

Even more, the Union Loop was a rectangular bridge, linking together in an unprecedented way the three parts of Chicago—the South Side, the West Side, and the North Side. Like the Brooklyn Bridge, the Union Loop was a connection. The Brooklyn Bridge joined together Brooklyn and Manhattan, and in creating that connection, it unified them and made them stronger. A decade and a half later, the elevated Loop joined together the three areas of Chicago, isolated from each other as they had long been, and broke down that isolation. Suddenly, it was easy and fast to travel from the farthest edges of one end of the city to the farthest edges at the other end.

The elevated Loop, in essence, transformed the individual elevated lines into a single network (although they would continue to operate separately for decades), and in doing that, it transformed those three sections of the city into a unified whole, into a union. It was no happenstance that it was called the Union Loop.

Indeed, the various sections of the elevated Loop even look like bridges. That shouldn't be a surprise, since each was built by a bridge-building company—the first, the Lake Street section, built by the Phoenix Bridge Co. of Phoenixville, Pennsylvania; the second, the Wabash section, by Pencord Iron Works of Pencord, Pennsylvania; the third, the Fifth Avenue (now Wells Street) section, by the Union Bridge Co. of New York City and Elmira Bridge Co. of Elmira, New York; and the fourth, the Van Buren section, also by Pencord Iron Works. Not only that, but the main reason the four sections look like bridges is that they were designed by the internationally renowned bridge builder John Alexander Low Waddell.

Like a Young Bull Elephant

The year was 1882, and John Waddell, just making a name for himself as an American engineer, was taking his new wife, the former Ada Everett, from her hometown of Council Bluffs, Iowa, to the site of his new job on the other side of the world—Tokyo. It was something of a honeymoon, since they left shortly after their July 3 wedding. Nonetheless, the move of six thousand miles from an Iowa town of about twenty thousand, where the daughter of a prominent local attorney had been courted by Waddell, to a westernizing but still very alien Asian nation was a drastic adjustment. So for company, the couple took along Waddell's older sister, Josephine.

The Japanese government, seeking to beef up the faculty of its newly established Imperial University of Tokyo, had hired the twenty-eight-year-old Waddell as the chairman of the civil engineering department. He looked forward to heading a large program but also expected to have time to do side jobs. Instead, he found that during his four years in Japan, the department never had more than twelve students, and as a foreigner, he couldn't find any private engineering work.

Never one to loaf, Waddell used his extra time to write two books. The first was *The Design of Ordinary Iron Highway Bridges*, one of the few books published in that era about bridge building. In fact, the book "became the seminal text at many engineering schools throughout the world, the 'gold standard' text on iron/steel bridge design." His second, though, *A System of Iron Railroad Bridges for Japan*, caused an uproar.

John Lyle Harrington, the editor of Waddell's collected professional papers and his business partner for several years, writes that the book was done at the request of university authorities. If so, they may not have known what they were getting into. On the first page of his introduction, the American engineer—now all of thirty-one and with a grand total of ten years of experience in the field—announces to the Japanese nation that its bridges have been built all wrong. What's needed, he writes, is for his host country to throw out its old ways of putting up bridges and adopt the American techniques that he details in his book.

"I hope you will excuse me," Waddell writes of his brash, blanket critique. Attempting to soften his harsh judgement, he tells the Japanese that it's not their fault. "The designs are not yours, but are the work of some present and former foreign employees of the Railway Department." The problem, as he sees it, is that these foreigners were English and not up to snuff compared with Americans.

Waddell goes on to list several "grave errors," such as spans that are too short and "the absolute lack of lateral bracing." He writes, "The trouble with most English bridges and consequently with those of this country, is that they are designed by railroad engineers, who have not made a special study of bridge designing, and are therefore incompetent to do the work entrusted to them."

A *System of Iron Railroad Bridges for Japan* was reviewed in the English-language *Japan Mail* on July 16, 1885, sparking a letters-to-the-editor controversy that lasted nearly a year. Waddell's critics were English engineers, and according to Harrington, they spent most of their time in attacks that were "almost venomously personal." The American, though, gave as good as he got, and like a young bull elephant, he trumpeted at one point, "Into the merits of the case not one of the writers of the letters in the *Mail*, attacking my book, has dared to enter. An open, scientific discussion is, apparently, the very last thing my opponents desire. They know that it would make patent to the world the radical deficiencies of the old English system of bridge building."

Waddell's blunt language in the book and in his letters to the *Japan Mail* apparently didn't affect his standing with the Japanese leaders. In 1888, two years after Waddell's return to the United States, Emperor Meiji bestowed on him the Order of the Rising Sun, with the rank of knight commander. All the newspaper bickering came to an end with Waddell's departure from Japan, but it was a preview of a later controversy that would spark when, with similar blunt talk, the then-middle-aged engineer wrote about his design for Chicago's Union Loop.

"Not Known for His Humility"

Although frail as a child growing up in small-town Canada, John Alexander Low Waddell developed "a robust constitution" when, at the age of sixteen, he took a ten-month trip on the clipper ship *N. B. Palmer* to China and back. Later in life, he became a big-game hunter and deep-sea fisherman, writing frequently for publications devoted to those pursuits. A thickly built man of medium height, Waddell was "quite stately with his white hair [and] a long brushy moustache." He was a fastidious dresser and found great enjoyment in attending formal occasions with his hair ornately curled and, to the amusement of some of his colleagues, with many of his medals festooned on the chest of his tuxedo, including the Japanese Order of the Rising Sun.

Waddell, a man "not known for his humility," certainly left his mark on Chicago, designing the elevated railroad Loop in the final years of the nineteenth century. The structure he gave Chicago is arguably the most distinctive visual element in the city's downtown—and in any city's central business district. With its airy steel framework and its looming presence over the city-scape and its trains rumbling twenty feet overhead, the elevated Loop says "Chicago" in a most physical and visceral way. But you won't find Waddell's name in a history of Chicago. And it's a rare account of the city's transit system and central business district that mentions him.

Even civil engineers, who honor him as a seminal figure in their field, overlook this part of his career. Waddell's design of the Union Loop, his later role as an authority on the construction of elevated railroads, and the standards he set are all overlooked in biographical profiles of Waddell by the American Society of Civil Engineers, the Dictionary of American Biography, and the professional journal of structural engineers, *Structure* magazine, as well as in books and articles that discuss his career.

Throughout his sixty-three years as a civil engineer, he designed more than a thousand bridges and other structures, but none more significant than the elevated railroad Loop in Chicago. None have been used by as many people on a daily basis for more than a century as his Union Loop. None have played as significant a role as a cultural force for unifying a city as his elevated Loop has for Chicago. Although often viewed in the past as the city's ugly duckling, the Union Loop staked out and helped create and preserve the downtown common ground shared by all Chicagoans. It has anchored Chicago's central business district, enabling the downtown to withstand the storms of demographic, social, and lifestyle shifts that have laid low many other municipalities.

Yet when Waddell died in New York City on March 3, 1938, at the age of eighty-four, his role in designing Chicago's elevated railroad Loop more than four decades earlier was ignored. Waddell was, the *New York Times* stated, "one of the leading bridge engineers of the United States." In the *Chicago Tribune*, he was identified as the inventor of the modern vertical lift bridge. Neither newspaper mentioned his Union Loop. Indeed, those obituaries only scratched the surface of Waddell's myriad achievements. Like Yerkes, he was a larger-than-life figure.

During his long career, Waddell was decorated by four foreign governments (China, Italy, and Russia in addition to Japan), as well as by his fellow engineers. He was a three-time winner of the Norman Medal of the American Society of Civil Engineers for original papers contributing to the advancement of the practice of engineering (1909, 1916, and 1920), a feat that has been duplicated just once. He was, in addition, the only recipient of the Clausen Medal of the American Association of Engineers for distinguished service in the field (1931).

He was deeply respected, honored as a bold innovator, and described as a "genius in the art of bridge building." He was seen by many as "the father of twentieth century bridge design in America." And more than six decades after his death, Waddell was described by a twenty-first-century admirer as "an inspiration to an entire generation of bridge designers."

Waddell designed elevated train structures in Chicago and consulted on those in Boston when these two cities were two of the most populous and crowded in the world. Yet like many men and women of his era who made their marks in huge metropolises, his beginnings were distinctly small-town.

On January 15, 1854, Waddell was born in Port Hope, a Canadian community of about twenty-five hundred souls on the northern banks of Lake Ontario, sixty-eight miles east of Toronto. His father, Robert, an Anglican from the Irish city of Newry in what is now Northern Ireland, immigrated in his late teens to Canada in 1831. His mother, Angeline Jones, was born in New York City, the daughter of Colonel William Jones, a War of 1812 veteran who served three years as the sheriff of New York City and County, as well as a term in the state legislature. Angeline was twenty-one when the couple married on November 25, 1852. Robert was nearly twice her age. John was the second of three children and the only son. When the boy was eleven, Robert Waddell, following in the footsteps of his wife's father, won appointment as the high sheriff of what was then the United Counties of Northumberland and Durham, and the family moved a few miles east to the slightly larger town of Cobourg, the government seat. In that post, John's father was responsible for the administration of the court system, as well as court security.

A year after his ocean voyage, the now-vigorous John Waddell left the family home again to travel three hundred miles southeast across the border to begin classes at Rensselaer Polytechnic Institute in Troy, New York. Founded in 1824, Rensselaer was the first school in the United States to confer civil engineering degrees, and it bestowed one on Waddell in 1875. In his first jobs, Waddell designed buoys and other maritime structures for the Marine Department of the Dominion of Canada and was involved in the construction of Canada's first transcontinental railroad, the Canadian Pacific Railway. Then, for three years, beginning in 1878, he was back at Rensselaer as an assistant professor in geodesy, descriptive geometry, and rational and technical mechanics. It was there that he authored papers on a variety of subjects and developed a reputation as a theoretician.

In January 1881, Waddell was hired as chief engineer with Raymond and Campbell, a bridge-building firm headquartered in Council Bluffs, and "developed his lifelong love for designing large bridges, a passion that would one day establish him as one of the world's great bridge builders." Following his tenure in Japan, Waddell returned to the United States, and in January 1887, he opened a private engineering practice in Kansas City, Missouri. Over the next half century, he was involved in the design and construction of hundreds of bridges, lighthouses, elevated railroads, and other structures on at least five continents. By 1912, halfway through his career, Waddell had already engineered $50 million worth of projects—the equivalent of more than $1 billion today. Four times in his career, Waddell took on partners as protégés, including his son Everett, who staffed a New York City office for him until the young man's death in 1920. (Waddell and his wife also had a daughter and another son.) A grieving Waddell then moved to New York, his base until his own death.

Waddell and his firms designed more than two hundred bridges in Mexico alone, as well as bridges in Cuba, New Zealand, Canada, China, Japan, Italy, and Russia. They built bridges from one end of United States to the other—from Connecticut to California, from Louisiana to Oregon, from Virginia to Kansas. Six or more of their works spanned the Missouri River, and at least two stretched across the Mississippi. They designed two of the three bridges that link the New York City borough Staten Island with New Jersey: Outerbridge Crossing, connecting the island to Perth Amboy, and Goethals Bridge, joining it to Elizabeth.

Many of these structures became official or unofficial landmarks for their communities and are still in use. At least thirteen are listed in the National Register of Historic Places, including the following:

- the Colorado Street Bridge, a 1,486-foot-long concrete arch bridge spanning the Arroyo Seco in Pasadena, California (1913), known for its eleven beaux arts arches, ornamental clustered light posts, and iron balustrade
- the Detroit–Superior Bridge (officially the Veterans Memorial Bridge), a 3,112-foot-long through-arch bridge over the Cuyahoga River in Cleveland, Ohio (1918), which links Detroit and Superior Avenues and was, for a time, the largest steel and concrete reinforced bridge in the world
- the Winant Avenue Bridge (also called the Route 46 Hackensack River Bridge), a double-leaf bascule bridge, featuring four octagonal concrete towers and spanning the Hackensack River in Bergen County, New Jersey, at Newark Bay (1934), at the former site of a rope-tow ferry that had operated since colonial times

"Struggling with the Gallant Tarpon"

Despite a heavy workload, Waddell turned his wide travels across North America and around the world to his advantage, taking several weeks off each year for fishing and shooting, often while on his way to or from one of his projects. According to a short biography by one of his partners, John Lyle Harrington, in 1905, "He is acquainted with every part of this continent where good sport is to be had. He has caught the tarpon in the Gulf of Mexico; the bass, pickerel, and muskellunge in Wisconsin and Minnesota, and the salmon in Canada; has shot deer in Arkansas, deer and elk in the Rocky Mountains, and small game in many sections of the country."

Waddell wrote frequently for *Forest and Stream*, a New York City–based magazine about hunting, fishing and other outdoor activities, founded in 1873. According to the magazine's editors, his articles on fishing were "intensely practical," as one would expect from a professional engineer, and had "less of the poetry of angling and more of the useful, instructive and definite description of tackle and modes of fishing."

Still, Waddell could also wax poetic about the playful pleasures of sport hunting and fishing, which he saw as essential to his health and well-being. He must have been on to something. Even though he was born in the 1850s, when a male child who survived infancy had a life expectancy of fifty-eight, he lived more than a quarter century beyond that. In 1903, Waddell spoke about the importance of recreation and relaxation at the conclusion of an address he gave to the graduating class of Rose Polytechnic Institute (now the Rose-Hulman Institute of Technology) in Terre Haute, Indiana, and repeated, a short time later, to the graduates at Rensselaer Polytechnic Institute:

> By this time you all have probably come to the conclusion that you have been listening for the last half hour or more to an old fogy, who thinks that there is nothing in life worthy of consideration but work, work, work, and who can talk on nothing but technical subjects. If this be so, I by no means blame you, for you would seem to have reason on your side; nevertheless, you would be entirely in the wrong, because I am a firm believer in legitimate relaxation of every kind, and in a man's getting all the pleasure he can out of life.
>
> Perhaps, too, I could talk of things that are far from technical, such as hunting the great game of the Rocky Mountains, canoeing on lake and stream, the shooting of rapids, travels in foreign countries, gunning for wildfowl in the marshes, sports afield with dogs and gun, fly-fishing

for trout in the streams of the far North, and struggling with the gallant tarpon on the waters of the Gulf of Mexico; but it was not to discuss such subjects as these that your president brought me here, so I shall desist, only remarking that the more you mix these things and other sports and amusements in with your work, the better will it be for you both physically and mentally, the longer will you live, the more will you accomplish, the more satisfactory will be the results of your work, the better men and citizens will you become, and the more interesting and agreeable will you prove to all with whom you are thrown in contact.

Chicago first felt the imprint of John Waddell in 1894 when his newly invented vertical lift bridge was erected over the Chicago River at Halsted Street, just north of Archer Avenue—known later to readers of Peter Finley Dunne's Mr. Dooley columns as "the red bridge," the gateway to the hard-scrabble neighborhood of Bridgeport.

Throughout most of the nineteenth century, nearly all large movable bridges in the United States were swing bridges. In a swing bridge, the span pivots horizontally ninety degrees on a center pier to create two lanes for boats to pass. But in 1890, the Harbor and Rivers Act gave the federal government, through the War Department, jurisdiction over navigable waterways and resulted in a twelve-year period in which Chicago was the international center of bridge innovation. "No other city in the world experimented [during this period] with as many different moveable and bascule-type bridges as Chicago," writes Chicago bridge historian Patrick T. McBriarty.

The problem with a swing bridge was its center pier, which the Chicago Vessel-Owners' Association called "a great obstruction to navigation" in its efforts to obtain a different sort of structure at Halsted Street. Waddell's design solved that problem by having the bridge platform—in this case, a 130-foot-long, cedar-block-paved section of Halsted Street—rise slowly between two metal towers, like an open-air elevator. Not only did this eliminate the center pier, but it also provided enough space under the raised platform to permit the tall masts of sailboats to pass below.

General John Moulder Wilson, the chief of engineers of the U.S. Army, described it as a "freak," more outlandish than any bridge he had ever seen in his career. Nevertheless, fourteen years after the bridge went into operation, Mayor Fred A. Busse included the structure as one of the "Seven Wonders of Chicago." Meanwhile, Waddell with one of his protégés, John Harrington, had refined the design, and vertical-lift bridges, particularly for railroads, proliferated across the nation and around the globe in the early twentieth century.

Brute Physical Labor

At noon on Labor Day, September 6, 1897, motorman John O'Brien opened the throttle, and his four-car elevated train pulled out of the Fifth Avenue station at Lake Street for a test run around the recently completed elevated Loop. For this very informal check of the structure, fifteen or so officials of the Lake Street Elevated line were on board, including General Superintendent Frank Hedley and President Delancey H. Louderback, Charles T. Yerkes's right-hand man.

They expected a relatively quiet ride around downtown Chicago on this fourth annual celebration of the national holiday. But it didn't turn out to be all that quiet. As Louderback and the others rode in the three passenger cars behind motor unit No. 101, office workers, shoppers, and others who were in the central business district saw the train making its circuits and wanted to get in on the action. "The impression was created," wrote the *Tribune* the next day, "that the loop was at last in operation, and the platforms along the line soon were filled with people anxious to take a ride." Fifty Lake Street Elevated employees had to be dispatched to the stations to clear the platforms and turn other would-be riders away.

Over the course of two hours, O'Brien's train made three trips around the Union Loop, as the officials examined each switch, turn and signal. "I am more than satisfied with the trip," said Hedley, adding, "We made all kinds of speed, and the running was as easy as on an old track bed." Less than a month after this Labor Day ride, the Union Loop went into operation, culminating four years of financial and political razzmatazz by Charles Yerkes. It was also the culmination of two years of brute physical labor, often interrupted by legal disputes and workforce troubles, to erect the Loop's steel superstructure.

That labor got underway in late summer 1895, when scores of workers, using plans drawn up by Waddell, began to rip out the Lake Street pavement near the south branch of the Chicago River to extend the elevated line eastward and then, at Fifth Avenue (now Wells Street), to start constructing the foundations of the new Union Loop structure. Through the fall and winter, the steel structure continued to move east to Wabash Avenue, where on March 29, work started on the first of the Union Loop's four curves.

A few days later, laborers began to fashion a second curve at the west end of the Lake Street extension, where the western section of the Union Loop would head south along Fifth Avenue. Then, in late November, Joseph Downey, the city's public works commissioner, issued the permit for construction to

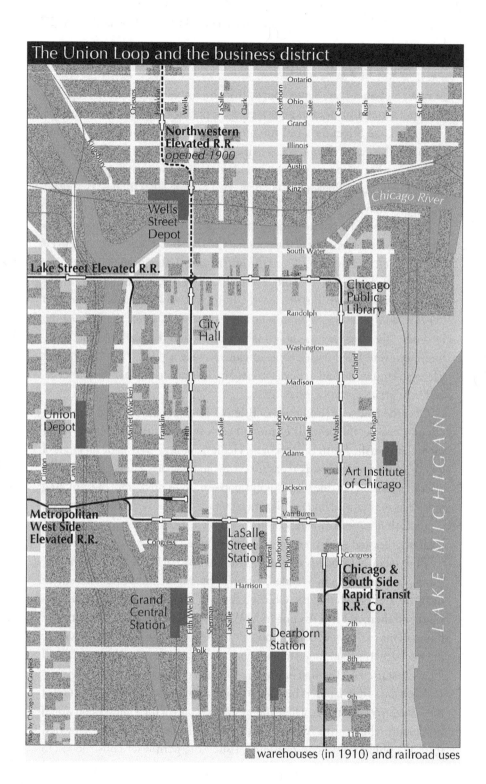

The Union Loop and the business district

Orleans
Franklin
Wells
LaSalle
Clark
Dearborn
State
Cass
Rush
Pine
St Clair

Ontario
Ohio
Grand
Illinois
Austin
Kinzie

Northwestern Elevated R.R. *opened 1900*

Wells Street Depot

Chicago River

South Water

Lake Street Elevated R.R.

Lake

Chicago Public Library

City Hall

Randolph

Washington

Garland

Market (Wacker)
Franklin
Fifth
LaSalle
Clark
Dearborn
State
Wabash
Michigan

Madison

Union Depot

Monroe

Adams

Art Institute of Chicago

Clinton
Canal

Jackson

Van Buren

Metropolitan West Side Elevated R.R.

Congress

LaSalle Street Station

Federal
Dearborn
Plymouth

Congress

Chicago & South Side Rapid Transit R.R. Co.

Harrison

7th

Grand Central Station

Fifth (Wells)
Sherman
LaSalle
Clark

Dearborn Station

Polk

8th

9th

11th

LAKE MICHIGAN

Map by Chicago CartoGraphics

warehouses (in 1910) and railroad uses

begin on the final section along Van Buren Street, including the curves that would connect it with the sections on Wabash and Fifth. It was the curve connecting Van Buren and Fifth that, completed on January 30, 1897, was the final piece of the elevated rectangle.

When finished, the elevated Loop had 11,200 linear feet tracks composed of steel rails and wood ties treated with creosote. The tracks rode atop four steel beams, called stringers, with typically two stringers per track and two tracks in a span. These stringers were supported, at intervals of thirty to fifty feet, by bents. A bent consisted of two steel columns and a steel cross girder spanning between them and arching over the street. A bent weighed eight thousand pounds and was erected on the previously constructed foundations. Once two bents were built, stringers could be erected in the span between them.

The stringers and bents were connected firmly together with a multitude of rivets. Under the process, a small cylindrical piece of steel was heated to incandescence at street level and tossed to a worker high on the structure. The worker caught it in midair with a funnel-like metal container or a thick glove, similar to a catcher's mitt. The red-hot piece was inserted through the precisely prepared and aligned holes in two or more steel plates. It was then hammered through the holes, forming the domelike shape of a rivet head. As the rivet cooled, it shrank and brought the connected steel plates tightly together.

"A lot of small pieces of steel were put together to make an overall lattice-work kind of structure," said George Krambles, the general manager of the Chicago Transit Authority (CTA), in a 1977 interview. "The steel columns that support the structure and the girders that run underneath the tracks also have this zigzag type of construction." In a way, Krambles said, building the elevated Loop was like putting together a jigsaw puzzle. "Back in the 1890s, when labor was cheaper than materials, it was economical to build this way because it saved on steel. Today it would just be too expensive to have iron-workers fitting all those little pieces together."

On Van Buren, the columns for the bents were set into the sidewalks, giving the structure a width of fifty-two feet over the street and providing free passage of up to four lanes of traffic. But shop owners along Lake, Wabash, and Fifth didn't want their sidewalks blocked, so the columns there were constructed in the street, twenty-four feet apart, allowing two lanes of traffic under the structure, as well as a parking lane between the columns and the sidewalk curbs. Once the final curve was completed, officials hoped to have passenger trains operating on the tracks in three months, but instead, because of legal disputes, workforce troubles, and contract negotiations with the three elevated companies, it took until October 3.

From the start, the structure was a major presence in the central business district, unique then as it is now, distinctive and unavoidable, as an industrial scholar wrote nearly eighty years later: "The Union Loop, a massive web of riveted steel girders and shining tracks, arches over busy city streets, passing close by the windows of tall buildings on either side, and insistently threads its way through downtown Chicago."

In his Union Loop design, Waddell included many innovations, such as his decision to dispense with tower bents as supports for the columns. Tower bents or, as Waddell called them, "bracing towers" were in use at the time and remain in use today in many sections of Chicago's elevated track structures outside of downtown, as well as elsewhere in the nation. Typically located twice per city block, tower bents reinforce the columns with diagonal and horizontal bracing. Picture an X between the columns, with a steel piece across the bottom just above ground level and a stringer or another steel piece across the top. This bracing arrangement is used from column to column within a bent and from bent to bent, thus creating a kind of box or tower of support, hence the name tower bent.

In a structure without tower bents, an accelerating or decelerating train causes the platform to sway in ways that are felt by passengers. However, if Waddell had included these bracing towers downtown, generations of Chicagoans would not have had the ease and freedom that they have enjoyed in walking—jaywalking—readily midblock from one side of the street to the other under the Loop structure. Waddell determined that the compactness of the Union Loop made the tower bents unnecessary. Since the distances between the stations were small, trains didn't develop much speed going from one to the next and, as a result, generated less sway in the structure.

Nonetheless, to a young visitor from downstate Galesburg, Carl Sandburg, the future poet and Abraham Lincoln biographer, the elevated Loop seemed to shudder with the passing trains: "I walked every block in the Loop, watched the frameworks of the Elevated lines shake and tremble and half expected a train to tumble down to the street." The structure, however, never did actually "shake and tremble" in a manner that a passerby could see because Waddell had designed the four corners of the Loop rectangle to absorb what stresses the moving trains did generate. Even so, those stresses were—and are—still felt at the corners of the Loop, as James Harper, present-day chief engineer for the CTA, explains: "In the Loop, longitudinal loads are absorbed by the four corners of the Loop, but some of these forces actually ripple around the entire Loop. When a train comes into Wells and Lake, you can feel it at the [junction] tower at the other corner of the Loop."

"Radically Wrong"

Waddell had never before designed an elevated railroad structure, so in July 1894, when he was hired by Yerkes to draw up plans for the Union Loop and the seven-mile-long Northwestern Elevated Company line, he launched on a thorough study of the methods and principles employed for elevated roads. The result was a fourteen-thousand-word paper Waddell presented on February 17, 1897, to the American Society of Civil Engineers at its meeting in New York City, which—no surprise to anyone familiar with the uproar in Japan—took the entire industry to task. Indeed, it sparked forty-one thousand words of comments and critiques by thirty-four other engineers, which, in turn, spurred Waddell to devote twenty-six thousand words to rebuttal. In all, the controversy prompted nearly ninety thousand words of discussion, or just a little fewer than are in this book.

Never one to pull his punches, Waddell began his paper by noting, in his second sentence, "For some years the author had felt that the methods in vogue for constructing elevated railroads were radically wrong." Indeed, later in his paper, he added, "The results of this investigation, made by the author and his assistants by examining the principal elevated roads of the East and those then in operation in Chicago, as far as the designing of metalwork is concerned, amount simply to the accumulation of a great mass of information exemplifying 'how not to do it.'"

In what he termed "an exhaustive discussion," Waddell looked at just about every aspect of the question, such as the loads that were carried by an elevated train, the proper system for bracing an elevated structure, the type of wooden floor for a platform, the fashioning of rivets and rivet holes, and on and on. For instance, he asserted that carelessness in punching a rivet hole often left the opening too small, and that it didn't help to enlarge the hole with a rotary cutting tool, called a reamer. Indeed, he proclaimed, "the use of a tapered, flexibly connected reamer is all humbug."

Among the "faulty details" of existing elevated structures, Waddell argued that there weren't enough rivets and there were too many expansion joints. The technique of setting a cross girder unattached onto two free-standing columns was "extremely faulty," and the reasoning behind it "fallacious." He noted that the lack of adequate bracing on elevated structures, particularly in New York, meant that platforms would shimmy and wobble, even when a train was still far away: "The practical effects of this fault can be seen to best advantage by standing on one of the high platforms of one of the elevated railroads in New York City. The vibration, by no means small, from an approaching train can be felt when it is yet a great distance. Some may claim that this vibration is not injurious; but they are certainly wrong." In fact, later, responding to his critics, Waddell expanded on this point:

> If anyone doubts the advantages of putting a little extra metal into the columns and fixing them at both top and bottom, let him stand for a while on one of the platforms of the Union Elevated Loop of Chicago and note the vibration, then try the same experiment on a number of elevated railroads of New York and Brooklyn, and compare the results.
>
> He would probably be considerably surprised; for he would find hardly a tremor on the Chicago road, while on some of the Eastern roads the vibration would be so great as almost to prevent him from writing legibly in a note-book.

What especially angered Waddell was that the manufacturers provided shoddy materials and workmanship, no matter what the designs for an elevated structure called for. One manufacturer told him, "It has been hitherto the general opinion that almost any kind of structure in respect to design, quality of material, and workmanship will suffice for an elevated railroad." Another, presented with Waddell's plans and specifications, complained, "Why, your requirements in regard to details and workmanship are as rigid as if you were about to build a railroad bridge." To which Waddell responded, "Yes. I consider this structure to be just as important as any railroad bridge ever built."

In contrast to the aggrieved replies of the English engineers to Waddell's book on Japanese railroads, the experts who weighed in on his elevated-railroad paper respectfully discussed in great detail many of his points. Nonetheless, Waddell used his rebuttal to their comments to elaborate on one of his themes and open a new area of discussion. Stepping back from the mass of details that his paper and the responses had dealt with, Waddell made a sweeping assertion: "The true reason why elevated railroads have been so unscientifically designed in the past is that, as a rule, the designing has been left almost exclusively to the manufacturing companies, which being more interested in profits than in anything else, naturally detailed the metal-work so as to have it go through the shops quickly and erect readily; and all considerations of scientific design appear to have been ignored because of these requirements."

The proof of this, he wrote, was what happened to him in Chicago. When contracts were being let for the first leg of the Union Loop along Lake Street, as well as for the Northwestern Elevated, "the strongest kind of pressure," Waddell wrote, "was brought to bear upon the president of these companies to induce him to set aside the author's plans and specifications." Moreover, they sought to persuade him "to adopt others submitted by bidders on the plea that the latter were the same as those used for the New York and Brooklyn elevated railroads, which roads represented practically the *ne plus ultra* of both design and manufacture."

Technically, the president of the two companies was Delancey H. Louderback, the top aide to Charles Yerkes. However, in a case such as this, the final decision wouldn't have been Louderback's. It would have been up to Yerkes, and the financier stood behind the designer and his plans. As Waddell wrote, speaking of himself in the third person, "Thanks to the sound business policy of the president, [Waddell] was finally successful in having both his plans and his specifications adopted and adhered to."

⬅ 11. Inside and outside the Loop

Yone Noguchi, a young, enigmatic Japanese poet and friend of the San Francisco literati, found the deafening clamor of Chicago's downtown, especially the Union Loop elevated trains, hard to stomach. During a visit to the city in 1899–1900, Noguchi was astonished by the "dangerous procession of street cars—cars above my head, cars under my feet, cars everywhere" and proclaimed, "Chicago is the noisiest city in America!" Indeed, the twenty-five-year-old wrote, "If the most noisy place is hell—surely Chicago must be hell."

The Union Loop had been in operation for only two years, but from the start, it seemed to bring a particular shrillness to the cacophony of the city's central business district. Also writing in 1900, Albert Fleury, a French painter who had moved to Chicago twelve years earlier, noted that an artist visitor from back home experienced the noise, the constantly moving cable cars, and the elevated trains as "brutal, immense, overwhelming," leaving him with "the feeling of a nightmare." Fleury also offered his own observations: "The sky is of iron, and perpetually growls a rolling thunder; electric lights are emitting burning sparks; below are wagons of every size and kind, whose approach cannot be heard in the midst of the noises; and the cars, with jangling voices which never cease, cross and recross."

These oppressive metaphors would echo down the decades and continue today, as modern Chicagoans gripe about the rumble of an elevated train overhead interrupting their conversations on a downtown sidewalk. In 1947, Nelson Algren wrote about "the southbound El thunder[ing] its disdain overhead, plunging down the neon wilderness." Thirty years later, architect Harry Weese, a fan of the elevated Loop, said:

> The entire elevated structure vibrates and resonates. It's like a gigantic tuning fork. Then there's the direct sound produced by each elevated train, somewhat like a bass viol. The viol's strings are like the el car's wheels—the strings start vibrating, the wheels start vibrating, and the sound travels through the bridge to this resonant box, the car. . . . In my order of sound, I say the squeal is worst. The click is more annoying than the rumble; it just keeps clicking. The el roar swells up like thunder and then goes away. You can adapt to the roar.

Such harsh, dissonant, invasive, inescapable sound was high on the list of reasons that critics sought to have the elevated Loop torn down—even before it went into service. Three weeks before the city's elevated lines began carrying passengers around the Union Loop, Colonel Richard Price Morgan, identified as "the father of the elevated railway," told the *Tribune* that the city was sustaining a great injury by letting the structure obstruct downtown streets. The reporter, whose newspaper had published its own complaints a week earlier, noted, "It is no news to the Chicago public that the Union Loop structure, with its noise and jar, its midnight at noontime under it, and above all its supporting columns, cutting off nearly two-thirds of the roadways, is a tremendous and all-pervading nuisance."

It wasn't just that the harsh sounds were unmelodious, according to the 1909 *Plan of Chicago*. They also cut into productivity. "Noises, ugly sights, ill smells, as well as dirty streets and workshops or offices, tend to lower average efficiency," argued the *Plan*, coauthored by Daniel H. Burnham and Edward H. Bennett and published by the Commercial Club of Chicago. And nothing was as bad as the noise of the elevated trains and the streetcars in the central business district, which the influential urban-planning document described as "excruciating." Indeed, the report went so far as to call such harsh dissonance "evil." Even so, the radical reshaping of Chicago's landscape, particularly its downtown, that the *Plan* envisioned didn't call for tearing down the cacophonous steel structure, the source of so much "evil."

Instead, the *Plan* proposed quadrupling the Union Loop in size.

"No Single Factor in the History of Chicago"

The *Plan of Chicago* wasn't the first voice to call for expanding the amount of land bounded by the elevated tracks, although all previous proponents had sought a much less extravagant increase of the area inside the Union Loop. Despite the complaints about the noise and obstruction, and despite the periodic demands for demolition of the elevated structure—which continued for decades—many civic leaders, particularly those in real estate, argued that a larger Union Loop would be a huge benefit for Chicago. And make some well-positioned businessmen a lot of money.

To understand this, it's necessary to go back many years, well before the elevated rectangle was completed and put into operation. Chicago real estate dealers were acutely aware that new transportation lines, no matter the type, had a direct impact on land development. In January 1884, for instance, two years after the inauguration of cable car service linking the South Side and downtown, a *Tribune* story pointed out that property values along that Chicago

City Railway line had increased in value. Seven years later, in discussing a proposal to replace the cable company's loop in the central district with one on a different route, a railway official said, "The scheme will help real estate around the [company's] loop, with a tendency towards developing retail spaces on Randolph street and Wabash avenue."

Once Charles Yerkes successfully negotiated the agreement of the city's elevated lines to build what came to be called the Union Loop, speculation began to focus on the impact that the structure would have on the value of real estate in the central business district. Work was underway in late 1895 on the extension of the Lake Street line to Wabash Avenue, the northern section of the loop, but nothing had started yet on the other three sides. In fact, word had just leaked out that Yerkes would set the location of the southern section along Van Buren Street, instead of farther to the south along Harrison Street, sparking his head-to-head showdown with Levi Z. Leiter.

On October 30, an ad hoc group of West Side leaders stepped into the middle of that fracas to urge the use of Van Buren, arguing that extending the loop to Harrison would hamper business growth in their area. The reason: real estate dealers, investors, and other businesspeople expected that the elevated loop would form the borders of Chicago's central business district, determining how future development downtown would proceed. The farther south the loop extended, the more new construction would be concentrated in that direction, meaning less growth to the west.

The *Tribune* reported that at the meeting of West Siders, former alderman Oscar M. Brady predicted that the elevated loop would boost the value of property inside the rectangle of tracks by 50 to 100 percent, adding, "He thought it obvious enough to every one that, if the loop ran on Harrison street, the business district of the South Side soon would be extended that far, and all the business that formed that extension would be subtracted from the actual growth of the West Side. On the other hand, if the business district was confined by running the loop on Van Buren street, the business district would spread westward instead of southward."

For two years before the Union Loop went into operation, the real estate market in the central business district was at a standstill. For one thing, the location of the loop's southern section was up in the air for months. Even though Yerkes won the city's approval for the line on Van Buren in July 1896, he was tied up in the courts by Leiter until October, when he got the go-ahead from the Illinois Supreme Court. For another, everyone expected property values within the loop to rise in value, but no one was sure how great that increase would be. For instance, in late December 1895, a *Tribune* reporter wrote, "Many capitalists are postponing intended investments until the effects of this improvement are more determined." Four months later, Owen F. Aldis, a prominent real estate dealer and an owner of property along Wabash Avenue, said, "Down-town real estate and rents will be greatly benefited by the loop in my opinion. . . . Within the loop all property will undoubtedly be increased in value, and rents may be raised as a result. Outside business will be greatly retarded in its growth."

Property owners, investors, and potential buyers were holding their breath. The owners of land in the area encompassed by the steel-and-wood rectangle were "not anxious to sell unless at prices much above the actual value at the present time," reported the *Tribune* a year before the Union Loop went into service.

Once elevated trains were running along the Union Loop, the structure's impact was immediately evident. Businesses wanted to be inside the loop rectangle, and they were willing to pay to get there. Indeed, they competed for spots in the thirty-nine city blocks encompassed by the structure, driving up rents and sales prices. Looking back four years later, a *Tribune* reporter wrote:

> It is an entirely safe statement to make that no single factor in the history of Chicago has operated to draw lines of property demarcation so sharply as has the loop, with the "magic circle," as it is frequently called, having generally come to be recognized as making the division between inside and outside property. Not to the extent, of course, of placing property just outside it in the same class with that two or more blocks away, but a definite line it certainly has established to the detriment of contiguous outside property, and to the corresponding advantage of property just inside.

This was clearly illustrated by a real estate deal involving Leiter a year after the Union Loop went into operation. Since 1892, the Siegel, Cooper & Co. department store had been renting Leiter's building on State Street, from Van Buren to Congress Street. But now, just as Leiter had feared, the location was deemed inadequate because it was just outside the "magic circle" of the elevated tracks. So Siegel executives spent the fall of 1898 vigorously working to arrange a move to one of three corners in the area encompassed by the loop structure—the northwest corner of State and Monroe Streets or either the southeast or southwest corner of State and Adams Streets.

That, however, would have left Leiter high and dry, holding an empty eight-story structure that covered half of a city block in what was thought of as an undesirable location. So a month later, Leiter gave the store a new lease at a reduced rent. Instead of paying $2.65 million over the next ten years, the store's rent would be only $2 million. That meant a total savings of $650,000, or the equivalent of just under $20 million in today's dollars.

The drama was replayed nine years later, when Siegel, Cooper & Co. spent many months making plans to move to an in-loop spot on State Street between Washington and Randolph Streets. Leiter had died three years earlier, but his estate gave the department store a similar sweetheart deal—a twenty-five-year lease at only a "small advance" over the $200,000 the firm had been paying. That lease would have continued until 1937, but Siegel, Cooper & Co., evidently the victim of its parent company's financial mismanagement, went under in May 1918. Its outside-the-loop location probably didn't contribute much, if anything, to the store's demise. Fourteen years later, the building became the flagship store for Sears, Roebuck & Co., which prospered there for more than half a century.

"The Himalaya Mountain Peaks of the Loop"

Following the Union Loop's construction and in the decades since, entrepreneurs, real estate investors, visitors, government officials, and scholars have groped for metaphors to describe the impact of the elevated structure on the central business district. "A steel girdle around the business section" is how geographer Harold M. Mayer and historian Richard C. Wade describe the elevated Loop in their 1969 book, *Chicago: Growth of a Metropolis*, adding that "it unmistakably defined the core of Chicago's central business district and identified the desirable and prestigious locations." In his 1996 book *City of the Century*, Donald L. Miller writes that the Union Loop created "one of the most densely packed commercial cores on earth."

The Union Loop and the quarter square mile that it enclosed "is the heart of Chicago, the knot in the steel arteries of elevated structure which pump in a ceaseless stream the three millions of population of the city into and out of the central business district," wrote Harvey Warren Zorbaugh, a University of Chicago sociologist, in 1929.

Data compiled by Homer Hoyt for his classic of urban history, *One Hundred Years of Land Values in Chicago*, show that in 1892, the value of the property in the city's greater downtown—the one and a half square miles bounded by Lake Michigan, the main and south channels of the Chicago River, and Roosevelt Road—was $350 million, or 23 percent of the land value in the whole of Chicago. Two decades later, in 1910, after the construction of the elevated Loop in the center of that greater downtown, land was worth $600 million. What that meant was that despite a series of several national recessions, the central business district now represented 40 percent of the city total.

Indeed, according to Hoyt, the new elevated lines and the Union Loop boosted retail business on State Street to such an extent that despite an "otherwise extreme depression," land values there actually rose somewhat. In fact, in 1906, the *Economist* asserted that there was "nothing in the world so valuable as State Street frontage." Hoyt has his own metaphor for this dominance of the central business district, centered on the area inside the elevated Loop: "If the land values in Chicago were shown in the form of a relief map, in which the elevations represented high land value, a picture of startling contrasts would be disclosed. In the center would be the Himalaya Mountain peaks of the Loop, but on all sides except along the high ridge running north along the lake, there would be a descent into the deep valleys of the blighted areas."

Those metaphorical heights were mirrored by the construction of scores of new skyscrapers and other tall buildings inside—and outside—the Union Loop tracks. In fact, according to George E. Hooker, the civic secretary of the City Club of Chicago, not only was the property inside the elevated rectangle valuable, but it was also intensely crowded *because* it was valuable. In a report to the Second National Conference on City Planning and the Problems of Congestion, held in Rochester, New York, in 1910, Hooker wrote that probably no other city in the world had so many "important social functions" crowded into such a small space as Chicago did in its downtown:

> Within an area of less than a square mile [which included the land within the Union Loop and the land around it] there are found the railway terminals and business offices, the big retail stores, the wholesale and jobbing business, the financial center, the main offices of the chief firms of the city, a considerable portion of the dental and medical professions, the legal profession, the city and county government, the post office, the courts, the leading social and political clubs, the hotels, theatres, Art Institute, principal libraries, the labor headquarters, and a great number of lesser factors of city life.

By contrast, Hooker wrote, such businesses and services were "scattered" along a three-mile stretch from the Bowery to Fifty-Ninth Street in New York, along a two-mile line from Copley Square to North Station in Boston, and along the four miles between Victoria Station and Aldgate Pump in London.

Chicago's central business district, as it evolved and grew after the Great Fire of 1871, was contained in the area bounded by the natural barriers of the lake and the river, as well as by the dense collection of railroad yards south of Harrison Street. Although there was still plenty of room for new buildings, similar businesses tended to want to group together, as geographer Michael P. Conzen notes: "Retail shopping focused north-south along State Street (following the establishment there of Marshall Field's great department store immediately after the fire), finance to the west along LaSalle street, hotels and cultural institutions on the east facing the lake along Michigan Avenue, and a government precinct around City Hall in the northwestern sector." As a result, landowners with sought-after locations saw the development of the skyscraper in the 1880s as a way to boost their profits. According to historian Donald L. Miller, the skyscraper wasn't simply an attractive addition to a city's skyline but also "a machine for turning land into money."

With the opening of the Union Loop, the most valuable and most profitable real estate was suddenly within the circuit of its tracks. Investors and business owners wanted to be located within this "golden circle," and anyone erecting a building wanted it to be able to serve as many people as possible. "The great value of Chicago down-town ground encourages these monstrous structures which resemble towers more than buildings," the *Tribune* wrote in 1902. The result was congestion upon congestion, as Hooker explained:

> When it was found that the high building, with its excellence in general appointments, promised better returns on the price of the lot than a low one, the prices of lots mounted. This rise has been in many cases startling, not to say fabulous.
>
> Such a rise in value means that a given lot is predestined to that much more intensive occupation in order to pay income on that value. The purchaser, under the plea of an innocent holder and of vested interests, insists upon his right to put the land to that use, and does so. In other words, the district suffers from the operation of a vicious circle, in which an increased value arises from an increased density of occupation and an increased density of occupation from increased value.

A total of eighty-seven buildings of 10 or more floors, all served by the nearby Union Loop, were erected in the greater central business district between 1898 and 1927. Forty-three of those, averaging 17.5 floors per structure, were constructed in the area encompassed by the Union Loop. The other forty-four, averaging 16 floors, went up in the outer parts of the central business district. While nearly the same number of skyscrapers were built inside the Union Loop as outside of its tracks, those inside were taller and crowded more closely together.

The owners of the buildings within the "magic circle" benefited from being cheek by jowl with many other businesses, as well as being in the middle of the thick pedestrian streams of shoppers, office workers, and tourists. It was cheaper to erect a tall building outside of the elevated Loop, but the structure would be more isolated. For that reason, most of the forty-four in the outer area—which covered more than five times as much land as inside the rectangle of tracks—were clustered as close to the elevated Loop as possible.

Between 1893 and 1901, the maximum height allowed by the City Council yo-yoed—from 130 feet up to 155 feet, then back down to 130 feet again, and then up to 180 feet. Architectural historian Thomas Leslie writes that "two objections to skyscrapers had gained traction in political circles: tall buildings increased fire problems, and their bulk deprived neighboring lots and streets of sunlight and fresh air." While such concerns were legitimate, he observes that "they tended to be voiced by aldermen who benefited from a greater spread of high land values."

Alderman William Mavor, who introduced the ordinance in 1901 to increase the height limit, told his colleagues, "The limitation to ten stories [130 feet] was a mistake, made when the Council was trying to check the tendency to congestion in the down-town district." A year later, as the nation and Chicago began to come out of a decade of hard economic times, "the City responded to pleas from developers by raising the limit to 260 feet [about 20 stories]," Leslie writes. Nine years after that, the limit was dropped to 200 feet, and then in 1921, it was again raised to 260 feet.

Within the Union Loop rectangle, new office buildings of all sizes tended to be constructed near each other, as data collected by social scientist Earl Shepard Johnson show. Between 1895 and 1915, most of the construction of office buildings within the Union Loop (fifty-one of seventy-one) took place along its eastern edge, between Dearborn Street and Wabash Avenue, and through its center, between Madison and Monroe Streets. Over the next twenty years, the majority of new office buildings (twenty-seven of thirty-eight) were erected along the western boundary of the elevated Loop, between Clark and Wells Streets.

Yet if some saw the elevated Loop as a "magic circle," Hoyt notes that for others, it was "a Chinese Wall" that blocked growth of the downtown. "It is a notorious fact," wrote Julian Street, less than twenty years after the Union Loop went into operation, "that the business and shopping district of Chicago is at present strangled by the elevated railroad loop, which bounds the center of the city." That sentiment was echoed by a *Tribune* reporter who wrote in 1911, "Without any good or sufficient reason, this iron ban came to be accepted as marking the line of demarcation between desirable and undesirable property in the business district. . . . A general belief prevailed among business men that a location outside the loop was the indubitable evidence of business inferiority and decadence, and, as a result, it was shunned by many merchants who at the same time groaned at the high and advancing rents they were compelled to pay for locations inside the 'magic circle.'"

In fact, such complaints were somewhat exaggerated. For instance, the *Tribune* reporter's diatribe came in a story about how construction was starting to occur outside the tracks of the loop, in part because it was easier to find property there and cheaper as well. Although the majority of office building construction between 1895 and 1915 was inside the Union Loop, Johnson's figures show that twenty-two were erected in an area east of the tracks—bordered by Wabash Avenue, Randolph Street, Michigan Avenue, and Van Buren Street. Similarly, in the next two decades, a cluster of thirteen office buildings was constructed in the five-block area northeast of the elevated Loop.

"Tightly Girdled within Itself"

Although the elevated Loop was "designed to afford magnificent relief to the town," it had "drawn a belt about its waist," complained writer-businessman Edward Hungerford in 1913, adding, "the loop has acted against the growth of the city, has kept it tightly girdled within itself." Well, then, why not get a bigger girdle? That was, essentially, the question that entrepreneurs, business leaders, and real estate investors had been asking since the turn of the century.

In August 1901, real estate dealer Frederick S. Oliver wrote a column in the *Tribune* calling for an extension of the southern section of the Union Loop to Harrison Street, an increase in the land encompassed by the tracks by a third. Five months later, Alderman James Patterson introduced a resolution in the City Council to extend the elevated Loop even farther south to Polk Street. This would have increased the amount of land enclosed by the elevated structure by 50 percent.

Real estate dealers heartily endorsed Patterson's plan. "An extension of the loop to Polk street would be beneficial all around," said Joseph Donnersberger, a former president of the Chicago real estate board. "The area within the loop now is altogether too restricted for the amount of business transacted." W. D. Kerfoot, who had been selling land in Chicago for nearly half a century, said, "Once the extension was made, it would help all property within the loop, change the character of Clark street completely, and relieve the awful congestion of business in the down-town district."

Yet for anyone dealing in property sales, whether buying or selling, an expansion of the elevated Loop wasn't really about congestion. It was about making money, as W. A. Merigold, another veteran real estate man, acknowledged: "The sooner the extension is made to Polk street, the better it will be for all kinds of business within the loop. In the past the increase in values on down-town property has benefited the few, but others would come in for their share when the change was made. Everybody, in fact, would be benefited."

Not exactly everybody, however. Take the business owner operating a department store within the boundaries of the Union Loop. It would be clear that adding more land to the blocks encompassed by the elevated structure would open up new areas for development and new businesses that would compete with the merchant's firm for customers. Similarly, the owners of property or a building within the elevated Loop would know that any expansion of that loop would increase the value of the property in the added area—and would reduce or, at the very least, limit the increase in the value of their own real estate. In both cases, the store owner and the property or building owners would be hurt financially and unlikely to welcome the idea.

The Patterson proposal was still being debated four months later, but by that time, it was one of several ideas for addressing the congestion of the elevated trains. A second idea was to double-deck the elevated Loop. A third proposed adding a section of elevated tracks between Wells Street and Wabash Avenue on Monroe Street to create, in essence, two loops in the same amount of space. A fourth, backed by Mayor Carter Harrison II, would have extended the elevated Loop all the way to Taylor Street, doubling the size of the land inside its tracks.

A committee of the owners of land south of Van Buren Street was organized to lobby for a loop extension to Polk or Taylor, but by October 1902, they had to concede they were stymied. General F. H. Winston, the committee chair, said the group had decided to abandon any more efforts on stretching the elevated Loop to Taylor, and would focus instead on Polk. However, the committee also acknowledged that the Metropolitan Elevated, one of the four companies operating on the Union Loop, was "not at all friendly to the extension," because earlier in the year, it had spent $770,000 for property for a separate terminal for part of its traffic. Although never spelled out, it appears that the four elevated companies would have been expected to pay for any extension.

The committee seems to have given up fairly soon after this. Nonetheless, real estate dealers continued to lobby throughout the rest of the century's first decade for an extension. And in 1909, the much-ballyhooed *Plan of Chicago*, made public on the Fourth of July, must have seemed the answer to their prayers. Known as the Burnham Plan, for its primary author, Daniel H. Burnham, the document was a milestone in city planning—the first attempt to create a comprehensive blueprint for a city and its region and a model for such documents for municipalities and other governments, large and small, worldwide. Indeed, historian Carl Smith writes that it was the single most important step in the development of urban planning and in the recognition that an essential role of municipal government is to anticipate, plan for, and shape the future.

And it was a beautiful object in and of itself. "As carefully thought out as it is, the *Plan of Chicago* makes its first appeal to the senses, not the mind," writes Smith. "Like many of D. H. Burnham and Company's buildings, it exudes a forthright and foursquare gravitas." The *Plan*'s main text of 124 pages is adorned with dozens of gorgeous illustrations of Chicago, not as it was in 1909 but as it might become. "[Fernand] Janin's hushed black-and-tan elevation of the Civic Center folds out to reveal a vision of an ideal neoclassical cityscape dominated by an elongated dome forty or more stories high that dwarfs the other significant structures supporting and surrounding it," notes Smith. "[Jules] Guerin's skill with a limited but expressive range of color—mainly from pastel beiges and blues to deep violet and brown—and with perspective leads us into a more serenely civilized place than we have ever known."

For the past century, the *Plan* has been the roadmap for reshaping the city and its region—from the creation of North Michigan Avenue and the construction of Wacker Drive to the establishment of the Cook County Forest Preserve District, from the widening of scores of streets to the building of Navy Pier. Burnham's plan played a key role, along with the efforts of mail order magnate Montgomery Ward, in developing Grant Park as the city's front yard and in converting nearly the entire length of its 30-mile lakefront into public land available for anyone to use.

But the *Plan*'s proposal to radically expand the size of the Union Loop received little or no attention when it was published nor very much mention over the next hundred-plus years. That's surprising, since it really was radical. On page seventy-three of the *Plan*, Burnham and Bennett—and the Commercial Club—envisioned a new elevated Loop that would run along Canal Street on the west, Thirteenth Street on the south, Wabash Avenue on the east, and Lake Street on the north. Gone would be the portion of the Union Loop along Fifth Avenue (now Wells Street) and Van Buren Street. Instead of the elevated Loop encompassing a quarter-square-mile area, it would have enclosed a full square mile of land—quadrupling the real estate benefiting from the loop's embrace. In part, the proposal was aimed at bringing the elevated Loop near to—but not too close to—the Civic Center, the new central focus of the city that Burnham envisioned at Halsted and Congress Streets.

Even more, it was part of Burnham's effort to give the downtown room to grow and "maintain the Loop's business dominance over the city and region," according to urban historian James T. Lemon. "In short," he added, "the plan's key concern was to strengthen the centre to encourage office development and alleviate congestion." Chicago's central business district was "distinctive" because "unlike New York and London, Chicago's CBD did not split into two. The plan would open the way for an even more extensive central district, not a new major secondary one."

Chicago's investors, business leaders, and government officials—who would be the ones who ultimately had the responsibility to put the *Plan*'s proposals into action—were all for making the downtown as strong as possible. They endorsed and brought to fruition, for instance, the *Plan*'s proposal to replace the ugly, crowded South Water Market Street along the southern shore of the Chicago River's main channel with a double-decker roadway that allowed delivery trucks to bring their merchandise to the basements of buildings, relieving some congestion at street level. This new street, completed in 1926, was named for Charles H. Wacker, who played a key role in promoting and enacting many of the *Plan*'s provisions. Two decades later, work began on a north-south extension of Wacker Drive along what had been Market Street to Harrison Street, thus achieving one of Burnham's goals of providing a way to get around the central business district without going through it. This project was easy for the power elite to like because it made business easier, more efficient, and more profitable.

But the idea of expanding the elevated Loop all the way to Canal and Thirteenth Streets was part of what might be called the fantasy element of the Burnham Plan. Anyone glancing at the two beautiful Guerin watercolors inserted between pages 108 and 109 of the *Plan* would notice something striking. The two scenes depict areas south and west of the central business district—with every building except for the forty-story Civic Center of equal height. It was as if Burnham were trying to replicate the radical renovation of Paris that Baron Georges-Eugène Haussmann carried out between 1853 and 1870.

Never in the *Plan* is Chicago's forest of downtown skyscrapers shown, and as these two images suggest, Burnham seemed to be arguing that skyscrapers had no place in the new areas to be developed inside and beyond the expanded elevated Loop. This was part of Burnham's vision for Chicago as it might become, but it certainly wasn't Chicago as it was in 1909. Chicago entrepreneurs had extensively displayed their desire to maximize the use of their land to the nth degree by building as high as their money and the market and the law would permit them. They weren't likely to sit still for the sort of regimented height displayed on these pages. Moreover, anyone owning property or operating a business inside the quarter square mile encompassed by the elevated Loop was even less likely to endorse a quadrupling of the loop's footprint than they were to agree to extend the southern section to Taylor Street, Polk Street, or even Harrison Street.

The *Plan's* idea for this extreme expansion of the elevated Loop was probably dead on arrival. Nonetheless, in 1911, the elevated Loop expansion was included in the 137-page *Wacker's Manual of the Plan of Chicago*, written by publicist Walter D. Moody and named for Wacker, the first chair of the Chicago Plan Commission. The *Manual* was designed to be a not-so-subtle piece of propaganda used in civics classes through Chicago's public and private schools to explain the need for bringing the *Plan's* provisions to reality.

Moody, Wacker, and the rest of the *Plan's* boosters knew that implementation of the document would take decades and that today's schoolchildren would be tomorrow's voters. In addition, they expected the students to explain to their parents the importance of these improvements. Although a reprint of the *Manual* in 1915 included the loop expansion, it was gone from a revised edition, published the next year, never again to be seriously considered.

This charcoal drawing of the elevated tracks along Wabash Avenue is by
French artist Albert Fleury, who in 1900 wrote of the Loop, "The sky is of
iron, and perpetually growls a rolling thunder." Image and quote from *Brush
and Pencil* 6, no. 6 (1900): 277, 280.

The elevated Loop—
with its thicket of
girders rooted in the
street pavements, and
its mass looming over
pedestrians, and its
rumbles and screeches
crowding the open
air and penetrating
buildings along its
border—was a major
presence for anyone
downtown, as can be
seen in this postcard
image of Wabash
Avenue. Photo from
the collection of
Bruce G. Moffat.

The Union Loop was a rectangular bridge, linking in an unprecedented way the three parts of Chicago—the South Side, the West Side, and the North Side—and transforming the city into a unified whole. "Union Elevated Railroad: Union Loop, Wells, Van Buren, Lake Streets & Wabash Avenue, Chicago, Cook County, IL, 1968," *Historic American Engineering Record*, Library of Congress Prints and Photographs Division, Washington, DC, https://www.loc.gov/item/il0389/.

The elevated Loop, seen here from the intersection of its Lake Street (*foreground*) and Wells Street sections, is woven so deeply into the physical fabric of Chicago's central business district that it can't ever be seen in its entirety. "Union Elevated Railroad: Randolph-Wells Street Station, Randall & Wells Street, Chicago, Cook County, IL, 1968," *Historic American Engineering Record*, Library of Congress Prints and Photographs Division, Washington, DC, https://www.loc.gov/item/il0387/.

On a sunny day, the steel girders of the elevated Loop provide Chicago's downtown with the beauty of shifting shadows. Author's photo.

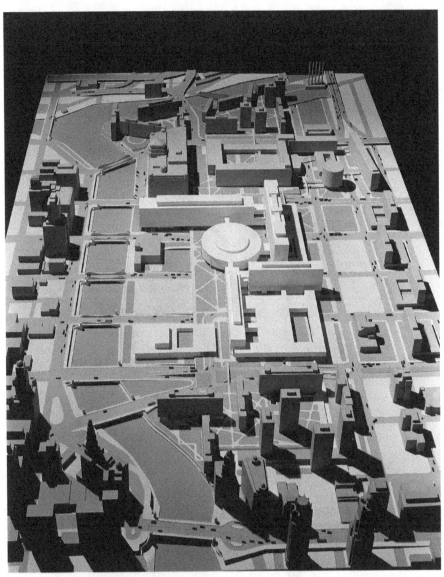

On March 16, 1954, officials and reporters gathered for the unveiling of this model of the Fort Dearborn Project, which, according to the *Chicago Tribune*, was "an architect's dream of what a modern city should be." If built, it would have been the death knell of the city's Loop. Chicago History Museum, Hedrich-Blessing Collection, HB-17153-F; Clayton Kirkpatrick, "Outline Vast Civic Center!," *Chicago Tribune*, March 17, 1954, 1.

For much of the twentieth century, there was no better place to be on a New Year's Eve than at State and Randolph Streets in the center of the Loop, where crowds, such as this one greeting the first day of 1937, could swell to 100,000 or even 150,000. 1937/*Chicago Tribune* Photo Archives/TNS.

John A. L. Waddell argued that earlier elevated structures shook and shimmied because of sloppy and inadequate riveting, so he designed the elevated Loop with myriad rivets tightly connecting its large and small steel plates. Author's photo.

"I would estimate that 75 percent of the original structures remain today," says James Harper, present-day chief engineer for the Chicago Transit Authority. Author's photo.

Only a decade old in about 1907, the elevated tracks, here on Wabash Avenue as seen from Monroe Street, had already become a visceral part of life in Chicago. "Wabash Ave., Chicago, Ill." (Detroit Publishing, ca. 1907), Library of Congress Prints and Photographs Division, Washington, DC, https://www.loc.gov/item/2016813806/.

After more than 120 years, the elevated Loop remains a looming presence in the city. Author's photo.

For more than a century, in its loud, gritty, ugly-duckling way, the elevated Loop has shaped and saved Chicago and has united the city, its region, and the vast, endlessly diverse collection of cultures, faiths, classes, races, incomes, dispositions, preoccupations, enthusiasms, ideologies, ages, and genders who call themselves Chicagoans. Photo by Steve Kagan.

← 12. The Name "Loop"

Hobart Chatfield-Taylor's book *Chicago*—published in December 1917, with evocative black-and-white illustrations by Lester G. Hornby—was a valedictory to his hometown. Chatfield-Taylor and his wife, Rose, major figures in Chicago's high society, were preparing to move to their newly built Italian villa in the Montecito area, just outside of Santa Barbara, California. Both had been born in Chicago and, although they traveled the world, had always been residents of the city and its wealthy northern suburbs. In fact, Rose was the daughter of Charles B. Farwell, who had served four terms in the U.S. House of Representatives for Chicago-area districts, and one term as U.S. senator from Illinois, while her uncle John had operated a major dry goods store in the downtown area for more than half a century, at one point taking on Marshall Field and Levi Z. Leiter as junior partners.

Chatfield-Taylor, now in his early fifties, was a gentleman writer who, because of an uncle's bequest, was independently wealthy. In the midst of the social whirl of balls, fetes, dinners, and masquerade parties, he found time to write—producing novels, histories, and biographies of seventeenth-century French playwright Molière and eighteenth-century Italian playwright Carlo Goldoni. Just two years earlier, he had joined with a small group of midwestern literati, including Hamlin Garland, Harriet Monroe, and Vachel Lindsay, to establish the Society of Midland Authors and was promptly named its first president.

Chicago was more than just a goodbye note to the city; it was also something of a billet-doux to a place that Chatfield-Taylor clearly loved. On its opening page, Chatfield-Taylor describes how he stood with the world-famous French actress Sarah Bernhardt on the balcony of a Chicago hotel, a year or two after the turn of the century: "The moon had laid a silver trail across the lake, the buildings of the city loomed shadowy in the night. Below us blazed the lights of Michigan Avenue; from its pavement came the rumble of many cabs speeding to places of revelry. A moment of silence had come to appease the fatigue of speaking in a foreign tongue; but it was broken by the surpassing woman beside me. 'I adore Chicago,' she exclaimed. 'It is the pulse of America.'"

The core of Chatfield-Taylor's book is its second chapter, "The Heart of Chicago," a paean to the city's lively, teeming, frantic downtown, known simply as the Loop—"a cauldron of human endeavor by day, a pleasure spot by night," and "literally, as well as metaphorically, the heart of the city." Chatfield-Taylor notes that, technically, the Loop is that part of the central business district that is "encircled by the ugly posts and girders of the elevated railways." But in fact, for him and for many, it was a term that could also be used to cover the areas around the elevated Loop structure.

It's an indication of the high respect with which the author regarded the Loop that he capitalized the word. For many decades, there was no consensus on whether to treat the word as a name and write it with an uppercase L or to consider it not "official" and therefore not worthy of the honor of capitalization. Indeed, the *Tribune* didn't start to capitalize the word when it referred to the downtown until the late 1940s, and even then, the capitalization wasn't consistent.

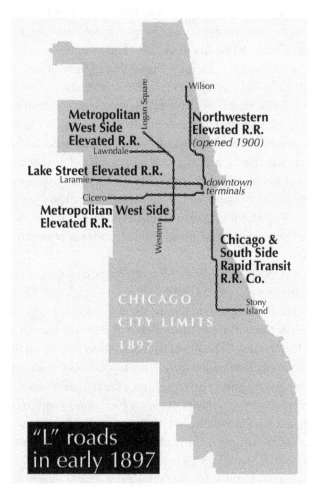

Metropolitan West Side Elevated R.R.

Northwestern Elevated R.R. *(opened 1900)*

Lake Street Elevated R.R.

Metropolitan West Side Elevated R.R.

Chicago & South Side Rapid Transit R.R. Co.

Wilson

Logan Square

Lawndale

Laramie

Cicero

Western

downtown terminals

Stony Island

CHICAGO CITY LIMITS 1897

"L" roads in early 1897

Ever since its incorporation, Chicago has been divided into three sections by the Chicago River, Chatfield-Taylor writes, noting that these sections "view each other askance and mingle but little." The Loop, however, "is a neutral land" where Chicagoans from the three sections

> transact business by day and enjoy themselves by night, and because the trains of the elevated railways run around it, instead of through it and out again, as they do into the Wall Street district of New York, it is called the "Loop." . . .
>
> When the office buildings and stores vomit them into the streets at nightfall, they hang to straps in surface, steam, or elevated cars, until they reach the houses and flats they designate as home; but no sooner is the soot washed from their faces than a goodly proportion of them hasten back to the Loop again, for here are the clubs, theatres, restaurants, and hotels, as well as the banks, offices and department stores.

Chatfield-Taylor was writing two decades after the opening of the Union Loop, and by this time, the name Loop had been firmly attached to Chicago's downtown. In the city's lexicon, Loop meant both the elevated Loop and the downtown—but most often, now, when it was used, it referred to the downtown. That's what Ernest Hemingway had in mind when he used the word "loop" as a synonym for "downtown" in his six-hundred-word "A Very Short Story." In the story's final sentence, he wrote, "A short time after, [the subject of the story] contracted gonorrhea from a sales girl in a loop department store while riding in a taxicab through Lincoln Park."

"I Call It *The Bean*, Too"

The naming of Chicago's central business district as the Loop didn't happen all at once. It was a progression in which hundreds of thousands of people took part, albeit without much conscious thought. From one perspective, this can be viewed as something unimportant that happened by accident. A quirk, a blip, a twitch in the history of the city.

On the contrary, the christening of the downtown as the Loop was extraordinarily significant to Chicago. The step-by-step evolution of the name wasn't a random fluke. Rather, it occurred because Chicagoans recognized—were, in a way, awed by—the impact of the new elevated Loop in their lives as a startlingly useful transportation system, as an unavoidable physical structure, and as a key dividing line between the center of wealth and activity and the rest of the city.

It's not that anyone sat down and decided that this would happen. A close look at the way the new name of Chicago's downtown emerged shows how the organism of a city responds to a sudden change in its physical and mental landscape—how the people of that city reorient themselves to new realities, including completely new travel patterns and completely new ways of deciding the value of real estate and completely new ways of seeing the city.

Most names, of course, are bestowed. Modern Americans, for instance, are given their names by parents at the hospital where they are born. A new high school is usually given the name of some local, national, or international hero. A land developer sets up a network of streets within a subdivision and gives each a name. Such names, however, don't necessarily remain forever. Marion Morrison is an example of the many actors who take stage names—in his case, John Wayne. Similarly, Natalie Hershlag became Natalie Portman.

Not all schools keep the names with which they're christened. On July 17, 1927, Chicago labor leaders gathered to dedicate a new elementary school at 123rd and State Streets in honor of Samuel Gompers, the first president of the American Federation of Labor. Unions and their members were a major political force in the United States at that time, so giving the school the Gompers name was a smart political move. More than eight decades later, labor was much weaker, and the African American vote in Chicago was crucial. So in 2014, the Gompers name was stripped off the school in favor of Jesse Owens, the black track star who had won four gold medals at the 1936 Olympics in Berlin. Another school, just a block south of Gompers, had been named for Owens, a major hero in Chicago's African American community, but it had been among forty-nine underutilized schools closed by the Chicago Board of Education.

Yet another example of name-changing occurred in Chicago in the early twentieth century. Between 1880 and 1900, Chicago's population more than tripled—from 503,185 to 1,698,575. Much of that population growth was achieved through nineteen annexations, in which such towns and villages as Hyde Park, Rogers Park, Austin, Norwood Park, and Lake View were added to the city. This caused a problem, however—a multiplicity of duplicate street names. For instance, in 1901, Chicago had nine Sheridan Streets, nine Forest Streets, ten Oak Streets, thirteen Washington Streets, thirteen Center Streets, and fourteen Park Streets. So over the next three decades, Edward Brennan, a private citizen with the backing of the City Club of Chicago, spearheaded an effort that resulted in the renaming of hundreds of city streets to eliminate duplications.

All these examples involve conscious choices. Sometimes, though, the public bestows a different name—on a work of art, for instance, or a building—and ignores the "official" name in favor of its own.

Consider the larger-than-life marble sculpture of a nude couple embracing that Auguste Rodin displayed publicly in 1898. He called it *Paolo and Francesca* because he was depicting the star-crossed thirteenth-century Italian lovers Francesca da Rimini and Paolo Malatesta. However, when *Paolo and Francesca* (also called *Francesca da Rimini*) was unveiled, the public gave it the name it's had ever since: *The Kiss*.

The same thing happened in Chicago between 2004 and 2006, when a 110-ton stainless-steel sculpture was being erected in the Millennium Park section of Grant Park, just east of the elevated Loop. The Indian-born British artist Anish Kapoor called his work *Cloud Gate*, but much to his initial irritation, the public decided, on its own, to call it *The Bean*, and in common parlance, at least, it's been *The Bean* ever since. In fact, so apt was the public's name for the work that in 2017, Kapoor acknowledged, "I call it *The Bean*, too."

The Bean and *The Kiss* illustrate instances when large numbers of individuals—thousands, hundreds of thousands—made a common decision without consulting one another, without even thinking very much about it. These artworks reverberated in the minds of viewers in such a similarly deep way that the name was called up, as if it had always been there. *The Bean*—well, it looks just like a huge stainless-steel bean. With the Rodin sculpture, when the first viewers looked at it, *The Kiss* seemed the only name for it. (This also happened with a sculpture that Rodin named *The Poet*. The public, though, has called it *The Thinker*.)

Pablo Picasso may have been on to something when, working on a commission from the architectural firm of Skidmore, Owings & Merrill, he completed the model for a 162-ton, 50-foot-tall sculpture to be erected in the plaza of the Chicago Civic Center, now known as the Richard J. Daley Center. The artist, who refused any payment for the sculpture, didn't give the work a name. But ever since its unveiling in 1967, it's been called *The Picasso*.

Names have power, and this is something that a company will try to capitalize on by bestowing its name onto a large, tall, impressive building. As cultural historian Neil Harris notes in *Building Lives: Constructing Rites and Passages*, "In the case of office buildings, the name can testify to the size, wealth, and prestige of a major corporation. Speculative structures frequently entice major tenants by the promise of naming the new building after them. As a major space-user, the renting corporation reaps the additional publicity."

The same principle is at work when the naming rights for a sports stadium are sold. U.S. Cellular Field, home of the Chicago White Sox, was an advertisement for a wireless telecommunications network—a corporation that, in

2003, was willing to pay millions of dollars to turn the baseball park into a kind of billboard. In 2016, the name was changed to Guaranteed Rate Field after that mortgage company bought the naming rights. Here again, the public often has its say. U.S. Cellular Field was called the Cell by White Sox fans. That happens with skyscrapers as well. Writing in 1999, Harris pointed out that "what is now the Amoco Building, once the Standard Oil Building, is familiarly called Big Stan, in distinction from Big John, the John Hancock, a few blocks to its north." Shortly after *Building Lives* was published, the Amoco structure's name was changed yet again, this time to the Aon Center—but people still call it Big Stan.

A century ago, the Fuller Company learned, to its chagrin, what could happen when thousands upon thousands of minds individually focus on a structure—in this case, the image of a structure not yet built—and unilaterally, unequivocally, albeit unconsciously, agree on what it should be called. The firm, which was in the business of building skyscrapers, hired Chicago's Daniel H. Burnham to design a twenty-two-story headquarters in New York City on an unusual triangular piece of land bordered by Fifth Avenue, Broadway, and Twenty-Second Street. It would be called the Fuller Building, an apt advertisement for the construction company.

Alas, when the *New York Herald* published, on June 2, 1901, a front-page drawing of the new building, the caption read, "Flatiron Building." And ever since, it's been the Flatiron Building. In her biography of the structure, urban historian Alice Sparberg Alexiou wrote, "The image really did resemble a monster version of the cast-iron object found in everybody's kitchen. And what a strange location—a little triangular lot in the middle of an intersection!—for this strangely shaped new skyscraper. People were talking about the Flatiron Building—the name entered the popular lexicon—even though it hadn't yet been built. It didn't yet exist, but it was already famous."

Officials of the Fuller Company weren't happy, however. Calling the structure the Flatiron Building didn't promote their business as they'd planned. Also peeved were the members of the Local 2 union of ironworkers, one of whom wrote in *Bridgemen's Magazine*, "To call the magnificent structure now being erected . . . by the Fuller Company the Flat Iron building is decidedly a misnomer. It looks a great deal more like a 20-deck Irish man-of-war sailing up Broadway." No question, from the right vantage point and with the right frame of mind, the Burnham-designed building could be thought to resemble a tall sailing ship. But the worker's image never resonated with the public the way the name "Flatiron Building" did. And still does.

A Physically Imposing, Steel-Girdered Fact of Life

The New York–based Butterick Publishing Company, founded in the aftermath of the Civil War, made its name and its money selling graded sewing patterns, tissue paper dress forms in a variety of standard sizes. Some patterns were available each month in the women's magazine that was published by the company from 1896 through 1937, known during most of those years as the *Delineator.* But anyone looking for a wide range of Butterick patterns had to buy them over the counter at clothing, dry goods, and other stores.

In Chicago in the first decade of the twentieth century, Butterick patterns were sold at nearly a hundred locations, including the city's major department store, Marshall Field & Co. But at some point in early January 1907, Marshall Field stopped carrying the patterns. To get the word out to Butterick customers—and to keep any sales loss to a minimum—the company took out a series of three large display ads in the *Chicago Tribune.*

The first, published on January 10, was headlined "BUTTERICK announces that its Patterns can no longer be found at Marshall Field & Company." It included a list of all the places where the patterns could still be purchased, grouped by area: Suburban, North Side, West Side, South Side, and a fifth, which included three large department stores (the Fair, Mandel Brothers, and Siegel-Cooper & Co.) and was listed as "The Loop."

Twelve days later, a similar advertisement was published, but in the meantime, Butterick officials had apparently decided that mentioning the loss of Marshall Field as an outlet might not be good publicity. So in this ad, the company announced that its patterns could be found "ONLY with merchants given below *On the Loop*"—at the Fair, Mandel Brothers, and Siegel-Cooper—as well as at the scores of shops throughout the rest of the city and suburbs.

The final ad was run twenty days later, and it was identical to the second, but with one change. In this ad, the reader was told the patterns could be found "ONLY with merchants given below *In the Loop.*"

In the space of just over a month, Butterick's ad writer illustrated the complicated nature of the name Loop, its complex relationship to the central business district, and the lack of consensus on how to use the name, and also hinted at the evolution of that name.

The phrase "On the Loop" could have been employed anytime on or after October 3, 1897, when passenger trains began running on the Union Loop elevated structure. It was clear that to be "on" the Loop was to be next to it. The Mandell Brothers and Siegel-Cooper stores did, in fact, border it in this manner, although—advertisements were never expected to be absolutely accurate—the Fair was a block away.

"In the Loop"—that was also clear to Chicagoans from the beginning. It meant being inside the circuit of the Union Loop, and that was true of the Fair and Mandell Brothers. Siegel-Cooper, in Levi Z. Leiter's building just south of the elevated structure on State Street, was, technically, outside the Loop.

Both were efforts to clarify the phrase used in the first ad, "The Loop." That phrase, which obviously didn't refer to the elevated structure itself, was used in this case as a synonym for "downtown" or the central business district—as a shortened version of "the Loop district." But seemingly, the company bosses weren't comfortable with that. Hence the "on" and "in" the Loop phrasing in the later ads.

It took a long time—more than a decade—for Chicagoans to come to grips with the presence of the Union Loop in their lives. In terms of transportation, it was an immediate hit. But the elevated structure was much more than a transportation artery. Its impact was much greater than that of the two sub-way lines, which, more than four decades later, were built into and out of the downtown area. Those underground lines were hidden from view. Their riders knew the lines were there, but at the surface, the city went about its business without giving the subways a thought. That's still the case.

A better comparison for the Union Loop is the Chicago River. Imagine if the area now occupied by Chicago did not have the river running through it. Getting from one part of the flat prairieland to another would be just a matter of walking or riding there. Now picture what it would be like if the river were suddenly plopped onto the landscape. In a snap, all previous patterns of movement would be disrupted. Not only would the river be a physical barrier between one section and another, one that would require a bridge or a boat to cross, but it would also be a demarcation, a border. The main channel, the north branch, and the south branch would be lines across the prairie, creating separation—in fact, creating sections. Chicago has a North Side, West Side, and South Side because of the river. Those "sides" wouldn't exist without the river.

Few Chicagoans spend much time boating on the river and its branches. Yet the river touches every person in the city. Major streets go over the river on bridges, which in cold, wet weather can freeze over more quickly. Smaller streets that meet the river, however, don't cross over. They come to a dead end. In the same way that the Lake Michigan shoreline is a border on the east edge of the city, the river is an edge to many neighborhoods. Throughout much of Chicago's history, the river, especially its south branch, was an open

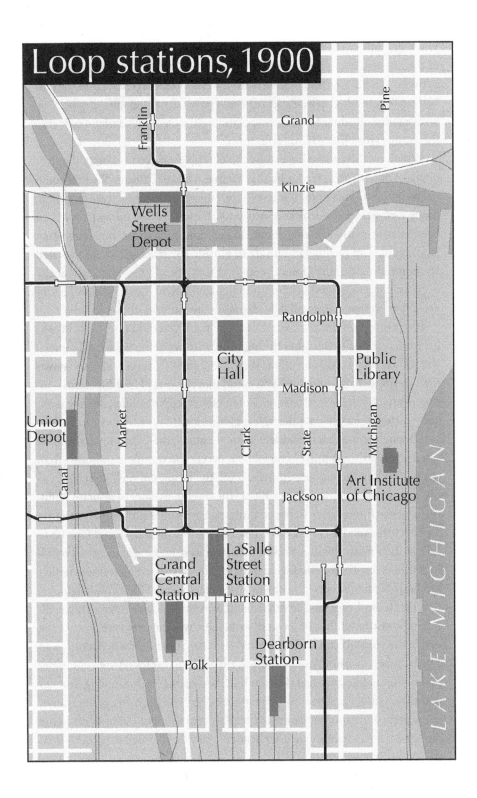

Loop stations, 1900

Pine

Grand

Franklin

Kinzie

Wells
Street
Depot

Randolph

City
Hall

Public
Library

Madison

Union
Depot

Market

Clark

State

Michigan

Canal

Art Institute
of Chicago

Jackson

LaSalle
Street
Station

Grand
Central
Station

Harrison

Dearborn
Station

Polk

LAKE MICHIGAN

sewer, and human development turned its back on the waterway. An example of this is the Civic Opera Building's five-story blank facade along the river between Washington and Madison Streets. Antipollution efforts over the past half century resulted in a cleaner river, and proximity to the waterway became an attraction, leading to the incorporation of "river" and similar words into the names given to areas and structures.

Whether Chicagoans have sought to play up their connection to the river or play it down, the waterway has been a major fact of Chicago life that could not be ignored. That's how it was with the Union Loop once it was completed. Since well before the structure was built, Chicago's real estate people had been talking about, thinking about, and scheming about the meaning—that is, the value—of having land inside or outside the rectangle of the elevated structure. But once the Union Loop went into operation, it was a physically imposing, steel-girdered behemoth that, like the river, was a substantial, unavoidable presence, immediately changing the patterns of everyday life.

It was more porous as a barrier than the river; you didn't need a bridge to get from one side to the other through the shadows of the tracks and girders. But it was clearly a demarcation. When you got off a train and came down the two stories to ground level, you could move in one of two directions—in, toward an intense concentration of stores, offices, opportunities, amusements, and bustle, or out, into a quieter, less glitzy locale.

Although only about twenty feet above the street, the Union Loop structure ran above nearly two miles of downtown streets and was more imposing than the city's tallest skyscrapers. At street level, the facades of such skyscrapers as the seventeen-story Monadnock Block, the seventeen-story Marquette Building, and the fifteen-story Reliance Building gave only a hint of their majestic architecture. You had to make a conscious effort to step back and look up to take in their many floors, and even then, you were looking at these tall buildings from a less-than-advantageous angle. They were best seen from another tall building set far enough away to give a clear view of their full height.

The Union Loop, on the other hand, was unavoidable. Move in any direction—north, south, east, or west—and there was the structure down at the end of the street. If you had any errand on Lake Street, Wabash Avenue, Van Buren Street, or Fifth Avenue (now Wells Street), you found yourself under and in the middle of a steel skeleton that, because of the lumbering thunder of the trains and the squealing of their steel wheels on the turns, seemed alive, like a prehistoric monster come to life. Rare was the spot out-of-doors in the downtown area where you neither heard nor saw the elevated structure—even so, you knew it was there.

The Union Loop was such a presence downtown that it was a reference point. A *Tribune* reporter, writing a story on a plan to asphalt every downtown street, employed the elevated structure, although it was only two months old, to help readers understand the area to be paved: "Picture to yourself every trolley pole and cable slot, every car track with its accompanying ruts and pools of muddy water, every cobblestone and stone crossing cleared off from every inch of all the streets within the district marked off by the Union Loop."

Store owners used the elevated Loop to attract customers and direct them to their doors. Less than two weeks after the Union Loop went into operation, the Rock Island railroad took out a large display ad to crow that its station was "the Only One on the Loop." A few months later, James Wilde Jr. & Co., a menswear concern, took out an ad to alert customers, "Stairs from the Loop Elevated Trains Right to Our Door." The reverse also occurred. For instance, the New Era Furniture & Carpet Co., promoting itself as "The Store of the Wage Earner," ran an ad that stressed its low prices. As if to prove the point, the store, located on State Street, three blocks south of the elevated structure, noted that it was "Out of the High Rent Loop District."

Writing "within the district marked off by the Union Loop" or "lying within the Union elevated Loop" quickly grew cumbersome. So in the space of a few months, the most often used phrase was simply "within the loop." However, even then, another phrase was bubbling up in the language patterns of Chicagoans. A synonym for "downtown" had long been "business district." So it isn't surprising that the area circumscribed by the elevated Loop began to be called "the loop district."

What is surprising is that the first use of that term in the *Tribune* occurred just two months after the Union Loop began operation. The December 19, 1897, story concerned the impact of rapid transit on the city's property values, particularly the effect that the "loop circle" was having in "the business district" and "the downtown business district." About a third of the way through the fifty-five-hundred-word report, an extremely long article for the newspaper in those years, the reporter discussed the woes of owners with property "outside of the loop district."

While that was an indication of the significance of the Union Loop, "loop district" didn't catch on at first. It wasn't until nearly a year later that it was used again in the *Tribune*, in a story about commuters riding trains from the suburbs "into the union loop district." In late 1899, three articles employed the term; two dealt with property assessments, and the third made reference to the next meeting of a group of potential pawn shop owners to be held "somewhere within the 'loop' district."

By the early 1900s, usage of "loop district" to describe the area inside the elevated rectangle—and also as a synonym for the downtown—began to pick up speed. It appeared dozens of times in the *Tribune* pages in 1904 and 1905. It was a neat shorthand way to talk about a complex subject, and Chicagoans knew what it meant.

"All Roads Lead to the Loop"

Even as this was happening, the start of a simultaneous shift was underway toward an even shorter, simpler term for the downtown. As 1904 dawned, some city people were beginning to refer to the central business area as simply "the loop." Tracking this usage is more difficult since, at the beginning, at least, there was ambiguity about whether someone referring to "the loop" meant the elevated structure or the area inside it.

For instance, in early 1904, a real estate column by Marvin A. Farr, a former president of the Chicago Real Estate Board, opened this way: "Once it was said, 'All roads lead to Rome.' Now in Chicago, 'All roads lead to the loop.' For some years this has been true. Trade and capital have poured into this vortex until it has come to a belief that whatever one's wants they can only and must be supplied 'downtown.'" This was a clear use of "loop" for "downtown." Still, Farr didn't appear to be completely comfortable with the term, inasmuch as he also used "downtown" once, "central district" once, and "business district" twice.

As time went on, "loop" was employed more and more—and more comfortably—as a synonym for "downtown," although often both words were used, as well as, at times, "central business district" and "business district." Indeed, "within the loop" was increasingly replaced by "in the loop." This was significant because the use of the preposition "within" called to mind the elevated structure, even when "loop" was a substitute for "downtown." When the preposition "in" was employed, the Union Loop wasn't conjured up. "In the loop" meant "in the downtown," no question.

A breakthrough came in April 1907, when the *Tribune* published a long story about the city's crowded downtown, titled "Chicago's Loop Is the Busiest Spot on Earth." This euphoric bit of boosterism employed "loop" dozens of times, with only a single mention of "downtown." For instance, the article declared, "On many days the population of the loop is not less than a million people," and asserted, "The loop is unique in that members of nearly every profession in existence are to be found there." Nonetheless, the reporter still felt the need to make reference in the article's opening paragraph to the elevated Loop structure: "If it were possible for an inhabitant of Mars to discover through a big telescope the busiest and most congested spot on the face of the globe, he might hesitate for a few moments about Wall street and its vicinity, but it is certain he finally would pronounce the space bounded by the Union elevated Loop, Chicago, to be far and away the leader in this regard."

Another, perhaps more significant milepost was passed in the *Tribune*'s New Year's Day issue for 1912. In the two stories that the newspaper printed about the celebrations the night before, there were three mentions of the "loop" and two of the "loop district." The articles made no reference to the elevated Loop at all and did not feel the need to use "downtown" or "business district," either. By January 1, 1912, the evolution of the term "loop" was complete.

Over the course of fourteen years, the significance of the Union Loop structure—its unavoidable presence on the urban landscape, its looming presence—had impressed itself on Chicagoans. In reaction, hundreds of thousands of people began employing the word "loop" in their talk and writing in ways that they had never done before. These people didn't set out to rename the city's downtown. But that was the result.

Indeed, the renaming was so thorough that the use of the word no longer required the hearer to think of the elevated trains on their wood-and-steel structure. By 1912, people rarely meant the Union Loop when they employed the words "within the loop" or "in the loop" or the "loop."

In an odd bit of linguistic alchemy, the elevated Loop lost sole ownership of its name in this process. As a result, over the past century-plus, a Chicagoan using the word "Loop" might be referring to the rectangle of elevated tracks that encompass the downtown. Most often, though, through all those decades and still today, when city residents, workers, and visitors mentioned "the Loop," they meant the downtown. The name is shared by the elevated structure and the downtown—but Chicago's downtown holds the lion's share.

Part Four

The Heart of Chicago

← 13. "My 'Other Neighborhood'"

A century ago, J. Ogden Armour's wealth was estimated at more than $125 million—the equivalent of about $2.5 billion today. Nonetheless, the lifelong Chicagoan had a mournful existence. "I don't suppose," he said after an economic fall from grace, "I shall ever be happy. Perhaps no one ever is."

Armour was thirty-seven when his father died in 1901, leaving him to run Armour & Company, the family's meatpacking business on Chicago's South Side. A year later, he lost his only sibling, Philip Jr. Even as Armour took the helm of the firm, he and his wife were frantic to find a treatment for their seven-year-old daughter, Lolita, who was born with both of her hips displaced. In 1902, they brought to Chicago the head of the department of orthopedic surgery at the University of Vienna, Dr. Albert Lorenz. His operation was a success. Later, as an adult and one of the wealthiest women in the United States, Armour's daughter went on to have a bumpy life during which she married four times.

Armour was successful in building and expanding the family business into an international concern, benefiting greatly from government contracts during World War I. In the aftermath, though, with those contracts canceled and much of the globe caught in economic hard times, the bottom fell out of his business. "I lost money so fast," he said, "I didn't think it was possible"— reportedly losing an average of a million dollars a day for 130 days. (Untouched by the losses were the fortunes that he had set aside earlier for his wife and daughter.)

In 1927, with only about $2 million left, Armour was on vacation in London when he was struck by typhoid and died of pneumonia. His obituary in *Time* magazine noted that, recently, when he'd said he didn't expect ever to be happy, Armour had added, "But the thing that would make me happiest just now would be to know that I could get roaring drunk and wander about the loop for two days without anyone paying any attention to me."

For Armour, the Loop—Chicago's downtown, encircled by the elevated Loop, rooted by the elevated Loop—was a special place, a place he knew well enough to find his way, even if intoxicated. It was also a place, he acknowledged ruefully, that offered anonymity to nearly anybody, except someone as well known as he was. Indeed, the Loop *was* a special place for everyone living in the city and its suburbs, as well as the many visitors, such as writer Edward Hungerford. In 1913, Hungerford described the contrast between "the blue waters of the lake" and the elevated Loop structure—"the noise, the dirt, the street darkened and narrowed by the over-shouldering constructions of man." And he described the variety of riders on the elevated trains rumbling above the downtown streets:

> Pressing her nose against the glass of a window that looks down into surpassingly busy streets, over-shadowed by the ungainly bulk of an elevated railroad, is the bent figure of a hatless peasant woman from the south of Europe—seeing her America for the first time and almost shrinking from the glass in a mixture of fear and of amazement.
>
> Next to her is a sleek, well-groomed man who may be from the East—from an Atlantic seaport city, but do not be too sure of that, for he may have his home over on Michigan avenue and think that "New York is a pretty town but not in it with Chicago." You never can tell in the most American and most cosmopolitan of American cities.

At a third window, Hungerford wrote, was "a man who has come from South Dakota," where he had "a big ranch up in that wonderful state. You know that because last night he sat beside you on a bench in the dingy, busy office of the old Palmer House and told you of Chicago as he saw it." Chicago's Loop with its hotels and restaurants and stores and amusements and offices and promenades and diversions belonged to the man from South Dakota, and the one from New York (who might just have been from Michigan Avenue), and the "hatless peasant woman" who, looking upon the downtown hustle and hum, was "seeing her America for the first time." Just as it belonged to J. Ogden Armour.

"A Jekyll-and-Hyde Sort of Burg"

The Loop was the focus of Chicago, and what focused Chicago on the Loop was the elevated Loop, which defined, delineated, demarcated the downtown and helped crystallize it as the quintessence of the city. As in many American cities, Chicago's business center, its downtown, wandered in the nineteenth century—from South Water Street to Lake Street and then to State Street. When, two decades after the elevated structure was completed, Hobart Chatfield-Taylor called the Loop the city's "neutral land," he understated its importance. Once the Union Loop tracks and girders were in place, the area inside that rectangle was the center of the Chicago universe.

This centering of the city had begun with the cable car lines that brought workers and shoppers into the downtown from far out in the city. But the lines dropped passengers off at different places, and being at street level, they were relatively inconspicuous and never functioned as dividing lines the way the elevated Loop structure did. What the elevated structure did was to anchor the downtown within its multigirdered embrace. This stopped the tendency of the central business district to shift and wander as the years went on. The elevated Loop was, in a way, a huge signboard pointing to the area within its circuit, identifying this place as special, significant, and vigorous.

The Loop—the downtown within the rectangle of the elevated tracks—was and remains for Chicagoans, as longtime newspaperman Bill Gleason wrote, "my 'other neighborhood.'"

> When I came back from World War II, I was in the Loop almost every day. In the late '40s and early '50s, the Loop was the mecca—the Loop was alive—even after Midnight. People would come out of the hotels, particularly in the nice weather, because air conditioning wasn't a big thing yet, and socialize. Men would be outside talking about baseball, horse races, politics—anything you can imagine.
>
> I was so excited about being in the Loop. . . . I also remember the omnipresent noise of the "L" and the things that might fall on you from the elevated trains and tracks, like pigeon droppings.

To some extent, every well-functioning downtown serves this purpose, but in Chicago, the elevated Loop tightly focused the pulsing heartbeat of the city's center. As historian Sam Bass Warner Jr. writes, "To a degree perhaps not equaled since the 1830s and the heyday of the Broadway promenade in New York City, the downtown district became *the* city for Chicagoans. It was the place of work for tens of thousands, a market for hundreds of thousands, a theater for thousands more." The Loop, Warner notes, "functioned as the symbol of unity and pride" for Chicagoans, who by 1950 numbered more than three million, as well as for another million people in the suburbs.

Over more than 120 years, the relationship of Chicagoans to the Loop has evolved. The city's downtown is exciting and bustling in the third decade of the twenty-first century in different ways than in the middle of the twentieth. Once crammed with department stores and shoppers, the Loop is now filled with college students and tourists. It is home to affluent condo dwellers and a destination for theatergoing suburbanites. It's had its hard times and survived them. However, even in years of adversity, the Loop has been a special place

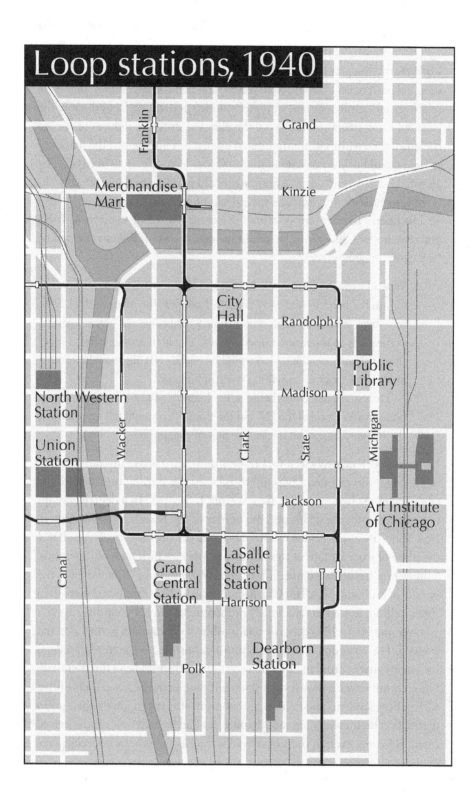

Loop stations, 1940

Franklin

Grand

Kinzie

Merchandise Mart

City Hall

Randolph

Public Library

North Western Station

Madison

Union Station

Wacker

Clark

State

Michigan

Art Institute of Chicago

Jackson

Canal

Grand Central Station

LaSalle Street Station

Harrison

Polk

Dearborn Station

for Chicagoans. It is the one small spot of land that has been shared by all the city's citizens—indeed, by all the people of the vast metropolitan region. In this way, the Loop has played an essential role in unifying Chicago, in giving Chicagoans a communal identity.

This importance of this cannot be exaggerated. The Loop—the downtown encircled by the elevated tracks—has served as a common ground for the citizens of a Chicago that has been divided from its start. As one late twentieth-century writer noted, the elevated Loop "defines and unites the center of the city."

"A City Perpetually Divided"

From 1830, Chicago has been divided by geography, divided by heritage, divided by railroad tracks and viaducts, divided, in a multiplicity of ways, in its own self-concept. The Loop has provided a core from which the city's many physical, intellectual, and cultural divisions are bridged and kept from flying apart, like shrapnel, in shards and fragments.

In his epic prose-poem, love-hate letter, *Chicago: City on the Make*, Nelson Algren called the city a "Jekyll-and-Hyde sort of burg" and "Old Seesaw Chicago." For him, it was a place of interwoven, intergrown contrasts, of tenderhearted do-gooders such as crusader Jane Addams and violent hustlers such as mobster Al Capone—a city that "forever keeps two faces . . . one for hustlers and one for squares."

This gnostic combination of sharp darkness and bright light was noted with caustic humor by *New Yorker* writer A. J. Liebling. In a series of mid-twentieth-century articles, collected in his book *Chicago: The Second City*, Liebling turned his skeptical eye on Chicago's history of boosterism and braggadocio, noting that in 1857, for instance, an editorial writer for the *Tribune* looked forward to the day when the city's "last rival in the race for greatness is left behind." Indeed, turn-of-the-century commentators fearlessly asserted that by the 1950s, Chicago would be the world's great city and home to thirteen million people.

They were wrong. As Liebling wrote, the city had fallen ten million short of that population mark. Despite high hopes, it wasn't the largest city in the world. Or even in the United States. And its hold on second place was coming under increasing threat from Los Angeles. Nonetheless, Liebling pointed out that Chicagoans had found a way to still keep bragging—by boasting of being worse than anywhere else:

> People you meet at a party devote a great deal more time than people
> elsewhere talking about good government, but they usually wind up

the evening boasting about the high quality of crooks they have
met.

At every social gathering, abuse is heaped upon the head of every
politician in public view, the standard complaint being that the fellow
is not sufficiently idealistic. The male guests carry five-dollar bills
folded in their drivers' licenses. Upon being stopped by a traffic policeman, they present the license, the cop takes the fin and returns
the license, and the transaction is closed.

Robert Merriam, an honest alderman, told Liebling, "Chicago is unique. It
is the only completely corrupt city in America." When the writer mentioned
a few other morally compromised places, Merriam became defensive: "But
they aren't nearly as big."

It was a strange kind of triumphalism. If Chicago couldn't have the clean-
est government, it could claim the dirtiest. If none of the city's sports teams
were perennial contenders, Chicagoans, for much of a century, could boast
of how hapless the Cubs baseball team was. Liebling called this Chicago's
"first-or-nothing psychology." And he saw it as ambivalence in the face of a
lost legacy of anticipated greatness.

Yet it was deeper than that, older than that. Chicago has always had a multiple personality. As the meeting point of East and West—its reason for existence
from the beginning—Chicago has always been looking in two directions at
once. Chicago is the largest city located on a continental divide. Rain falling
on the West Side of the city and in the western suburbs drains down the Des
Plaines River into the Mississippi River system, while the water from showers
closer to the lakefront flows east into the Great Lakes and St. Lawrence River.

It wasn't the puny Chicago River and its harbor that drew Native Americans, French traders, and later, American pioneers to this area, but the
relatively easy portage, called Mud Lake, that linked the Chicago with the
Des Plaines River—and linked the continent's Eastern Seaboard with the
Gulf of Mexico. This was the reason, too, for the Illinois & Michigan Canal,
which, when completed in 1848, connected Lake Michigan and the Illinois
River at Peru, Illinois. From the start, Chicago and its people developed a
character comfortable with dualities—with good and bad, beauty and grime,
rich and poor, old and new. The duality of Chicago's birth as the intersection
of the moneyed East and the frontier West was intensified by the duality of
its rebirth.

Within forty years of Thompson's subdivision of land, Chicago had grown
into one of the most important cities in the nation, ranking fifth in population.

Then the Great Fire of 1871 erased all of the city's central business section—its banks, its newspapers, its department stores, its government facilities. None-theless, with the help of eastern capital, that downtown area was well on its way to being rebuilt before the first anniversary of the blaze.

Chicago was essentially re-created from scratch. It was reborn out of the ashes, a phrase that, ever since, has been continually repeated. And the city's death and resurrection was endlessly celebrated, such as in the odd praise for the blaze in *Industrial Chicago* twenty years after the catastrophe:

> The fires of October, 1871, came to blot out forever the works of forty years, in the south and north divisions of the city, to destroy the little that was beautiful as well as the mass that was odious in the eye of art.
>
> Those fires were fortunate events for the Garden City, as a whole, and none profited directly by them, so much as art and architects, for the flames swept away forever the greater number of monstrous libels on artistic house-building, while only destroying the few noble buildings, of which Old Chicago could boast. The doings of the fire-god here in 1871, were quick and sure, as Whittier expressed it:
>
> > "On threescore spires had sunset shone,
> > Where ghastly sunrise looked on none;
> > Men clasped each other's hands, and said:
> > The City of the West is dead!"

Of course, the whole point was that Chicago wasn't dead. The fire had cleared away the ugliness and made room for the beautiful. It was an exam-ple of what scholar Ross Miller describes as Chicago's core identity—"an ingrained and finally institutionalized schizophrenia." The city, he writes, coped with the holocaust of the Fire by embracing it and, from that, came to embrace all its many incongruities: "It was not as if Chicago was the only American city with dark recesses. . . . Only in Chicago's case there was a certain pride in the city's divided nature because of its faith in an eventual coherence that would vindicate the struggles. . . . A city that seemed perpetu-ally divided was employing its inherited contradictions to prevail. . . . Instead of trying to resolve its divisions like the cities of the East Coast and Europe, it would make the conflicts the basis of its identity."

The Center Holds

A quarter of a century after the fire, the new elevated Loop formed a psychic core where Chicago could find stability amid its chaotic identity clashes, where the central business district that came to be called the Loop could serve as the calm eye in the center of the constant storm of jarring divisions.

One such division—the great drive in executive suites to make money and the great violence on the city's mean streets that could flash out at a moment's notice—was highlighted in *Chicago: The History of Its Reputation*, an examination of the city's first century, written during the Prohibition-driven gang wars of the 1920s. In their introduction, Lloyd Lewis and Henry Justin Smith noted that the city had been "studied, loved, hated, praised and denounced" and complained that its amazing growth from the hamlet that Thompson platted to one of the world's major cities had been overshadowed by its dark notoriety: "Chicago, to some people, means brute force; it means ruthlessness and even menace. Its 'blood-and-thunder' reputation has girdled the earth, outstripping again and again the fame of its herculean business enterprise. Almost from the beginning this has been true."

Another sharp contrast was apparent in one of the most prominent events in Chicago's history, the World's Columbian Exposition of 1893, a six-month-long international fair that drew more than twenty-seven million visitors to a 690-acre site on the South Side. Its nearly two hundred large, elaborate, but temporary structures, mostly neoclassical in design, were coated with white-painted staff (a mixture of plaster, cement, and jute fiber) that gleamed so brightly that the collection was nicknamed the White City.

It was a fairy-tale place of order, cleanliness and backward-looking elegance that was the antithesis of the actual Chicago with its grimy laborer neighborhoods, its gruesome stockyards, its polluted river, its smoke-filled skies, the noise and clutter and chaotic movement of its downtown. The "schizoid spirit" of this endeavor, as social scientist Anselm L. Strauss expressed it, was the juxtaposition of the fair as an ideal of beauty and purity with the everyday city of ambition, avarice, and unsightliness.

Two days before the end of the fair, Mayor Carter Harrison told a group of visiting mayors, "The World's Fair is a mighty object lesson, but, my friends, come out of this White City, come out of these walls into our black city. When we get there, we will find that there is an object lesson even greater than the World's Fair." For Harrison, the "black city" was a place of great economic drive and business energy. But whether the mayor realized this or not, the phrase also called to mind all that was dingy and squalid and noxious about Chicago, including its soot-covered buildings and the huge disparity between the lives of its rich and poor.

While wealthy Chicagoans, such as J. Ogden Armour, lived in the distant suburbs and employed strikebreakers to crush efforts of workers to improve their lot, those workers, most of them immigrants, were among the many Chicagoans scraping by and living in crowded, rat-infested hovels, at the mercy of the powers that be, as Upton Sinclair detailed in his novel *The Jungle*.

One of those real-life immigrants, Patrick Prendergast, a twenty-six-year-old mentally disturbed office seeker, went to Harrison's home a few hours after the "black city" speech. He was admitted into the vestibule by a maid who went to wake the napping mayor. When Harrison came into the hallway, Prendergast pulled out a .38-caliber revolver and shot him three times. The mayor died in less than an hour. Nine months later, in what historians have called a political murder, Prendergast was hanged for the slaying.

All these dualities—Chicago as enterprising and violent, as dying to the fire and being reborn from it, as the White City and the black city—had their roots in the physical nature of the city. Not only did Chicago sit on the continental divide, but it was divided into three parts from its birth. The Chicago River was the reason for this division. While the mouth of the waterway was an attractive spot for early pioneers, there was no consensus on where the community that became Chicago would find its center.

Jean Baptiste Point DuSable, a trader of French and African descent, built a home in the 1780s on the north bank of the river's main channel, just east of what is now Michigan Avenue, and is celebrated as the first long-term non-native resident of the area. In 1804, U.S. Army troops, under the leadership of Captain John Whistler (the grandfather of painter James Abbott McNeill Whistler), constructed the log-built Fort Dearborn on the south bank. However, two decades later, the focus of the still nascent settlement was at the junction of the main channel with the river's north and south branches.

In 1829, Mark Beaubien erected the Eagle Exchange Tavern, later known as the Sauganash Hotel, on the east side of the river's south branch, a short distance below the main channel. The greatest concentration of settlers, though, was on the western bank in an area that came to be called Wolf Point. Six years earlier, James Kinzie and David Hall had built a tavern there, noteworthy for a wordless sign featuring a painted wolf that hung from a nearby tree branch. Over the next decade or so, the tavern was run by a series of proprietors and called several names: Wolf Point Tavern, Wolf Tavern, Rat Castle (for its infestation of rats), and Old Geese's Tavern. In addition, the area had a church, a school, and various log cabins.

So DuSable and some earlier pioneers settled in the area that became the city's North Side, while Fort Dearborn and the Sauganash Hotel were on the future South Side, and the bulk of the hamlet was in what's now known as the West Side.

When James Thompson laid out the streets of the future city, he ignored the lakefront. He was engaged in what geographer Michael P. Conzen calls "premature platting," the drawing of lines across a large, empty and relatively flat space of land. In effect, Thompson was using these lines to transform this untouched, generally unsettled area into real estate, into relatively uniform sections that could be easily bought and sold.

Starting on the east at State Street, he mapped out nine blocks on the north side of the river, twenty-two on the west side, and twenty-seven on the south side. Of the fifty-eight blocks on the Thompson plat, twenty-seven, or nearly half, had some access to one or more of the river's three channels. State and Madison Streets, which in the future would be called the busiest corner in the world, formed the bottom, southeast corner of the map—and was open country, as was much of the land Thompson subdivided.

For nearly two centuries, Chicago's three sections—the South Side, West Side, and North Side—have been like fraternal triplets, closely related and yet different and separate, as if three separate cities were stitched uncomfortably together by a long-forgotten treaty. "During all the years of our early childhood," wrote Arthur Meeker, born in 1902 to affluent parents on Prairie Avenue on the Near South Side, "we seldom went to other parts of the city. The Loop . . . we shared in common; but each residential quarter was self-sufficient. Even the far South Side seemed to be a long way from Prairie Avenue. . . . The West Side I cannot recall ever seeing. As for the North, it, too, appeared incredibly remote."

The river "was a force for division," writes historian Henry Binford, adding that the waterway "raised formidable obstacles to travel between the three segments of town. The first few decades of Chicago's history as a settlement are full of tales of ferries begun and abandoned, bridges erected and then washed away in spring floods."

Each section has evolved on its own, connected to but independent of the others. Each has had its economic ups and downs. The South Side, for instance, was the boom area of the late nineteenth century. For one thing, it could be reached from the East by land—and later by railroad—without having to cross any of the channels of the Chicago River. Passengers from lake ships who landed at South Water Street could reach the north and west sections only by one of a dozen wooden bridges in use by 1871 or by ferry. The same was true with merchandise unloaded there.

In addition, the South Side was the beneficiary of the first cable car route and then the first elevated railroad line, transportation improvements that spurred housing construction. Also boosting real estate development was the

1893 World's Fair. Nonetheless, as cable car and, more important, elevated railroad service expanded to the West and North Sides, the playing field among the city's three sections was somewhat leveled.

One common trait the three sections shared was the presence of the very rich and the very poor, sometimes simultaneously in the same small area. For example, on the South Side, many of the richest Chicagoans, including Marshall Field, Potter Palmer, and Philip Armour, Ogden's father, lived on Prairie Avenue, from Sixteenth to Twenty-Second Street (Cermak Road today), at the end of the nineteenth century. Meanwhile, just three blocks to the west was the city's red-light district, the Levee, home to brothels, gambling dens, and vices of all sorts.

Prairie Avenue, however, started losing its allure after 1885, when Potter and Bertha Palmer moved to the North Side. By the turn of the century, the area was at the northernmost edge of the Black Belt, the long, thin section of the city that, because of racism and restrictive covenants in deeds and leases, was the home of most of the city's African Americans, many of them working class or impoverished.

On the Near West Side, wealthy families had fancy homes near Union Park at Ashland Avenue and Washington Boulevard. The home where Carter Harrison lived and was assassinated was on Ashland, just two blocks south of the park. Eventually, though, the area was dominated by factories and the overcrowded homes of laborers and their families, including "two-story wooden dwellings, rear tenements, and jerry-built flats." The Near West Side had long been a major point of entry for immigrants, and the housing there was run-down, worn out, and ill maintained. In 1917, Hobart Chatfield-Taylor wrote, "One must be truly an old Chicagoan to recall the time when the shady streets which lie west of the river vied in social standing with any in the city. Here factories now belch their smoke upon the mansard roofs of dilapidated tenements that once were the mansions of wealthy citizens."

It was a slum, very much like the slum, similarly filled with immigrants attracted by nearby factories, on the Near North Side, cheek-to-jowl with the Gold Coast, where, wrote sociologist Harvey Warren Zorbaugh in 1929, waves of immigrants—"Irish, Swedish, German, Italian, Persian, Greek, and Negro"—settled for a time and then gave way to another group. "But each has left its impress and its stragglers, and today there live on the Near North Side twenty-nine or more nationalities, many of them with their Old World tongues and customs."

Within a mile of this slum, called Little Hell, was the Gold Coast, which the Palmers had helped found four decades earlier, an enclave of the very rich, including the home of Cyrus H. McCormick and a residential building with seventeen-room apartments at a monthly rent of $1,000 (the equivalent of about $15,000 today).

The Fragmenting of the Grid

The contrasts between Little Hell and the Gold Coast—and the similar ones on the West and South Sides—are indications of another divisive element of the cityscape of Chicago, its fragmentation. That fragmentation was a key reason the city needed the strength and weight of the elevated Loop and the Loop downtown to serve as the solid, secure anchor of the city's many clashing cultures, mindsets, and ways of life.

On a map, Chicago's street grid seems to flow seamlessly in all directions. From an airplane, Chicago has the appearance of endless straight lines and right angles, creating a mosaic of rectangles. Yet appearances, as Michael P. Conzen notes, are deceiving: "The popular belief is that Chicago is America's quintessential city with a vast, uniform street grid. This is completely wrong. Not only do the rivers interrupt street continuations in both cardinal directions, but diagonal arterials, railroads, freeways, industrial zones, parks, airports, and other large institutions block continuation on countless occasions."

The landscape of Chicago, as it has developed since Thompson's plat of 1830, has become far less a grid and much more a maze as a result of all those human-made diagonals that slice through all those right angles, as well as the parks and other large pieces of land that block the unimpeded flow of streets. Indeed, Conzen points out that except for a handful of major streets, such as Western Avenue, the more than 150 other north-south streets "all suffer at least one major blockage, many several, and large numbers dead-end ignominiously in both directions after only a few blocks."

The greatest diagonals, of course, are the North and South Branches of the Chicago River, which, along with the main channel, turned the city into "three giant wedges." This was heightened later, when the Illinois & Michigan Canal and, subsequently, the Sanitary & Ship Canal extended the South Branch to the Des Plaines River. Each wedge was further subdivided by the railroad tracks that barreled into the downtown area from the north, west, and south, acting like a wall between one side and the other, between what became one neighborhood and another. Much later, the expressways would act in this same way, dividing one portion of land from another. The diagonal streets—some of which, such as Ridge and Vincennes Avenues, were initially Native American trails—didn't function as much like a wall between communities, but they did slice through many of the grid's rectangles, leaving odd-shaped blocks.

This fragmenting of the grid and the landscape encouraged the creation of tightly contained communities, often characterized by a common heritage, language, religion, employment, or a combination of those. Chicago became known as a city of neighborhoods because of this proliferation of communities. Mike Royko, the quintessential Chicago newspaper writer of the second half of the twentieth century, called these communities "neighborhood-towns" and "ethnic states," adding that even with your eyes closed, you knew where you were by "the odors of the food stores and the open kitchen windows, the sound of the foreign or familiar language, and by whether a stranger hit you in the head with a rock."

And Chicago's divisions have always gone well beyond these "neighborhood-towns." Consider that the city, with its 2.7 million people, is divided into fifty wards, with an alderman for each. By contrast, the 4 million people of Los Angeles are represented by only fifteen council members. Indeed, A. J. Liebling quipped, "The city of Chicago, on the west shore of Lake Michigan, is less one town than a loose confederacy of fifty wards. . . . Communication between the residents of the different wards is further limited by the pronounced tendency of immigrant groups in Chicago to coagulate geographically."

In the 1920s, University of Chicago sociologists looked at how community ties within the city were affected by the grid and disruptions in the grid and determined that Chicago was made up of seventy-five community areas (later increased to seventy-seven). Those designations are still in general use today, although other, later demographers mapping the city have identified more than 170 neighborhoods.

This fragmentation of Chicago's physical, social, and cultural landscape not only divided one Chicagoan from another and one neighborhood from another but also made maneuvering through the cityscape, at times, a dangerous endeavor. Bernard Judge, who grew up in Chicago in the middle of the twentieth century and later was the city editor of the *Chicago Tribune*, recalled, "I totally knew the boundaries of my neighborhood and my parish in terms of where it was safe to go and where it might not be." With his usual flair for the often politically incorrect language of Chicago's streets, Royko explained that Chicagoans tended to stay in their own neighborhoods for self-preservation: "Go that way, past the viaduct, and the wops will jump you, or chase you into Jew town. Go the other way, beyond the park, and the Polacks would stomp on you. Cross those streetcar tracks, and the Micks will shower you with Irish confetti from the brickyards. And who could tell what the niggers might do?"

Given the city's balkanization, Chicago could easily have been a prime illustration of the phenomenon that William Butler Yeats noted in "The Second Coming," his 1919 poem: "Things fall apart; the center cannot hold." In Chicago, however, the center did hold. The center—the downtown that, with its steel girders, the elevated Loop anchored—served as the unifier despite all the divisions of a heavily divided city. And not just the city, but the metropolitan region as well.

"A Special Occasion"

"The pulsing heart of the Chicago region," wrote economist Robert A. Walker in the mid-twentieth century, "is the 'Loop.'" The city's downtown—the area embraced by the rectangle of elevated railroad tracks—contained the greatest concentration of economic might in the metropolitan region, the greatest concentration of jobs, the greatest concentration of public officials, and the greatest concentration of people with power to make things happen. But, more, it was a magical place to visit for people from the neighborhoods and suburbs, like going to a foreign country—"an exciting place" and "an exotic and wonderful place," recalled newspaperman Judge.

"So vital did the Loop district become [by the 1920s] that everyday life in Chicago appeared to revolve around going downtown," note Chicago historians Eric Bronsky and Neal Samors. For three-quarters of a century, the Loop, bordered by the elevated tracks, was filled with amusements, with movie theaters, with restaurants, and above all, with shopping. "The Loop was the mecca—the Loop was alive . . . a fairyland," said journalist Bill Gleason.

"The Loop," write Samors and coauthor Michael Williams in another Loop-related book, "seemed to have room for everybody in its best years—Minsky's Burlesque operated down the street from the stately Chicago Theater, while the arcades, tattoo parlors and flop houses in the south Loop never seemed to threaten shoppers to the north." Each neighborhood had its own shopping area, often with a large department store, "but nothing could compare with the selection and class of State Street's finest stores." Samors and Williams explain, "Shopping in the Loop was considered a special occasion in those years [the 1950s], and proper attire was worn by all, including children, who would be required by parents to wear their own 'best' clothes. Men wore jackets, ties and fedoras—and a sea of crisp, perfectly blocked hats could always be seen moving through the Loop. Ladies wore only dresses and skirts—pants were practically unheard of for women in those years."

In those years, "it was still a special thing to go downtown, especially on a date, since it was much more expensive," remembered television consultant Bob Dauber. "The Loop was just a special place for us to go—it was out of the neighborhood—an adventure—and it was upscale. It was less expensive to take a date to a neighborhood theater or club, but on special occasions, we went to the downtown clubs, like Mister Kelly's, the Black Orchid, London House and the Blue Note."

Working in the Loop felt special, too. "There is something about working downtown that gives you a swagger and makes you feel important," said attorney Gary T. Johnson, president of the Chicago History Museum, "and provides an extra status to what you are doing." Historian Michael H. Ebner writes, "The [Loop] district pulsated." Artist Mitch Markovitz had a homier take: "For being a big place, the Loop is really nicely contained and you feel cozy in it. It's like being in your own back yard, or knowing where all the bathrooms are in Marshall Field's—you don't have to think about it. I like the fact that you can look east and see a huge park and the lake. You might not necessarily see the water, but with no trees or mountains, you know there's a big open space."

Most Chicago neighborhoods, especially those identified with a particular ethnic or racial group, had the feel of a small town. Surprisingly, that was also true in the Loop because, unlike other big cities, so much business and activity were crammed into such a small space that everything could be reached with a quick walk. "People usually walk in the Loop rather than taking a cab, and there are very few downtowns where you can do that," said Gary Johnson.

> You are considered some kind of a wimp if you take a cab, even if it is a seven or eight block walk. . . . In other cities, people would always drive to where they were going and they would pull into garages in the building where they needed to be. But downtown Chicago always had little places you could go because people always were walking from place to place. I always found the most interesting places in the Loop located on the streets where the "L" was built.

State Street was a procession of stately department stores, starting with the majestic Marshall Field & Co., and then, farther south and a little less haughty, Carson Pirie Scott & Co., and then, south again and even less expensive, Goldblatt's, and finally, in the Levi Leiter building south of Van Buren Street, Sears, Roebuck & Co. But small, more humble storefront businesses, the nitty-gritty of everyday commerce, were scattered throughout the Loop, especially along the streets below the elevated structure (Wabash

Avenue, Lake Street, Wells Street, and Van Buren Street)—"barbers, tailors, shoe-repair shops, adult bookstores, hobo hotels, cut-rate cafeterias, sidewalk newsstands, a 128-year-old drugstore that sells leeches for drawing blood."

Sarah Bernhardt called Chicago "the pulse of America," and nowhere was that more apparent than in the Loop where crowds reflected the full spectrum of American life, from the J. Ogden Armours of the nation to the grubby workingmen on the way home from factory jobs, from liquor store clerks to corporate giants, from those who traced their ancestry to the founding of the city to those who had just arrived from seemingly every corner of the globe.

And this great diversity was reflected in the clientele of that mammoth State Street presence, the Marshall Field's store. While aiming to serve the carriage trade—those rich enough to arrive in their carriages and, later, limousines—Marshall Field's also sought to be "Everybody's Store."

Its celebrity customers included U.S. presidents Grover Cleveland and Theodore Roosevelt, Prince Henry of Prussia, and Hetty Green, who, because of her shrewd late nineteenth-century investments, was reputed to be the richest woman in America. Celebrities of a much different sort, the Everleigh Sisters and the madams of the city's other high-priced bordellos, were also to be seen strolling through the aisles. "They brought their girls with them sometimes," said longtime doorman Charley Pritzlaff, "and the girls were just as polite and well-behaved as their Madames. Nobody knew who they were but me, I guess."

The store's motto—"Give the lady what she wants!"—was reflected in the Marshall Field's merchandise, from the basement "lower price" section to the most luxurious silks. "Laborer's wife or society *grande dame*, Idaho general storekeeper or rich retailer," wrote Chicago historians Lloyd Wendt and Herman Kogan, "the customer was to be catered to, pleased, and gratified."

More than a few of those scouting out the offerings at Marshall Field's and other Loop stores were preteens who, through the first two-thirds of the twentieth century, came downtown on a bus or an elevated train on their own. Such unescorted children were part of the fabric of the everyday Loop population. Television consultant Bob Dauber, for instance, would head downtown on the elevated train at the age of nine for weekly piano lessons. George E. Kanary, a railroad historian, recalled taking the subway from Logan Square to the Loop to run errands for his widowed mother, who ran a neighborhood deli: "Because my mother at first operated the store by herself with only me to help her when I was home from school, she could not leave, and so it became my responsibility to shop for her, go downtown to pay her mortgage, things like that. I would often walk out with up to $200 in my pocket—this was in 1947, when I was not yet ten years old!"

Raymond DeGroote, a railroad enthusiast, was even younger when he took the Ravenswood visit his father in the Loop: "A seven-year-old kid going downtown by himself! . . . It wasn't scary at all, it was an adventure!"

Not all the children in the Loop without adult accompaniment were there for serious purposes. It was common in midcentury Chicago for clusters of preteen boys to come to the Loop to wander around what was, for them, essentially a huge playground, such as a group in the early 1960s from the Far West Side that included an eleven-year-old named David.

Somehow, during the afternoon, David got separated from his friends, but he wasn't worried. He still had a quarter, enough to get on the Lake Street train going out to Laramie Avenue. Alas, he boarded the Ravenswood instead, and once he realized his mistake—and now out of money—he walked back to the Loop along the tracks until he found Lake Street, and then walked west about seven miles through some of the city's rougher neighborhoods to finally reach home.

By this point, his parents were frantic, and when the boy walked in the back door, his mother burst into tears, hugging him and saying, "Why didn't you tell someone you were lost?" David's response: "I wasn't lost. I knew where I was."

Another group of four boys—who, as a joke, called themselves the Rutabaga Club—routinely would go to the Loop for a day of fun. They were altar boys together at Resurrection Catholic Church in the working-class neighborhood of Austin on the Far West Side—Jim Crimmins, Louis Demos, Larry Bobko, and Mel Mangan.

It was easy enough for them to get there by taking the Jackson Boulevard bus or the Lake Street elevated train, Crimmins recalled decades later, and the four went often. "We would just go downtown and look around, and not spend a dime except for carfare." They'd ride the elevators to the Skydeck at the top of the Prudential Building, then the tallest structure in the city. At Christmas, although they had little money, the boys would stroll aimlessly through Marshall Field's, haunting the toy department, in particular, while, to their amusement, store employees kept close watch on them.

Starting in 1958, when they were in the sixth grade and about eleven years old, they would choose a day every year, which they called the Rutabaga Day, to head to the Loop with their hard-earned savings from paper routes and other odd jobs—about $16—to splurge on a blockbuster movie, treats, and an all-you-can-eat buffet. "Blowing it all in a day seemed so wildly extravagant and so foreign from our usual way of operating." The day would involve a visit to the Planetarium, the Aquarium, or the Field Museum and a walk through Grant Park to Buckingham Fountain. And then, after their movie, it was on to the Blackhawk Restaurant on Wabash for the buffet in the Indian Room. "I remember these big plates and these big pieces of roast beef they would carve for you," Crimmins said. "We would spend an enormous amount of time there, go back three or four times, and then we would go somewhere else for dessert."

And then they'd return home, sated and on top of the world. "We felt like we had this city figured out." The key to Chicago, they knew, was the Loop.

← 14. Wandering Downtowns

More than likely, Mayor Martin Kennelly walked to the offices of the architectural firm of Skidmore, Owings & Merrill at 100 West Monroe Street. It was, after all, just two blocks south of City Hall, and the late winter weather was mild with highs in the forties. The newspaper reporters also probably walked, even Clayton Kirkpatrick from Tribune Tower on Michigan Avenue, a mile away. And the business leaders, too, such as Mark A. Brown, president of Harris Trust & Savings Bank, across the street at 115 West Monroe, and Hughston M. McBain, the chairman of Marshall Field & Co., four blocks away.

The Loop, like most American downtowns in 1954, was a walking place. You might have to take a cab to get somewhere in Manhattan or drive if you were heading to a meeting in Los Angeles. But part of what made an American downtown *downtown* was how close together everything was.

On Tuesday, March 16, the mayor and the business magnates and the reporters were converging on the Skidmore offices for the announcement of what Kirkpatrick would call a magnificent vision "to revitalize the heart of Chicago." Quietly developed by the city's economic power brokers over the previous four years, the Fort Dearborn Project was breathtaking in its scale and ambition, "grand enough," according to Kirkpatrick's front-page *Tribune* story, "to arouse the pride and fire the imagination of all Chicagoans."

The idea was to scrape clear a 151-acre tract just north of the main branch of the Chicago River, from Rush Street west to the north branch, and as far north as Ontario Street. To level this "largely urban wasteland pocked with decay," containing about forty city blocks. To sweep aside 513 warehouses, small factories, and aged housing structures and transform the resulting blank canvas into "an architect's dream of what a modern city should be." In place of those old nickel-and-dime structures, easily dismissed as blight, the Fort Dearborn Project envisioned a monumental high-rise development clustered around a multigovernment complex with a host of towers:

- a twenty-two-story federal building
- a thirty-story City Hall
- a twenty-two-story county building
- a twelve-story state of Illinois building

- a twelve-story Hall of Justice
- a two-story library
- a two-story Hall of Records
- a three-story municipal services building for such agencies as the CTA, the Chicago Board of Education, and the Sanitary District of Chicago (now the Metropolitan Water Reclamation District of Greater Chicago)

This hub of governance was the crown jewel of the vision, and the headline on Kirkpatrick's story was a shout: "Outline Vast Civic Center!" But there was much more. Also included was a Chicago campus of the University of Illinois to replace the derisively nicknamed "Harvard on the Rocks," the temporary site on Navy Pier where about four thousand students had been enrolled each semester since 1946. Instead of filing into those makeshift classrooms, future students would learn about Shakespeare, Einstein, and Freud in a collection of seven buildings, ranging from two to fifteen stories tall, including a gymnasium, theater, and athletic field.

And perhaps the vision's most radical element, the project called for a forest of new residential towers, ranging from ten to twenty-eight stories high, with a total of five thousand apartments. During a decade in which the population of the Loop, inside and along the edges of the elevated tracks, would fall by nearly 40 percent, the Fort Dearborn plan called for an infusion of thousands of new residents—not in the Loop but across the river on the Near North Side. Total cost: an estimated $400 million, or the equivalent of about $3.8 billion today.

Kirkpatrick—who, after a fifteen-year career as a *Tribune* reporter, would start his ascent up the newsroom ladder later that year, becoming the paper's editor in 1969—enthused that the project would result in "the most sweeping changes in the central business district since the fire of 1871."

That was certainly true, but not in the way that he or the big names behind the project anticipated. That day, Nathaniel A. Owings, who oversaw the preparation of the project's design, told reporters that the city "must either grow or become decentralized with the central core doomed to decay. Some outlet must be found to allow the Loop to grow." He was echoed by real estate promoter Arthur Rubloff, who had come up with the idea for the mammoth redevelopment. The project, he said, would work to reduce congestion in the Loop "without destroying it. In fact, it will anchor the Loop and stimulate further development on all sides." But Owings and Rubloff were wrong.

As history had shown, locally and in other American downtowns—and as the future would make even clearer in city after city—the construction of this gargantuan government–university–residential center on the north side of the river would have been the death knell for the Loop as Chicago's downtown. And it would have left the city much less protected against the drastic social changes even then taking place in the United States as the suburbs rose and thrived while the cores of old-line metropolises withered and died.

The proposed site of the Fort Dearborn Project was nearly identical in acreage to the land enclosed for the past half century by the tracks of the elevated Loop. And what the plan's boosters were proposing was the creation of a brand-spanking-new city center, just east of the developing upscale retail promenade along Michigan Avenue, dubbed by Rubloff the Magnificent Mile.

The Fort Dearborn Project, if built, would not have anchored the downtown Loop. It would not have revitalized this crossroads of Chicago, this second neighborhood of all Chicagoans, this unifying place in a city riven with divisions geographic, cultural, racial, and social. No, far from protecting the Loop from decay, this spectacular "architect's dream of a modern city" would have destroyed the heart of Chicago.

"Constantly on the Move"

"Downtown" is an American word for an American phenomenon. Europeans in the nineteenth century were fascinated by the downtowns in the United States where business activities were tightly clustered in a district that was set apart from residential areas. "If your caprice takes you down town," wrote one British diplomat to prospective visitors, "you soon find yourself in the very whirl and maelstrom of commerce and trade." Back home, by contrast, shops, offices, and homes were scattered together willy-nilly over the whole of the cityscape, often with merchants and other business activities on the first couple of floors of a building and apartments on the upper stories.

An American downtown was noisy, congested, and very busy. "Except for shoppers, many of whom went about their business in a leisurely manner, everybody was in a great hurry, rushing to and fro, trying to get as much done as possible," notes downtown historian Robert M. Fogelson. That whirl and rush was concentrated into a very small space, a fraction of a fraction of the city's total area. In late nineteenth-century Boston and Pittsburgh, for instance, this commercial center covered about a third of a square mile. In Chicago, the land inside the elevated Loop tracks was just a quarter of a square mile—roughly one-thousandth of the city's land area.

It was valuable for a business, especially one catering to the public, to be in the center of things, and downtown property owners could demand higher rent and sell for greater profits than on the district's edges or elsewhere in the city. As a result, there was a frequent call for an expansion of the downtown to include some less expensive land (although, of course, once this land was a part of the downtown, its value would rise). An example of this tendency was seen in Chicago during the first two decades after the completion of the elevated Loop. Recognizing the sharp difference in value between land inside and outside the elevated Loop, some real estate dealers and businesspeople stuck on the outside lobbied to elongate the rectangle of tracks southward to include more land—their land—within its "golden circle."

Fighting against such campaigns in Chicago and other cities were the entrenched interests—those who owned downtown land and those who already operated inside the downtown and benefited from its intense concentration. As Fogelson notes, "Even minor moves could mean major windfalls or wipe-outs because of the tremendous disparities in real estate values in and near the business district. 'I know real estate values,' said a Chicago alderman in 1910, 'and I can point out a piece of property in the loop worth $6,000 a foot and only four blocks away another piece that the owner couldn't sell for more than $500 a foot.'"

Although the downtown was clearly an important place, it had no standing in law and no official borders. It was the subject of a continual tug-of-war between those who wanted to stretch it here or there to benefit their land or operations and those who wanted to keep it tightly contained to benefit theirs. Consequently, the American downtown—while the center of power and financial might, filled with tall buildings, even skyscrapers—"was highly unstable because it was constantly on the move," writes Fogelson.

A downtown, by its nature, was prone to wander, to shift its center of gravity from here to there, to turn its back on a portion of its old site or on all of it, to stretch, to drift, to shuffle down this street or that, over here and then over there. At the end of the nineteenth and beginning of the twentieth century, the downtowns in New York, Seattle, and Portland, Oregon, moved north away from their original sites. In Philadelphia, the downtown moved west.

The story was the same in many cities, writes Fogelson: "Downtown St. Louis also moved west, leaving the East End virtually deserted. So did downtown Omaha, which spread along Douglas, Farnum, and Harvey streets from Tenth to Sixteenth street. Downtown San Francisco headed south from its original location near Portsmouth Plaza and then, as it approached Market Street, turned west. Downtown Los Angeles also drifted south, away from the site of the original pueblo." This continued through the first third of the twentieth century, until the Great Depression brought the construction of new commercial buildings—and the movements of downtowns—to a screeching halt.

Downtowns would shift for any number of reasons—all of which had to do with a financial jackpot for someone. For instance, Fogelson notes, there was "a tendency of fashionable retail stores to move in the direction of affluent residential sections." New transit lines or terminals often played a key role, as the Union Loop did in Chicago. In some cases, one part of a downtown would wither because the property owners there didn't want to spend money to maintain their buildings to keep tenants. And there were also cases when, through force of will, financial might, and readiness to risk big, a single power broker would bring about the movement of a downtown to a completely different place. That's what happened in Chicago in the middle of the nineteenth century.

Moving to State Street

In Chicago, as in most other American cities, the downtown wandered, even to the extent of being wiped off the face of the prairie by the Great Fire of 1871. In the three decades after James Thompson laid out the streets of the future city, the focus of business activities was fluid. But by 1860, most retail stores had put down stakes on Lake Street, while wholesaling took place a block north on South Water Street. One of those Lake Street stores belonged to Potter Palmer, and in the mid-1860s, the flinty commercial genius had an idea.

After getting his feet wet in the dry goods business in upstate New York, Palmer had come to Chicago, where in 1852, in his mid-twenties, he established the Potter Palmer & Co. dry goods store on Lake Street, just east of Clark Street. The enterprise was a quick success due to Palmer's many innovations, such as offering customers a money-back guarantee.

Not only did his store make money for Palmer, but he also found a way to turn a profit from the Civil War. As the potential for war loomed, he risked every dollar he had to buy up cotton and woolen goods, stockpiling them "in warehouse after warehouse." Once the war began and cut off the supply of Southern cotton, his merchandise netted him profits of more than $2.5 million, the equivalent of nearly $40 million in present-day dollars. After the war, he took on Marshall Field and Levi Z. Leiter as partners in his dry goods concern but soon sold out to them.

He had decided to go into the real estate business. As with the Civil War, Palmer was betting on the future. He recognized that the crowded, constrained Lake Street had outlived its usefulness as the center of the city's business district, and he gambled that he'd be able to determine the downtown's new home. As the *Tribune* wrote, "He was gifted with that foresight which not only enabled him to forecast with accuracy the trend of the growth of the town, but permitted him to do a great deal toward shaping the course it took."

In 1867, shortly after selling out to Field and Leiter, Palmer began buying up property along the "narrow, irregular" State Street, "little more than a wide alley," bordered by shacks along the sides and the open prairie to the south. He spearheaded an effort to widen the street and began replacing the shanties with large opulent buildings, including a grand, new six-story building that, in 1868, became the home of Field, Leiter & Co., and the first Palmer House, which opened in September 1871.

Persuading his erstwhile partners to relocate to State Street—and pay the largest annual rent ever in the city's history, $50,000 (the equivalent of about $900,000 in today's money)—was the masterstroke in Palmer's plan to remake the thoroughfare as the center of the new downtown. As historians Harold M. Mayer and Richard C. Wade note:

> The effects of these decisions were felt throughout the business com-
> munity, and the shift to State Street was sudden and dramatic. One
> contemporary thought the change so important and far-reaching that he
> called Palmer's work the "Haussmannizing of State Street," likening it
> to the rebuilding of Paris by Baron Georges Eugene Haussmann under
> Napoleon III. By 1869 thirty or forty stone-faced buildings had sprung
> up along the renewed street. Land values soared, and the commercial
> axis of the city, which had previously extended east and west along the
> river, assumed its present north-south orientation.

But what a single tough-willed, risk-embracing entrepreneur had been able to accomplish in three years, a natural cataclysm erased in thirty-six hours.

A New Downtown to the West?

On the night of October 8, 1871, a fire broke out in the O'Leary barn on the west side of the river, about a mile southwest of Palmer's palatial State Street buildings. Driven by gale-force winds, the blaze quickly jumped the river and thundered north, devouring three and a half square miles of the heart of the city, killing at least three hundred and leaving a hundred thousand people—a third of Chicago's population—homeless.

Within three weeks, Marshall Field and Levi Leiter set up temporary shop far to the south in a two-story, red-brick barn at the corner of State and Twenti-eth Streets, "stocked anew and rich with the various fabrics of two continents" in a relatively well-appointed space. Their chief competitor, John V. Farwell, had to make do with makeshift accommodations amid the burned shells of buildings on Michigan Avenue near Jackson Boulevard, where, he said, "our goods saved from the fire will be closed out cheap." Another competitor, Carson, Pirie & Co., set up its first postfire operations at its wholesale department on Lake Street, a block west of Reuben Street (present-day Ashland Avenue) and a mile and a half west of the river.

Soon, though, owners of the largest stores began to cluster together into a new business district a half mile west of State Street near the river's east bank, in an area damaged by the fire but cheaper and more easily cleared and developed. In mid-November, Farwell resumed somewhat full operations at his rebuilt warehouse on Monroe Street, east of Market Street. For Field, Leiter & Co.'s customers, the barn on Twentieth Street lost its luster, and the owners opened a second site in April a block north of Farwell. Carson, Pirie, by contrast, chose a location untouched by the blaze on Madison Street, a mile west of the river.

Chicago's downtown had wandered west. But the question was whether it would wander back. Certainly, a quick move back was out of the question, as Leiter observed: "If a store were erected upon our old quarters or near it, it would be of little or no value for occupancy for the coming year. The debris from the burned buildings is so great that it would prevent access of people, and the dust arising from it would destroy a stock of goods."

However, the new western downtown wasn't living up to the hopes of the general merchandise stores, because the core of their business, the lady shoppers, weren't happy about going to the new area to shop.

Again, Potter Palmer acted as a city shaper. He announced plans to build a second, even more elegant Palmer House to replace the two-week-old structure that had been leveled by the conflagration, and he set about establishing State Street once again as the business center of the city. To bankroll this effort, he sold his property at State and Washington Streets—the site of the Field, Leiter store—to the Singer Sewing Machine Company.

With Palmer focusing again on State Street, Field and Leiter decided to come back, even though their annual rent in the newly built Singer building would increase to $75,000 (about $1.5 million in today's dollars). On the second anniversary of the fire, the new Field, Leiter store opened at State and Washington, symbolic for the *Tribune* of "the mighty, splendid Chicago which took the place of that which perished . . . the wonder of the world and the beauty and ornament of the continent of America." Chicago's downtown was back on State Street.

"When a City Heart Stagnates"

Essentially, what a strong downtown does is provide an economic center of gravity for its city and region. As the central business district, it is "the city's principal magnet," writes urbanist Charles Abrams. That's what Potter Palmer made State Street into—twice. For two decades, State held sway, but as the nineteenth century was coming to a close, the advent of elevated railroads in Chicago resulted in a threat to the street's supremacy. Each of the city's three elevated lines (and any future ones) was prohibited by its city franchise from building into the downtown area. The result was that each had a terminal about a half mile from the corner of State and Madison Streets:

- the Alley "L" at Congress Parkway and State
- the Lake "L" at Madison and Market Streets
- the Metropolitan "L" at Franklin Street between Jackson Boulevard and Van Buren Street

This was inconvenient for riders who had to walk or take a cable car several blocks to get where they were going. And it was only a matter of time until some shrewd entrepreneurs realized that instead of requiring customers to trek to their store, they'd bring their store to the customers. In other words, each of those terminals could have functioned as an independent center of gravity—with the resulting development of three or four competing business districts or subdistricts, each primarily serving a different area of the city. The result would have been a weaker and much more complicated commercial economy for Chicago.

That never happened, however. When Charles T. Yerkes brought the Union Loop into existence in 1897, he gave the city and its business community a sharp refocusing that established the land and the activities within the rectangle of elevated tracks as the most important and quickly the most valuable in Chicago. The Union Loop anchored the business economy and acted as the city's center of gravity—its unifying force that brought into balance its myriad contrasts and contradictions. And that's where it stood for half a century.

But by the mid-1940s, the Loop, like other downtowns around the nation, was beginning to face an unprecedented competitive threat—the rise of suburbia. A decade later, when the Fort Dearborn Project was proposed to "revitalize the heart of Chicago," the full scope of this threat was being understood. "The downtown of department stores, retail districts, and popular entertainment," write urban planners Bernard J. Frieden and Lynne B.

Sagalyn, "survived through the end of World War II, when a new set of circumstances in the United States began to tear it apart."

During nearly two decades of economic hardship and war, housing construction had been slower than slow, but with peace, new federal funding, and millions of GIs returning to civilian life, pent-up demand fueled an enormous home-building explosion. Housing starts, which had averaged thirty thousand a year in the 1930s, leaped to one million in 1946 and to two million by 1950. And the vast majority of those new homes were in suburban and rural areas, where land was cheap, widely available in large tracts, and free of most building regulations. This exodus away from cities was accelerated in the mid-1950s by the establishment of the Interstate Highway System. New homebuyers and their families found suburban subdivisions much easier to reach with these new roadways—and jobs were easier to get to, as well. No longer was it necessary to live close to factories, offices, or public transportation.

Mayors and city business leaders felt betrayed because this rush to the suburbs was being aggressively encouraged by federal initiatives. As one study of Atlanta's declining downtown noted in the mid-1970s:

> Governmental policy has accentuated the decline of central cities in the United States because it has worked to subsidize the suburbs at the expense of the core cities. National policy has not encouraged the development of middle income housing in the central city. . . . The federal government, moreover, has positively encouraged the development of raw rural land for residential purposes because of its policies of providing both [Federal Housing Administration] mortgages, and of allowing mortgage interest payments to be deducted from a family's gross income for tax purposes.

As families found brand-new homes in brand-new subdivisions, city stores, big and small, followed their lead. The biggest of them landed in shopping centers established across the face of suburbia. They were called "centers" for a reason. They were new downtowns in terms of retail shopping and movie theaters, new economic centers of gravity. And where these retail malls were built, office construction followed.

This was an unexpected development in the longtime tendency of city downtowns to wander. In this case, however, the wandering didn't involve an extension of the central business district a few blocks in one direction or another. Instead, these completely new downtowns were being erected many miles away, draining the economic lifeblood of the old city centers.

Business were leaping from the city center out to new centers on virgin sites in the suburbs.

Consider that in 1958, Omaha's downtown was responsible for 22.4 percent of all retail sales in the metropolitan area. However, by 1967, its share had been cut nearly in half, falling to 12.3 percent. Yet as bad as that was, just five years later, downtown Omaha was responsible for only 6.7 percent of sales. The story was even gloomier in Phoenix. Despite nearly a hundred years of retail dominance, downtown Phoenix saw its share of the city's retail sales sliced nearly in half in just ten years—falling from 52 percent in 1948 to 28 percent in 1958. But much worse was to come. By 1972, the city's central business district accounted for only 3 percent of all sales.

"The decline of downtown retailing," writes urbanist William H. Whyte, "left a legacy of empty storefronts and those most depressing of sights—boarded-up department stores and movie theaters with blank marquees." What was at stake across the nation was the health and future not only of the downtowns but of the central cities themselves. As Jane Jacobs, the influential urban activist, writes, "When a city heart stagnates or disintegrates, a city as a social neighborhood of the whole begins to suffer: People who ought to get together, by means of central activities that are failing, fail to get together. Ideas and money that ought to meet, and do so often only by happenstance in a place of central vitality, fail to meet. . . . Without a strong inclusive central heart, a city tends to become a collection of interests isolated from one another."

Particularly depressing was the fate of the downtowns of two cities that, at one time, had been among the strongest in the nation—Cleveland and Detroit. In late 1978, Cleveland, once the fifth-largest U.S. city, defaulted on its federal loans, the first municipality to do so since the Depression, and one reporter bemoaned its fall: "You name it, and Cleveland had it until after World War II: Smart downtown hotels, stores, restaurants, night-spots, theaters, and all the other components of good city life." But the weight of urban ills and the flight of people and business to the suburbs became overwhelming. "Downtown suffered heavily, and physical blight spread over much of the city."

The story was similar in Detroit, where one reporter found "a virulent case of self-hatred" in 1976, explaining, "The streets of downtown Detroit are graced with proud new buildings, but there are no people. It is like a stage set without any actors. Fine restaurants and hotels are half empty. Offices are losing their occupants. Stores have moved, leaving vacant buildings in their wake. After 6 p.m., you could fire the proverbial cannon down the street without harming anyone."

"The Region Still Revolves around Chicago's Downtown"

The deterioration of downtowns in Detroit, Cleveland, Phoenix, and Omaha, as well as in scores of other cities across the United States, was there for anyone to see, and that's what the backers of the Fort Dearborn Project were trying to avoid in the mid-1950s. Yet by proposing the construction of literally a second downtown, the Fort Dearborn boosters were undercutting Chicago's greatest strength in the face of the suburban threat—the intense compactness of its Loop, provided by the rectangle of elevated tracks.

The suburban threat was serious enough, but as the coming decades showed, mayors, business leaders, and planners across the nation who developed or permitted to develop a "new" downtown, either as an extension of the old one or as an independent center, were undercutting the strength that compactness had brought.

That's what happened in Phoenix, urban affairs writer Alan Ehrenhalt notes, when, during the 1960s, officials despaired of creating a stronger downtown and instead sought to turn Central Avenue, a major street running north from the center, "into a fashionable boulevard of midrise office buildings and high-rise apartment buildings." That effort was relatively successful, but mainly what it did was "to empty out downtown even further. Central Avenue didn't bring many people into the city except to work at nine-to-five jobs, and it all but eviscerated what was left of the old downtown."

The story was similar in Washington, D.C., where, in the mid-1970s, urban planner Kenneth Halpern reported that the city's older downtown was in decline, "largely because federal policy has been dispersing federal offices across the Potomac to the Virginia suburbs." What building was going on at the time was in an area northwest of the downtown. "There seem to be many reasons why developers have shifted their attention away from the old core, including lower land costs and easier assemblage of land, but one reason stands out: the steady deterioration of the old downtown, culminating in the 1968 riots."

Chicago's Loop was facing all the same pressures as other American downtowns. And the fact that the Fort Dearborn Project, despite many of the city's power elite among its boosters, failed to get off the ground is a testament to the rootedness that the rectangle of elevated Loop tracks had long brought to the quarter square mile of land it enclosed.

While the *Tribune* editorialized that the project was "a wonderful dream," the newspaper took a wait-and-see approach. And there were those who were skeptical about the plan, believing that it was an effort to give some of its boosters, such as Marshall Field & Co., time to arrange "an orderly retreat to the suburbs." One businessman told political scientist Edward C. Banfield, "Well, these fellows are fighting a delaying action. They are smart enough to know that they can't reverse it, but they are trying to slow it down."

The project seemed to run counter to the ideas of F. T. Aschman, the executive director of the Chicago Plan Commission, who wanted to hem in the central business district between residential areas to keep it from "spreading out and dissipating itself." As Banfield reports, Aschman pushed compression as a concept to "preserve the high property values of the central district whereas lack of compression would encourage a gradual shift of valuable store and office properties out of the Loop and to the north."

In fact, there was a danger that moving the many government offices, including the courts, to the north side of the river would result in a vast migration of lawyers away from the Loop and into the North Side. And the first burst of opposition came from those attorneys. They didn't want to move. "Ten thousand lawyers had offices within easy walking distance of the city-county buildings," writes Banfield. "Courts and lawyers had to be close to each other; even if there were a place in the Project to which they could move, the lawyers would resist." Banks, which did frequent business with lawyers and the courts, were also opponents. So it was not surprising that within a month of the announcement of the project, the courts had been dropped from the plan.

Some prominent managers of major Loop buildings, including Graham Aldis, were also early antagonists, and they went so far as to organize the Committee for Government Buildings Downtown, a group that included leaders of the Chicago National Bank, the First Federal Savings and Loan Association, the Midwest Stock Exchange, and Carson, Pirie, Scott & Co., which, like most Loop department stores, feared a loss in sales if so many government employees were moved to the other side of the river.

In arguing against the project, Aldis asserted that it was important to make the Loop stronger, not weaker. As Banfield relates, Aldis contended that given national trends, downtown merchandising was going to move out into the suburbs. "The future of the Loop lay in office buildings—the Loop would continue to grow as a financial, legal, and management center; it would be disastrous, therefore, to dilute the concentration of office buildings—the Loop's real strength—by moving government buildings away." Ultimately, Aldis proved right. The development of Michigan Avenue as a shopping mecca and the profusion of suburban malls led, eventually, to the departure of all department stores from the Loop except Macy's, which replaced Marshall Field & Co.

What saved Chicago's central business district during the decades when so many other downtowns were withering was the concentration of government buildings, banks, and office buildings in the tight, crowded, compact area ringed by the elevated Loop tracks. There was just too much money invested inside that "golden circle" to walk away from, and there was just too much economic might in the Loop to permit the downtown to collapse.

Never did Chicago's downtown become as bleak, empty, and woebegone as many other formerly booming central business districts. As urban planner Emrys Jones notes, "The concentration of downtown office blocks, neatly contained in Chicago by the loop of the elevated railway, proved self-perpetuating." And when many downtowns across the nation began to come back as vibrant, vital city centers, the Loop was strongly positioned to lead the way.

In 2003, urban expert Robert E. Lang studied how the office space in thirteen large metropolitan areas was distributed among its primary downtown, secondary downtowns, edge cities (concentrations of business, shopping, and entertainment in suburban municipalities), and what he calls the "edgeless city," isolated office structures scattered hither and yon in the suburban sprawl.

Chicago was one of the few without competition from one or more secondary downtowns, and its Loop was one of two primary downtowns—the other was Manhattan—that still held more than half of all the office space in the region. New York had 56.7 percent, while Chicago had 53.9 percent. The next closest was Boston, where the primary downtown had just 37.4 percent, while in the ten other metropolitan areas, the central business district accounted for as little as 13.1 percent (Miami) of all office space. Lang writes, "Chicago captured the key idea of the monocentric metropolis, which held that the center structured the space for the rest of the region. Despite the recent emergence of substantial edge cities, the region still revolves around Chicago's downtown." And he adds that "Manhattan is so strong a core that it does a good job of holding the region together; the same is true for Chicago's loop."

The death knell for the Fort Dearborn Project came when Chicago's new mayor, Richard J. Daley, initially a supporter, turned against the plan, telling Banfield, "They took the city hall out of one place in Los Angeles and put it in another place and there's no development around it. What I want to know is: where's the best location for the people of Chicago? Are we going to discommode the people of Chicago for a real estate promotion?" In Daley's Chicago, that was it.

The Fort Dearborn Project had represented a major threat to the Loop. If carried out, it would have destabilized the city's economic focus and left it weaker in the face of increasing suburban competition. The mayor's rejection of key elements of the plan meant that the city's downtown had dodged a deadly bullet. However, the elevated Loop structure itself was about to face its greatest threat—from Daley.

← 15. Raze the Loop

CTA planning official Harold Hirsch had a ringside seat to the turn of events that saved the elevated Loop from the wrecking crew, and more than thirty years later, he could only marvel at how close a thing it had been. After all, a blitzkrieg of Chicago clout, backed by the expectation of federal funds, had been escalating for more than a decade. The elevated structure, characterized as ugly and noisy and gloomy, had been at the top of the hit lists of two mayors—Richard J. Daley and Michael A. Bilandic—and an entire Mount Olympus of Chicago movers and shakers. Two new subways—one under Franklin Street, near the south branch of the Chicago River, and one under Monroe Street, right through the central business district—would eliminate the need for the rectangular Loop. And they were seemingly as good as built.

Then, during the evening rush hour on Friday, February 4, 1977, a terrible accident on the Loop ratcheted up the intensity. A Lake–Dan Ryan train, heading around the curve at Wabash Avenue and Lake Street, slammed into the rear of a Ravenswood train awaiting clearance to go into the station at State and Lake Streets. The first three cars on the Lake–Dan Ryan train slowly jackknifed into the air and crashed to the street below. Eleven people were killed and 180 injured in the worst-ever accident on the city's elevated lines.

Even as the CTA was working to clear the wreckage and reopen the tracks, Bilandic stepped into a phone booth near the crash site and talked with President Jimmy Carter, emphasizing the city's need for federal money to demolish the Loop structure and replace it with the new subways. Three days later, the mayor met in Washington with Carter and U.S. transportation officials to plead for federal funding. Afterward, he told reporters, "I think we're going to get it."

By November, the outlook was dire for the eighty-year-old elevated Loop. "Those who want to save the el are now making their last stand," wrote Connie Fletcher in *Chicago* magazine. She added, "It is now the eleventh hour for the elevated. . . . Unless alternative measures are proposed and adopted, within ten years the Loop elevated, by law, will have been razed and replaced with a subway system."

Those trying to save the elevated structure were led by architect Harry Weese, but in August 1978, he acknowledged, "The Loop's elevated train, which gave Chicago's downtown area its name and structure, may be doomed." Seven months later, the drumbeat of demolition had grown deafening, as articles in the *New York Times* and *Christian Science Monitor* detailed the threats against the steel-and-wood structure. Associated Press writer Arthur H. Rotstein started his story, "The Loop, perhaps Chicago's best known landmark, may be doomed." Indeed, it appeared that, in the parlance of Chicago politics, the fix was in. Yet redemption of the elevated Loop was just over the horizon.

In a startling upset, the upstart Jane Byrne won the February 27, 1979, Democratic mayoral primary, which was tantamount to election in a city with few Republican voters. Chicagoans, angry over his mishandling of snow removal and traffic management during a January blizzard, rejected Bilandic, the candidate of the powerful Democratic machine.

Then, in another unexpected plot twist, two months into office, Byrne dropped all plans for the new subways and set into motion events that not only saved the elevated Loop but refurbished and strengthened it. "I was surprised and gratified," says Harold Hirsch, who had feared the chaos and inconvenience that the loss of the Loop structure would have meant to public transportation commuters. "You get used to 'whatever City Hall wants, it gets'—this steamroller." This time, though, the steamroller had been brought to a halt by the new chief executive on the fifth floor of City Hall. "You were allowed to do something more reasonable," Hirsch says.

"It Ought to Be Taken Down"

The saga of the saving of the elevated Loop is one that began more than three-quarters of a century earlier. It's a tale that came to its climax during a wild-and-woolly ten-month period in which "cultural provocateur" Harry Weese, like a white knight riding to the rescue, spearheaded a public opinion campaign on behalf of the long-denigrated transportation structure. The Loop's noise and blemishes could be dealt with, he argued. What was needed was to recognize that the Loop was not only useful, unique, and functional but also, in its gritty way, fun.

It's a story about city officials who were so adamant about razing the elevated structure that they bent over backward to disparage its historic significance—even to the point of asserting the falsehood that the city's downtown got its Loop name from the earlier cable car operations. It's a story about the nonprofit Landmarks Preservation Council (now Landmarks Illinois), founded in 1971 "to stop the demolition of significant buildings in downtown Chicago," going on record with what journalists described as an "extraordinary" declaration that the elevated Loop shouldn't be protected from demolition.

And it's a story about how the key point of contention of the months-long battle—whether the elevated Loop should be granted preservation protection by placement on the National Register—had been made technically moot by a quiet decision in an obscure bureaucrat's office in Washington, D.C., even before the brouhaha started.

The threats to the elevated Loop had begun decades earlier, even before it went into operation on October 3, 1897. During the final days leading up to inauguration of the four-sided transit hub, the *Tribune* published two stories and an editorial about how troublesome the structure and its in-street columns were. The first story began, "Chicago has a great down-town nuisance—one that for widespread vexation, trouble and even actual damage is unequaled throughout the city. This great public bother causes enough annoyance, enough delay, and enough real loss to earn the title of the champion nuisance in the recent history of the municipality. It is the Union elevated loop."

The newspaper's editorial called the structure "an awful mistake" that had "ruined" three of the four streets over which it ran. And this was followed by a lengthy interview with Richard Price Morgan, the "father of elevated roads," who denounced the Union Loop and asserted, "It all comes down to this question: whether or not the people of Chicago are going to submit to having their streets obstructed or not. If not, the present structure can be removed at a limited cost and another with side supports put in its place."

Chicago commuters had quickly fallen in love with the Union Loop, and it certainly helped bring shoppers to the central business district. Nonetheless, many downtown business leaders, particularly those on the four streets under the tracks, couldn't stop grousing. Indeed, a *Tribune* story published just three months after regular service began called the elevated structure "a cancer" and dreamed of a future date when it could be removed. It's one thing to dream, but by 1908, Fred A. Busse became the first in a series of Chicago mayors to call for demolition of the Union Loop and replacement with subways: "It ought to be taken down."

After that, it was open season on the Loop, as this list illustrates:

- 1927: A proposal for a unified transportation system for Chicago includes plans for several new subways, as well as a provision for the removal of the elevated structure.
- 1937: The Local Transportation Plan for the City of Chicago seeks subways and the demolition of the Union Loop.
- 1939: Razing the Loop rectangle is part of the transit plan of the Chicago Department of Subways and Superhighways.

- 1953: The decennial *Local Community Fact Book for Chicago*, with extensive data from the 1950 census, takes for granted the imminent demolition of the elevated Loop, noting, "The eventual completion of the subway system will eliminate the elevated structures, which gave the Loop its name, and produce further changes."
- 1954: Ralph Budd, the chairman of the CTA, announces that the agency's comprehensive plan for an extension of rapid transit (subway and elevated) services in the city calls for "replacing the old elevated structure in the Loop."
- 1957: Mayor Edward J. Kelly's plan to revolutionize public and private transportation includes "ultimate removal of the elevated loop."
- 1962: A CTA improvement program envisions new subways under Wells Street and Jackson Boulevard to "permit the razing" of the Loop. To show the expected result, the *Tribune* prints an aerial photograph of the corner of Lake Street and Wabash Avenue as it presently is along with a retouched version of how it would look with the train tracks and steel structure gone.
- 1963: Sworn into his third mayoral term, Richard J. Daley tells a crowd of a thousand supporters in the City Council chambers that as part of improving mass transit, he plans to tear down the elevated Loop.
- 1965: The CTA identifies as its "No. 1 project . . . the razing of the Loop elevated structure, an old eyesore."
- 1966: Daley appoints a committee of public officials to oversee the planning of a new downtown subway, and John G. Duba, the committee chair and the city's planning commissioner, says, "Our primary objective will be to carry out preliminary planning and related studies for a new subway to replace the old Loop elevated tracks."

That's where it stood as the 1960s segued into the 1970s. The elevated train structure was on borrowed time, on its way out, although no one seemed to know when it would be removed.

Saving the Elevated Loop—for the Time Being

Then, in a stunning move, Mayor Daley unilaterally ordered the Loop torn down as soon as possible. This astonishing decree from the most powerful public official in Chicago's history came in late December 1973 in private meetings with city and CTA officials. And since the replacement subways were not yet funded nor planned in detail—much less put into operation—it threatened transit pandemonium for tens of thousands of city and suburban commuters. Nonetheless, as of the turn of the new year, the mayor's order remained a City Hall secret. On the second day of 1974, at an unrelated ribbon-cutting ceremony, Daley hinted at his startling plans with a cryptic, seemingly offhand comment to reporters: "Tomorrow, we'll announce the removal of the elevated tracks over Wells Street."

A few hours later, however, the mayor hit the roof when he read a *Tribune* story that not only revealed his plans for the speedy demolition of the entire Loop but also chronicled the opposition to the idea from two sets of city-hired experts. That's what got Daley so angry—that the story by urban affairs editor Paul Gapp disclosed that two recent evaluations of Chicago's transit plans, by the consulting firms American Bechtel and DeLeuw, Cather & Co., insisted that the elevated structure shouldn't be removed until the new subway system was in operation. This was not the way Daley wanted the public to learn about his intention to reconfigure the cityscape of Chicago with a single bold stroke, and he ordered his press secretary to vehemently deny the truth of Gapp's story. Events over the next two days, however, proved the reporter's accuracy.

"Daley sees this only, as some kind of key to a renaissance of the Loop and an incentive to real estate developers, but there are serious dangers involved," one of Gapp's sources told him. Indeed, under the plan, the Lake Street elevated would terminate at State Street, the Evanston Express trains would dead-end at the Merchandise Mart, and the Ravenswood trains would be routed into the State Street subway, creating problems of scheduling and between-train spacing. Shuttle buses would be used to ferry riders from the new terminals to other parts of the downtown, but one transit official feared that commuters from Evanston and elsewhere would rebel against the inconvenience of a shuttle bus, choosing instead to use their cars, adding, "And once you've lost a transit rider, it's hard to get him back. We'll have a system that won't be able to absorb much of an increase in passengers even if the gasoline shortage becomes more acute." Not only that, but if the jury-rigged system worked, the source explained, it could end up convincing federal transit officials that Chicago didn't need U.S. funds for subways—and they'd never be built.

Worse news for Daley and his demolition plan came three days later, when Gapp revealed that the American Bechtel report warned that Chicago's downtown would become "a ghost town" if the Loop structure were removed before the building of the subways. Elimination of the elevated tracks, the report predicted, would result in a shift of major development away from the central business district to the Near North Side, close to the Michigan Avenue's Magnificent Mile shopping district—the area marked out a decade earlier for the ill-starred Fort Dearborn Project. In fact, instead of boosting development inside the Loop-bordered downtown, the plan for a Franklin Street subway had already acted as a magnet to pull new office center and commercial construction, including the Sears Tower, the new world's tallest building, outside of the downtown core.

In his article, Gapp noted that Daley's desire to rid the downtown of the elevated structure had long been well known: "It sprang from the belief that the elevated was a steel noose around a dying downtown in strong need of massive upgrading. It was strengthened by the exhortations of real estate men, some of whom believe dozens of old buildings in the Loop should be torn down as well."

Gapp's stories saved the elevated Loop—but only for the time being. Daley, as mayor and chairman of the Cook County Democratic party, had unrivaled, almost dictatorial power over not just the city government but also ostensibly separate agencies such as the CTA. In the midst of his fifth term, he had been the city's chief executive for nearly two decades. What he wanted to happen almost always happened.

So if he hadn't been derailed by an aggressive reporter, Daley would have announced in that first week of January 1974 that the elevated Loop was going to be torn down, and the City Hall "steamroller" would have immediately gone into action. And quickly, the structure would have been razed. Within probably weeks, Wabash Avenue, Van Buren Street, Wells Street, and part of Lake Street would have been cleared of the elevated's steel columns, and commuters would have had to find their way as best they could.

And as the American Bechtel report envisioned, the city's downtown would have become untethered from the spot where, bordered by the elevated Loop, it had served Chicagoans for eight decades—and would have started to wander and fragment, as was occurring with the central business districts of many other large American cities.

Moving ahead on the demolition of the elevated Loop without guarantees of federal funding for the subways wouldn't have been out of character for Daley and Chicago Democrats. For much of the twentieth century, the party had controlled the voting power of one of the largest cities in the nation and, because of that large electoral bloc, could make or break presidential candidates. Consequently, Democratic presidents and, to some extent, Republican chief executives, as well as senators and representatives, paid close attention to the wants and needs of the city leaders.

Daley was a master at this aspect of the butt and ram of national politics, and he had come to expect that eventually, from somewhere, the money he wanted for the project would be produced by the federal government. An example of that approach was the multi-billion-dollar Deep Tunnel Project, officially known as the Tunnel and Reservoir Project (TARP), which involved two phases—the first to create 109.4 miles of drainage tunnels and the second to create reservoirs that could hold 2.3 billion gallons of sewage and stormwater. The first phase provided some flood relief, but its main purpose was to link the city's sewer system with the future reservoirs. The project, overseen by another independent agency that Daley indirectly controlled, the Metropolitan Sanitary District (now named the Metropolitan Water Reclamation District of Greater Chicago), got underway in 1975. City and district officials expected that the tunnels and reservoirs, funded heavily by the U.S. government, would be completed by 1985 or, at the latest, 2000, but such hopes turned out to be ephemeral.

As the twentieth century drew to a close and the new century dawned, voting patterns in the nation shifted so that Chicago wielded much less clout, and successive presidential administrations of both parties were much less open-handed with federal largesse. Although the first phase of TARP was finally finished in 2006, the second isn't expected to be on line until 2029—more than half a century after the beginning of the project.

"It Never Should Have Been Built"

Daley's desire to sweep away the elevated Loop, shared by many of "the downtown Big People," was rooted in a complex mix of motives and prejudices, only partially explained by Gapp. And the intense drive to make it happen continued after December 20, 1976, when the mayor suffered a massive heart attack and died. Indeed, the arguments for eliminating the Loop rectangle continued to be put forward as, with the passing years, the Franklin Street subway seemed an inevitability, even though architect Harry Weese launched a last-ditch effort to find a way to protect—and change public perceptions of—the structure.

The idea that the elevated structure was a "steel noose" around the neck of the central business district was nothing new. It was a view that had been asserted over the lifetime of the Loop and even before it went into operation. The elevated structure "girdled" the downtown and was a "Chinese Wall" blocking expansion to such an extent that it "strangled" the business district. Indeed, Charles G. Gardner, executive director of the State Street Council, asserted that failure to demolish the Loop elevated "would be a choke-chain on our future development."

The historic role the Loop elevated had played in bringing shoppers, workers, and other Chicagoans into the downtown was given, at best, lip service.

And totally missed, even by those business and civic leaders who most bene-fited, was the influence the structure had in raising and maintaining property values in the downtown, its impact in unifying the city, and the way that it rooted the central business district so deeply that the district survived the effects of the suburbanization of the country after World War II.

Mid-1970s real estate interests, hoping for a building boom, were adamant about the need to demolish the rectangle of tracks. And that was evident in the public pronouncements of downtown leaders, such as the following:

- Ross Beatty, president of the Michigan Boulevard Association and manager of three important downtown properties: "The el is a liability. It should come down, and now, while everybody is talking about it. The el is bad for property values. It's a disaster."
- Arthur K. Muenze, president of Wieboldt Stores: "It never should have been built and the sooner we get rid of it the better!"
- Jack H. Cornelius, executive director of the Chicago Central Area Committee, a high-level lobbying group for the city's corporate leaders and developers: "Chicago's Loop elevated structure is one that is old, deteriorated, excessively noisy, one which blocks the light to the street, one on which the trains shriek like a banshee as they round curves, and one which drips rust on people and vehicles passing beneath it in bad weather. . . . Removing the Loop elevated structure will open up new development opportunities which, in turn, will result in the creation of badly needed jobs for inner city residents."

Conceivably, in his final sentence, Cornelius was referring to employment opportunities that would open up in new office buildings to be erected in the expected development boom. Yet most of those jobs would have been white collar in nature, not the sort that were likely to be open to the people of Chicago's poorest neighborhoods, where, because of a host of social factors, education levels were generally low.

More likely, Cornelius was envisioning construction jobs that would be available to laborers (although, in Chicago at that time, union membership was difficult for African Americans and other minorities in poverty to obtain). If so, he was talking publicly about something that had been generally kept private by proponents of the new subways, since the main beneficiaries would have been politically connected contractors and politically powerful labor unions rather than the general public.

The reality was that however much money might be earned by however many workers involved in such projects, the construction jobs would be temporary. They wouldn't provide a long-term economic boost to the workers or the metropolitan economy. As one preservationist facetiously wrote, "I know in this town that the Unions have the clout and what could be better serving them than a six-year 'make work project,' such as the Loop El coming down and the Franklin Street subway going in."

Architect Douglas Schroeder, who worked closely with Weese to argue for the preservation of the elevated Loop, contended that Democratic city officials were approaching the question with short-term motives of campaign money and votes. He asserted, "The basic thinking is: Get the money from the Feds and get those public-works jobs. It's also to take care of the contractors—they're the big [political] contributors—and that will get the money flowing into party coffers. The elevated versus the Franklin Street subway controversy is symptomatic of the way the city powers think. Their priorities are absurd and will contribute to the decline of downtown, not to its enhancement."

But if jobs weren't prominent in the public comments of city officials and downtown business leaders, absolutely unsaid was another key reason behind the move to demolish the elevated Loop and spark redevelopment: the heavy presence of African Americans in the downtown area, particularly after 5 p.m. As *Planning* magazine noted in late 1978, "Some critics of the project see it as 'black removal,' an effort to make the Loop so high priced and so uninviting to blacks that they will go back to their 'own' neighborhoods." Or as Daley biographers Adam Cohen and Elizabeth Taylor pointed out, "His City Hall worked hard to develop the city's infrastructure and buttress its downtown business district. . . . Daley worked with powerful business leaders to revitalize downtown by pushing poor blacks out, replacing them with middle-class whites."

For decades, Chicago's African American population had been forced by restrictive covenants in deeds, as well as by public policy and white violence, to live within certain clearly delineated areas. Major public housing developments, erected by the Chicago Housing Authority (CHA), had been constructed in these areas to house and contain low-income black people.

Ringing the downtown were black neighborhoods—an area on the Near North Side containing the CHA's Cabrini-Green development, a large area on the Near West Side, and a much larger, mile-wide expanse called the Black Belt, which ran from Eighteenth Street on the north to Seventy-First Street on the south. As the city's high-end shopping focus was shifting from the Loop to North Michigan Avenue, and as more metropolitan-area residents were shopping at suburban malls, the central business district was increasingly abandoned by white people after 5 p.m. and increasingly patronized by African Americans.

This frightened the Chicago's power brokers, who had so much money invested in the Loop and its real estate, and the city's politicians, who feared even greater white flight from the neighborhoods than had already occurred. For instance, in a speech to the Business Managers Association, developer Arthur Rubloff warned that the Loop was in danger of becoming "the Central Business District Slum." And one Realtor told a University of Chicago researcher, "Unless something drastic is done, you will write off State Street in fifteen years. And the minority groups will take over and then, no matter what the white people do, it can never be brought back, no matter what is done. And the whole goddam town will go to hell."

Nominated for the National Register

By July 1978, a year and a half after the deadly crash on the Wabash-Lake turn, Chicago officials were shifting into overdrive to take the elevated Loop down. Indeed, as Paul Gapp, still bird-dogging the issue for the *Tribune*, noted, they were "itching to build the new subway" so that the first half of the demolition of the structure—the elimination of the legs along Wells and Van Buren Streets—could be carried out. But during that month, two letters were sent and a government form was filled out that threatened to thwart the high hopes of City Hall and Chicago's major power brokers.

The government form was titled "National Register of Historic Places Inventory: Nomination Form," and it was filled out on July 14 by Harry Weese and Judith Kiriazis, the editor of *Inland Architect* magazine. In eight pages, Weese and Kiriazis used the form to argue that the elevated Loop was historically significant:

> Chicago's Loop and its Elevated are symbiotic. The Elevated creates the land values and therefore shapes development. It is a logical response to the necessities of the crowded city, an artifact of the imagination when architects and engineers were one and the same. It is archetypal, complete, . . . the nexus of the region its spreading branches cover. Functionally it is as vital as ever, the best of distributors. Like the San Francisco Cable Car, it is a symbol. It has also given downtown Chicago its geographical name: "The Loop."

They noted that the elevated Loop, completed in 1897, had been part of "the technological revolution of steel and electricity" and compared it with the Eiffel Tower, built eight years earlier.

Although unpublicized at the time, this nomination posed a danger to federal money that the city expected—and needed—to raze the elevated Loop and construct the two new subways. A month later, when the nomination became public knowledge, an official in the city's department of public works said, "We have to assume those funds might be lost." Placement on the National Register would give the elevated structure protection from being unilaterally altered or removed for a project involving the use of U.S. funds. But to get on the register, it would have to be approved by an arm of state government, the Illinois Historic Sites Advisory Council.

Once filed, the Weese-Kiriazis nomination set into motion the process under which the council took testimony and voted on whether to approve the structure. For the elevated Loop, that process took five months, and because of Weese and his allies, it involved a lively public debate on the question.

However, even before that debate began, two letters with a direct bearing on the question had been sent by federal bureaucrats. The first was written on July 5—nine days before the Weese-Kiriazis nomination—by Edward Fleischman, the chief of the planning and analysis division of the Urban Mass Transit Administration in the U.S. Transportation Department. Addressed to William Murtaugh, the keeper of the National Register, the letter requested an opinion on whether the elevated Loop was eligible for inclusion on the register.

Murtaugh responded twenty-three days later that the Loop structure, in fact, was eligible because of its importance in U.S. history and because of its form of construction. In an interview more than three decades later, Fleischman said he had asked for an eligibility determination as a normal step in the complicated process of approvals needed before federal money could be distributed.

Eligibility for the National Register was important because, under federal rules, it granted the same protection to a structure as placement on the National Register. In either case, a city, such as Chicago, seeking money for a project would have to show that the work wouldn't have "an adverse effect" on the designated structure. The city couldn't tear down the structure or change it in ways that would ruin the characteristics that made it significant.

Except it could. The federal law would protect an eligible or designated structure only so far, Fleischman explained. If the city could prove a case that the only solution to achieving the public good would be to alter or raze the structure, the wreckers could go to work. As one prominent preservationist wrote, "If the good to us all that would come from using federal funds for some project that would damage or destroy the elevated would be greater than preserving the L and not doing the project, then, good-by, L."

At the same time that Chicago officials were seeking federal funds to tear down the elevated Loop and replace it with two subways, they were also seeking another large infusion of U.S. cash for the redevelopment of an area called the North Loop, which included much of the land bordered by Washington Street, Wabash Avenue, Wacker Drive, and La Salle Street. This plan, much of which was eventually carried out, called for the demolition of a host of buildings, including four listed on the National Register. Three of those—the McCarthy Building, the Page Brothers Building, and the Delaware Building—had been erected in 1872 and were examples of the sort of buildings constructed in the immediate aftermath of the Great Fire of 1871. The fourth, just outside the delineated area, was the Reliance Building, completed in 1895.

Three of the buildings on the National Register survived, but not the McCarthy Building, on the northeast corner of Dearborn and Washington Streets. Despite its spot on the National Register, it was razed in 1989.

Murtaugh's determination that the elevated Loop was eligible for the National Register and the implications of that ruling never became widely known, although during the five months of controversy over putting the structure on the register, at least some of those involved in the issue were aware of it. For instance, two members of the Illinois Historic Sites Advisory Council—Carroll William Westfall, an architecture professor at the University of Illinois at Chicago, and Harold K. Skramstad Jr., the director of the Chicago Historical Society (now the Chicago History Museum)—said listing on the register was "a moot point" since Murtaugh's eligibility decision. Technically, that was true. However, in the arena of public opinion, the debate over the elevated Loop meant life or death for the structure.

The fact is that Harry Weese, like Paul Gapp before him, saved the elevated Loop—for a crucial few months. He was aided by four enterprising journalists who were able to look beyond the tear-it-down arguments of the city's establishment to the deeper implications of the debate: Gapp with his continuing coverage; Connie Fletcher in her 1977 *Chicago* magazine article, "The Loop El: Love It or Lose It"; and Hank DeZutter and Patrick Fahey in their 1978 *Chicago Reader* article, "Learning to Love the El with Architect Harry Weese."

The nomination by Weese and Kiriazis delayed any action until 1979, when Jane Byrne's surprise election changed everything. Of course, in the second half of 1978, no one knew that she was going to win. Neither did anyone know that in 1981, Ronald Reagan would be elected U.S. president, and federal funds for city projects across the nation would dry up.

But if Weese hadn't stirred up a brouhaha about the elevated Loop, the public would have gone about its business without thinking about the structure. As a result, despite the eligibility determination by Murtaugh, the way would have been open for city officials and Chicago's business leaders to work quietly to convince federal officials, such as Fleischman, and their bosses, such as Carter, that the public good, as they defined it, was more important than saving the elevated Loop.

If the city had been able to accomplish that, it would have moved quickly and decisively—as Daley had wanted to do four years earlier—to bring down two of the four legs of structure (Wells and Van Buren Streets), hoping and expecting that with the removal of half of the elevated Loop a fait accompli, federal officials would feel under pressure to give the money for at least one, if not both subways.

That was the fear of the CTA—that two of the four sections of the elevated Loop would be razed, leaving a structure in the shape of an L and thousands of commuters trying to find new ways to get where they needed to go. "We, at the CTA, started to get negative, [asking] 'What are you going to do with our riders?'" says CTA planner Harold Hirsch. The CTA was worried that the city would remove the two sections of the Loop structure before the Franklin Street subway was constructed, leaving many commuters far from their destinations. The coverage provided to riders by the agency—the way services linked together and covered a large area—would have suffered.

CTA officials, including executive director George Krambles, also worried that even if the Franklin Street project were carried out, the downtown public transit operations wouldn't link together until and unless the second subway under Monroe Street were built. Given that the money for the Franklin subway was so slow in coming, no one knew when, or if, funds for the Monroe Street line would be available. Hirsch noted that Krambles "wanted to preserve the coverage we had, the fantastic coverage. [He became] quietly in favor of retaining [the elevated Loop] once he could see there was a question of how long it was going to take to replace it. He didn't want to be told, 'It's partial, and learn to live with it.'"

It was a scary proposition for transportation professionals, Hirsch said. "We were negative, but we couldn't express that" because the ostensibly independent agency was controlled by City Hall. As a result, Krambles and other agency officials had to follow the script that Mayor Bilandic (and before him, Daley) had written.

"The 'Loop' Trademark"

Not so muzzled was Harry Weese. A hyperactive child when he was growing up on Chicago's North Shore, Weese, as an adult, was "an outside personality," vibrant, ebullient, given to hard drinking and frequent womanizing, and quick "to chafe at authority of any kind." In architecture, he "presented a humanistic alternative to the sterile, steel-and-glass buildings then being turned out by followers of Ludwig Mies van der Rohe," and in city politics, he was "Chicago's conscience," a preservationist and a "cultural provocateur" who "loved to harass Mayor Daley."

Daley was gone, and now, in 1978, Weese was gleefully harassing Bilandic and the rest of the city's power structure. City Hall's party line was that the elevated Loop was ugly, noisy, and even dangerous, but the effervescent Weese bubbled with admiration for the structure, calling it "aesthetically pleasing." He told two reporters for the weekly *Chicago Reader*, during a tour of the elevated Loop, that the structure was "a useful, vital system that's not only convenient but fun to use."

Not many people talked about the elevated rectangle as "fun." Weese also admired "the gracefully curved beams holding the tracks up" and even enthused about its rivets. As the threesome moved south on Wabash Avenue, Weese rhapsodized about the scene: "Every visual artist knows that the Loop creates beautiful patterns of light and shade. And practically speaking, on hot days many people prefer walking on Wabash to keep them out of the sun."

The reporters noted that for Weese, Wabash was "the greatest jaywalking street around," because its support columns in the street forced motorists to be more careful, enabling pedestrians to stand next to the columns in safety before going across.

A little later, while riding around the Loop and watching the flow of second-floor windows from one building to another, Weese told the reporters that Walter McCarter, who headed the CTA for its first seventeen years, "said subways were depressing, that people like the el because they like to see this. The el is tried and true."

In addition to nominating the elevated Loop for the National Register, Weese wrote op-ed pieces, held news conferences, and was always available with a colorful quote for a reporter's story on deadline. In September 1978, he dispatched two allies to the town of Carmi in southern Illinois to attend the meeting of the Illinois Historic Sites Advisory Council, at which testimony was taken on the National Register nomination. Also attending that meeting were three of the city's biggest guns: public works commissioner Marshall Sulloway, city architect Jerome Butler Jr., and planning commissioner Lewis Hill.

A month later, the City of Chicago submitted to the council a sixty-eight-page statement (plus supplementary letters and documents) titled "The Chicago Union Loop Elevated Structure: Reasons for Not Listing upon the National

Register." For a city that had long touted itself as one of the greatest in the world, Chicago was in the unusual position of arguing that the elevated Loop was neither locally nor nationally significant. That resulted in some awkward sentences, such as this one: "While it is true that the elevated railroad system had a significant role in the development of Chicago, it should be recognized that the Loop Elevated is a small part of this elevated system, and it was the total system that contributed to this development."

The city's statement asserted that there was "absolutely nothing unique in the design or structure of the Loop Elevated," even though the rectangle of tracks connecting several elevated lines together is the only one of its kind in the world. And it argued that the creator of the Union Loop, Charles T. Yerkes, was a corrupt and infamous character. And finally, the statement declared, "It is interesting to note from a historical perspective that the 'Loop' trademark actually was derived from the four cable car loops which operated in Chicago's downtown area between 1882 and 1906, long before the Loop Elevated became a reality."

It's conceivable that the city made that claim in good faith, but a more cynical reading of the document is suggested by the two sources that were cited, with specific page numbers, as proof of the assertion: Homer Hoyt's *One Hundred Years of Land Values in Chicago* and Alan R. Lind's *Chicago Surface Lines*. Both books mention the existence of cable car loops, but neither suggests that those loops—which, in fact, never circled more than a handful of blocks each—led Chicagoans to call the downtown the Loop.

"That was language we threw in there to sweeten it a bit," said Stephen E. Roman, a city planner who took part in the drafting of the statement, during an interview decades after the controversy. Roman described himself as agnostic about where the Loop name came from: "I couldn't figure it out from the things I read. You could interpret it in both ways."

"It Is Strange"

The headline in the Paul Gapp story in the *Tribune* of December 6, 1978, was startling: "Landmark Unit Opposed to Saving of 'L' Structure." In the article, Gapp wrote that the Landmarks Preservation Council (LPC) had taken the "extraordinary" position of, essentially, endorsing the city's plan to demolish the elevated structure. "Extraordinary" because, after all, the LPC was "best known for taking vigorous stands against the destruction of architecturally famous buildings." Gapp's report was based on a press release that said the group opposed putting the elevated Loop on the National Register because it obliterated the view of landmark buildings, caused "an economic hardship" for the owners, and "is in our judgement a transit elevated system like many others produced elsewhere in the world."

The announcement came less than two weeks before the Illinois Historic Sites Advisory Council was to meet to make its own decision on the elevated structure, and the *Tribune* editorial page, a strong proponent of demolition, trumpeted the LPC's stand as further proof that the Loop—with "its appalling ugliness"—needed to go.

The question of the elevated Loop, first raised on November 16 by LPC president Robert J. Piper, an architect and planner, was assigned to a task force and put on the agenda for the group's meeting at the end of the month. In advance of that meeting, board member Maurice Forkert, a graphics designer, weighed in with a memo strongly urging demolition.

For one thing, Forkert reported that in a telephone conversation, New York City preservationist Everett Ortner had told him that the tearing down of the elevated structures on Third, Sixth, and Ninth Avenues around 1940 "proved to be a most progressive factor for improvements in the city . . . [and] stopped further expansion of old slums." Moreover, "Nobody missed them." Beyond that, Forkert asserted that "the elevated noise and the shaking of the buildings during rush hours is so great that it affects the nervous system of the people and starts the re-creation of new slums of the future." In addition, the elevated lines "drastically reduce commercial property values . . . add greatly to noise and dirt in the city . . . [and] obscure many fine structures which would otherwise be much more desirable for public use and a visual credit to the city."

On November 29, the LPC board met and voted against National Register designation seventeen to one, with one abstention. The one dissenting vote was from Martin Tangora, a mathematics professor at the University of Illinois at Chicago (UIC), and the abstention was by Carroll William Westfall, apparently because of his membership on the Illinois Historic Sites Advisory Council.

"I thought it was an important part of the Loop, of the downtown area," says Tangora decades later, adding that the elevated structure "defines Chicago." The opposition, he believes, was rooted in the landmarks group's tendency to want to save architecturally significant edifices more than ones that were historically significant. In addition, "there was a feeling that we were there to save buildings" rather than other sorts of structures. At the next LPC meeting, Piper reported that "the City accepted LPC's position with enthusiasm."

Given the nature of Chicago's you-scratch-my-back-I'll-scratch-yours politics, the vote by the landmarks group could be seen as an effort to curry favor with city officials for repayment later on other preservation issues. Westfall, a UIC architecture professor and former LPC president, says he doesn't think that was the case. Even so, he notes that one politically connected board member at the time, attorney-developer Oscar D'Angelo, was in the habit of asking the preservationists, "What have you done to make Mayor Daley look good?"

One organization that wasn't pleased by the action was the National Trust for Historic Preservation. Mary C. Means, the regional director of the Midwest Office, took the LPC to task, writing that the vote "raised a number of questions in our minds, chiefly concerning the grounds by which you arrived at this unusual decision. Consider this a formal request for an elaboration of LPC's position. . . . We are therefore concerned that knowing of the National Trust's public support of the preservation of the Loop Elevated, LPC did not out of courtesy inform us in advance of what the *Tribune* editorially referred to as your 'extraordinary action.'"

In the twenty-first century, the 1978 vote is something of an embarrassment to Landmarks Illinois, the new name of the LPC. "It is strange," said Lisa DiChiera, advocacy director for the group. Bonnie McDonald, the group's current president, noted, "Now, the general public values the 'El' and the Loop as something uniquely Chicago. . . . Some on the board in 1978 recognized that the 'El' might have its own historic value in creating what we now term 'a sense of place.' But, that view was certainly controversial at the time." Landmarks Illinois and other preservationist groups have evolved since the late 1970s, she said, and now work "to advance the understanding that not only buildings, but structures (bridges, roads, water towers, etc.) and sites (landscapes, battlefields, etc.) advance community building, economic development, livability and sustainability."

"To Reject the Loop El Is to Reject Chicago"

Leading up to the December 14 meeting of the Illinois Historic Sites Advisory Council, at least two of the members circulated memos in favor of putting the elevated Loop on the National Register. "Would anyone here be prepared to disregard the historic significance, let us say, of the Brooklyn Bridge simply because there are other suspension bridges—even predecessors—elsewhere in the world?" asked Titus Karlowicz, an art historian and assistant dean at Western Illinois University in Macomb. He was responding to arguments from demolition proponents that the elevated Loop was just another elevated structure, like many elsewhere in the nation.

Karlowicz noted that the National Register question had been "rather thoroughly obfuscated by very dense rhetorical smoke." From his perspective, the elevated structure certainly seemed to fit the criteria for the National Register as "a significant and distinguishable entity." Indeed, he asserted, "a structure that encloses a rectangle of 5 blocks by 7 is certainly a distinguishable entity, however much its stations or structure system may lack of individual distinction. There is to my knowledge no other such structure."

Both Karlowicz and Westfall noted in their memos that CTA executive director George Krambles had asserted, in line with other city representatives, that the elevated Loop didn't meet the National Register criteria but also had made this statement that buttressed the efforts of those seeking to protect the structure: "The elevated loop itself has done more for Chicago's central business district than any other artery of transportation. It is significant that our downtown has popularly adopted the name 'the Loop' from this unique facility."

On December 14, as the Illinois Historic Sites Advisory Council met to consider the register nomination, William G. Farrar, a state preservation official, read into the record an eloquent, impassioned, and in places italicized statement on behalf of the council's staff:

> This staff has considered the nomination of the Chicago Loop Elevated to the National Register of Historic Places and has concluded that:
>
> - *no single structure* has played a more significant role in promoting and shaping the growth of that metropolis; that
> - *no single structure* is more clearly associated with the millions of men and women whose lives are recorded not in the pages of the *Social Register* but in the work of Theodore Dreiser, Ben Hecht, Richard Wright, Studs Terkel, or Saul Bellow; and that
> - *no single structure* could be more symbolic of the drive, the energy, the raw excitement characteristic of that unique place.
>
> To reject the Loop El is to reject Chicago.
>
> Finally, we respectfully submit that *no single nomination* would be a more convincing rebuttal to those who brand historic preservation a pastime of an elite group of socialites and scholars.

Despite such fervor, the motion to approve the elevated Loop for the National Register lost. The proposal needed to garner eight votes to achieve a two-thirds majority. In the vote, though, only six members voted to approve. Five members voted no. On December 29, Keith A. Sculle, National Register coordinator, sent Krambles the official notice that the Loop structure had been rejected.

The way was now open for Chicago officials to put on a full-court press to persuade the federal government to provide the subway money and permit the tearing down of the elevated Loop. Then came the surprise election of the elevated Loop's final savior, Mayor Jane Byrne. This was followed by her surprise decision, revealed on June 22, 1979, to give up on the subways.

At first, no one was sure what would happen to the elevated Loop, but four months later, Byrne established a committee of city, state, and federal officials to develop a master transportation plan for Chicago. When the committee moved too slowly, she locked them in the proverbial smoked-filled room, said Anne Haaker, a state preservation officer who took part. "Nobody was getting out of that room [in City Hall] until an agreement was reached. She was chain-smoking, and pretty much everyone else was smoking. I think we were pushing for more preservation than what happened."

The resulting plan, announced in November and later refined, gave the CTA free rein to rehabilitate, replace, or eliminate all but one of the Loop stations (Quincy/Wells) but protected the elevated structure from demolition.

The final version of the program, approved by Edward Fleischman for the federal government, stated, "The location and structural characteristic of the Loop Elevated Structure (trestle) shall remain substantially unchanged as a result of the Loop Elevated Rehabilitation Project and shall continue to function as a transportation facility. All structural elements of the trestle will continue to be tested for structural integrity and replaced, if necessary. New structural elements may be added or existing ones replaced or removed for safety or operational reasons." The elevated Loop had been saved—finally.

⬅ 16. The Loop, New Year's Day 2019

A half hour before midnight on New Year's Eve 2018, a CTA Brown Line train, nearly empty, marches south along the elevated tracks over Wells Street, goes around the curve, and then heads east above Van Buren Street, on its circuit of Chicago's downtown. More than three decades ago, historian Carl Smith described the elevated Loop as the "most distinctive of all man-made Chicago landmarks" and went on to add, "Riding the el as it rattles around the downtown is one of the few experiences that one can share with Chicagoans of eighty years ago." That's still true.

Riders on this train, late on the last day of the year, can look out onto some of the same buildings that a Chicagoan taking one of the first rides around the Union Loop would have seen—the Monadnock Building (completed in 1893), the Second Leiter Building (1891), the Fisher Building (1896), and the Old Colony Building (1894), as well as the Page Brothers Building (1872) and a scattering of smaller structures erected in the aftermath of the Great Fire of 1871.

But it's not just the sight of these buildings that links a twenty-first-century rider with one at the end of the nineteenth century. Even more, those riders are connected by their use of this stumpy 2.1-mile-long rectangle of railroad tracks running twenty feet or so above four downtown streets. For nearly a century and a quarter, a quintessential experience for a Chicagoan—or a tourist, for that matter—has been riding around the downtown on these tracks. In *Historic Preservation* magazine in 1980, Tom Huth described riding on the trains as a "heady experience," explaining, "The passenger, flying along at pigeon-roosting level, assumes the majesty of looking down. Peering into second and third-floor offices, the rider catches a fleeting glimpse of business executives in conference or perhaps an office worker eating a bologna-and-cheese-on-rye."

Marion Shearer, whose great-grandfather operated a carriage shop in the area that later became known as the Loop, wrote in 1978 that the elevated Loop should be designated a Chicago landmark. "How could I feel otherwise when five generations of my family have ridden on it and when I can watch my grandchildren enjoying every minute of a ride to the Loop?"

Nowhere else in the world is such a ride possible. Although the use of transportation loops is common internationally, often with highway bypasses that avoid a central city and with subways, such as the London Underground, aboveground train loops in a central city downtown are rare.

The Detroit People Mover, for instance, is a 2.9-mile circuit of the city's downtown, handling a daily ridership of 7,500, compared with the average weekday ridership of 150,000 on the elevated Loop in Chicago. The Metromover in Miami, which has been losing riders in recent years despite being free, averaged fewer than 29,000 a day as of September 2018. In contrast to Chicago's elevated Loop, the People Mover and the Metromover serve only their downtown areas, with no links to outer portions of the city. They aren't part of a complex and extensive elevated train system, and they don't knit together their metropolitan areas the way the elevated Loop does in Chicago.

Over the decades, the number of elevated stations on the Loop has changed, as have the cars which, in rush hour, are still jammed with commuters. The creosote-treated wooden ties have been replaced over and over. But the steel structure itself—its stringers and bents, its columns and girders—is, amazingly, much as it was back in 1897.

"I would estimate that 75 percent of the original structures remain today," says James Harper, present-day chief engineer for the CTA. Of the many physical structures that he oversees, the elevated Loop is the most important, and Harper estimates that at least once a day, he or one of the other CTA engineers consults the designs that, in a time when Chicago was still an adolescent city, John Alexander Low Waddell drew for the construction and maintenance of the Union Loop. "As an engineer," he says, "I very much appreciate the uniqueness and the attention to detail of what was done. He was trying to create something beautiful, not just put the steel where it made the most sense. It still impresses me every time I come to work and look up at the structure. There are four hundred thousand pounds of moving steel over our heads, and we take it for granted. There's this huge mass of steel supported over my head."

Such admiration for the elevated Loop was rarely expressed down the many decades, leading up to the structure's near-death experience at the end of the 1970s. Cries to tear down the steel-pillared, rectangular bridge began even before it was finished and were regularly heard from politicians, planners, and those who felt that its screeching wheels, rumbling trains, gloomy shadows, flocks of pigeons, and lack of frilly ornamentation were unsightly.

Yet even before architect Harry Weese came to the elevated Loop's rescue, thoughtful observers were beginning to see the structure as something other

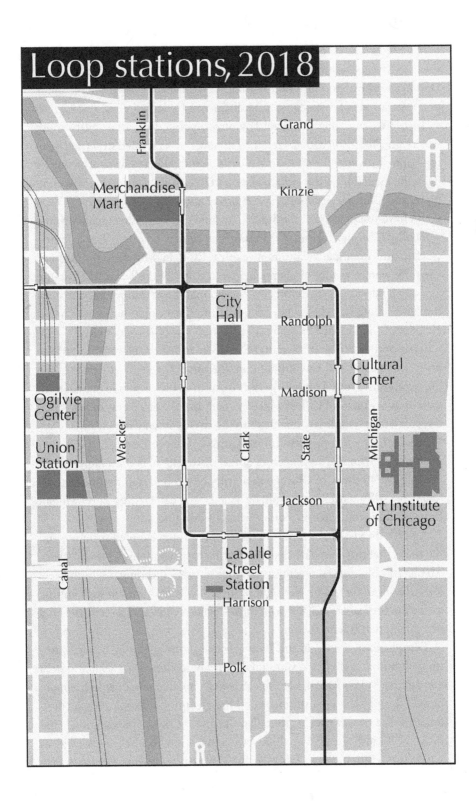

Loop stations, 2018

Franklin

Grand

Merchandise
Mart

Kinzie

City
Hall

Randolph

Cultural
Center

Ogilvie
Center

Wacker

Madison

Michigan

Union
Station

Clark

State

Jackson

Art Institute
of Chicago

LaSalle
Street
Station

Canal

Harrison

Polk

than a blight upon the cityscape. Indeed, in their magisterial 1969 history of the city, *Chicago: Growth of a Metropolis*, two eminent scholars—geographer Harold M. Mayer and historian Richard C. Wade—described the rectangle of tracks as "one of [Chicago's] most distinctive trademarks."

In 1984, geographer Michael P. Conzen pointed out that unlike other American cities, Chicago had retained its downtown elevated structure, turning it into "a major tourist attraction in its own right." A quarter of a century later, the evolution of the elevated Loop from pariah to attraction was complete, and Chicago historians Eric Bronsky and Neal Samors wrote, "Who could have imagined that the Loop 'L' would eventually become a revered symbol of Chicago?" James O'Connor, the former board chairman of the electric utility company Commonwealth Edison, told Bronsky and Samors, "As time wore on, a lot of people began to think of the Loop 'L' structure as a city landmark. It so identified Chicago that if you removed it, and even though it might have helped to beautify things, we would have lost a major element of what made Chicago different from any other major city."

Transportation expert Raymond DeGroote called the elevated Loop "the pride of the city," and David Bahlman, the former executive director of the preservationist group Landmarks Illinois, termed the rectangle of tracks "an extraordinary piece of Chicago history" that, like the cable cars in San Francisco, "gives extraordinary character to the streets down which it runs."

Another Chicago preservationist, Carroll William Westfall, the former chair of the School of Architecture at the University of Notre Dame, noted, "People like to think of Chicago as a gritty city. The Loop reminds people that here's still a piece." As a result, he added, "You can't write a novel without bringing it in. You can't do a movie without bringing it in."

Indeed, the visual and aural character of the Loop elevated structure and the trains that run on it have been like catnip to generations of moviemakers. All that rumbling and screeching, the huge tonnage speeding just twenty feet above heads of the actors, the sight of these horizontal lines of steel cutting across the vertical lines of tall buildings—together, they give a scene the kind of a punch that is hard to find.

Few places in the world still have elevated trains operating in such proximity to human activity, so shots taken anywhere along the elevated system are striking. When it comes to the elevated Loop, that punch is all the more powerful, since the steel structure and the gleaming trains provide a counterpart to the crowds packing the sidewalks and the skyscrapers soaring to the heavens. It's also a clear signal to viewers that a movie is set in Chicago, as writer Tom Huth noted in 1980: "As the cable car represents San Francisco, as the double-decker bus speaks for London, so the El gives shape and distinction to this place called Chicago."

In 1978, when Hollywood was just starting to use Chicago as a backdrop on a regular basis, Lucy Salenger, the director of Illinois Film Services, knew how important the elevated Loop was to attract those film crews: "I shudder every time someone talks about tearing down the 'L.' It's the one thing that every film company wants to see first. They love using it."

"A Pandemonium of Blurtings, Squawkings, and Bellowings"

The Brown Line train making its way around the Loop late on New Year's Eve is just leaving the CTA's new station at Washington Street and Wabash Avenue. As the train runs north, its cars clickety-clack over Randolph Street on the way to the curve toward the Lake Street station. Down below, the thick automobile and bus traffic on Randolph surges forward, only to cluster thickly at State Street. These vehicles are heading west on the one-way street. At State, a similar but thicker crush of cars is pointing north. The police have the southbound State Street lanes blocked at the Chicago River, where, at midnight, fireworks will celebrate the first day of 2019. Fireworks will also explode over the lakefront off Navy Pier.

On this night, the corner of Randolph and State is a crossroads. The westbound cars may be on their way to the junction of the Dan Ryan and John F. Kennedy Expressways to head north or south to New Year's Eve parties. Or perhaps they are heading to celebrations in the newly fashionable West Loop, west of those expressways. Parties in River North, the similarly fashionable neighborhood just north of the river, are the likely destinations of the northbound cars on State Street.

Few pedestrians are on the sidewalks, although ten teenagers in expensively casual clothing seem captivated by this intersection, crossing and recrossing as a group. Some are bundled up tightly against the thirty-five-degree cold, while others wear only a light jean jacket or no jacket at all. As the seconds tick down to midnight, the adolescents stride purposefully across State, heading east.

And then it's midnight. And the 114-year-old clock on Macy's (formerly Marshall Field's) is striking twelve. And all along State and Randolph, cars honk their horns while drivers seek to get a move on to wherever the next party is.

For much of the twentieth century, there was no better place to be on a New Year's Eve, no better party to find, than right here, right at this corner. This intersection of State and Randolph was the epicenter of the city's celebration. For hours ahead of the clock striking midnight, celebrants would gather up and down State until, by the time for the old year to end and the new one to begin, the crowd would sometimes swell to 100,000 or even 150,000.

Back on December 31, 1885, the *Tribune* reporter putting together the latest news under the headline "City Intelligence" for the next morning's paper started with a description of a society wedding earlier in the evening and a mention of the traditional watch services at eleven of the city's churches. And then, it appears, the reporter simply opened a window in the newspaper's offices on the southeast corner of Madison and Dearborn Streets to listen as the clock ticked down to twelve: "At 10 minutes to 12 o'clock last night a solitary steam whistle, very hoarse, awoke the echoes and most of the citizens within a half a mile of it with an unearthly roar. This was taken up by several hundred other steam whistles, which had apparently been simply waiting for a cue, and the chorus was swelled by crowds of merrymakers on the streets, who yelled themselves into perfect speechlessness as the old year went out and the new came in."

By the first day of 1893, the *Tribune* story about New Year's Eve led with the celebration—"Chicago's Down-Town Streets a Pandemonium of Blurtings, Squawkings, and Bellowings"—and then got to the watch services and sermons. This was the first of decades of front-page stories about the December 31 celebrations. Those New Year's morning stories about the partying the night before on downtown streets, particularly on State Street, became a staple of the *Tribune*'s coverage calendar.

During Prohibition (1920–33), the public festivities were a little less raucous on those seemingly rare occasions when authorities decided to clamp down and enforce the national ban on liquor sales. They weren't always so persnickety. Indeed, the banner headline in the *Tribune* about the party in the streets on December 31, 1928, was "Moist Hilarity Greets 1929." A photograph of the celebration—showing wide-smiling men in fedoras and caps, more than a few boys, and only a handful of grinning women, all packed tightly into a celebratory scrum—makes clear that by this time, State and Randolph had become the place to be on New Year's Eve for Chicagoans. And so it went, through the 1930s, 1940s, 1950s, 1960s, and into the 1970s. Each year, there'd be a front-page story, almost always with photos of the revelry under the Marshall Field's clock at State and Randolph.

By the late 1970s—the years when the elevated Loop structure was under the greatest threat of demolition—the *Tribune* turned away from the festivities downtown. By then, the newspaper had refocused its coverage to include large doses of news from the two hundred-plus suburbs in Cook County and the five collar counties where the bulk of the metropolitan population lived, as well as an even higher percentage of *Tribune* readers. It was also more involved in covering the nation and the world, dispatching reporters to chronicle stories from Washington State to Washington, D.C., and from Istanbul to Hanoi.

State Street had been turned into a mall, and on December 31, 1979, Jane Byrne became the first Chicago mayor to attend a New Year's Eve celebration at State and Randolph. Yet even with live music and mild temperatures, the festivities drew only 8,000. Seven years later, however, the crowd set what appears to have been an unofficial record, swelling to an estimated 150,000, many of whom were rowdies, harshly raucous, even violent. "It got downright dangerous," recalls Chicago cultural historian Tim Samuelson. "They were taking glass bottles [to the celebration] and throwing them in the air. It was an intimidating situation."

That's where it ended. The city banned any more partying on New Year's Eve on State Street. And celebrations moved inside at Navy Pier and other locations. At the end of 2015, an attempt was made amid much hoopla to establish a new tradition, featuring an outdoor countdown with a ball drop down the facade of the Hyatt Regency Chicago on the south bank of the Chicago River at Columbus Drive. Called Chi-Town Rising, the initial effort drew mixed reviews and was repeated only once, on December 31, 2016.

They Know They're in Chicago

In the first minutes of 2019, the drivers of cars, taxis, and buses are still trying to make their way through the intersection of State and Randolph to get somewhere else. No crowds of 100,000 or 150,000 smiling, yelling, happy Chicagoans, bundled up against the cold, are gathered here as in all those earlier decades in a communal celebration of the coming of New Year's Day. No "Blurtings, Squawkings, and Bellowings" of fish-horns and other noise-makers. No revolvers shot into the sky, no boom of a six-inch cannon, no beer bottles thrown in the air.

State and Randolph might be viewed at this moment as a forlorn place that time has passed by. Indeed, it might, on this night, be seen as an illustration of how far Chicago's downtown—its Loop—has fallen from the high importance it once held for the city and its region. Yet such a view of the Loop in the twenty-first century is too narrow. Zoom out, just a bit, from this small spot and consider what's going on all around it.

Out off Navy Pier, the sky is exploding with color and light as fireworks mark the new year. On the river, too, just east of Michigan Avenue, fireworks shoot up to the sky from a barge, watched by crowds lining the banks. At hotels that span much of the history of the city, well-dressed crowds of partygoers are welcoming 2019 with shouts, horn blowing, and midnight kissing. Cars, taxis, and buses may be passing through the State and Randolph intersection, but the odds are that many of the drivers and passengers are on their way from and to celebrations in and around the downtown. Far from a ghost town, the area inside the elevated Loop remains the epicenter of the metropolitan region, not just on New Year's Eve but throughout the year.

Even though much of the upscale shopping left downtown for North Michigan Avenue after the opening of Water Tower Place in 1975, the Loop has bounced back, still serving as the home of one of the world's most important financial districts, as well as a one-stop-shopping concentration of city, county, state, and federal government services and courts, while also being reinvented additionally as a bedroom community and a college campus. In list after list of the best downtowns in the United States, Chicago's Loop is there, a hip place to visit, to explore, and increasingly, to live.

In 1960, the U.S. Census Bureau determined that only 4,337 people resided in the Loop community area (the land inside the elevated tracks and surrounding it). Since then, the number sky-rocketed to 37,647, according to the bureau's population estimate for 2014–18. Many of those new downtown residents are affluent individuals, couples, and families drawn by the proximity to cultural institutions, such as the Art Institute of Chicago, the Loop theaters and restaurants, and the unparalleled Grant Park and Lake Michigan shoreline.

They are neighbors to tens of thousands of dormitory and day students at a growing number of colleges and universities. They are neighbors, too, to the millions of tourists each year who find the Loop one of the city's great attractions. In 2018, Chicago attracted nearly fifty-eight million visitors, up 33 percent from seven years earlier. These tourists are drawn to Chicago's lakefront, its Magnificent Mile, its river cruises, and its sports teams. But when they are walking in and near the Loop and hear a Brown, Green, Orange, or Purple Line train barreling over their heads or see one nearby or far away making its lumbering rounds along the tracks—or, even more, when they are riding in one of those trains—they know one thing for sure: they know they're in Chicago.

A Forest of Very Tall Buildings

A few hours later, after dawn on the morning of January 1, 2019, you could fly a plane over Chicago, and what you would see is a forest of very tall buildings along the lakefront in an area running north-south from Congress Street to

North Avenue and west from the Lake Michigan shoreline anywhere from a mile to two miles inland. Skyscrapers continue to be built inside the rectangle of the elevated Loop and even more, nowadays, in a growing area along its outer edges, particularly in the River North area and along Michigan Avenue. Interestingly, much of the area covered by this looming thicket of towers was included in the 1830 map on which surveyor James Thompson subdivided the land that became the city of Chicago.

Take a similar flight over Manhattan, and you'd see something very different—two forests of skyscrapers, one at the southern tip of the island near the Brooklyn Bridge, the other up in the area south of Central Park. There's a reason for that, according to *New York Times Magazine* writer James Traub: "Manhattan has no center. . . . If you asked a New Yorker for directions to 'the center of town,' he would be bewildered, and might, for want of better, send you to Times Square, or Columbus Circle, which are simply nodal points that New Yorkers pass through, often at their peril." Chicago, though, does have a center.

Back in 1917, Hobart Chatfield-Taylor wrote that the Loop—the downtown inside the four lines of the elevated Loop rectangle—was "literally, as well as metaphorically, the heart of the city." Three decades later, Nelson Algren described the elevated Loop as "the city's rusty heart." Like Algren's "broken nose" on a woman, the elevated Loop is the seeming flaw that has been transformed by time and affection into a mark of beauty. It is, like Algren's Chicago, "never a lovely so real."

Today, after a century of good times and bad—of growth, stagnation, confusion, and reinvention—Chicago's Loop is crowded with office workers, tourists, college students, shoppers, homeless beggars, financiers, judges, preachers, lawyers, bicyclists, and cops. After the commuters go home, the sidewalks are still busy with high-rise residents walking dogs, mothers pushing strollers, groups of teens on a lark, and suburbanites lining up for the latest theater offering from Broadway. And it leads writer Edward McClelland to ask, "Why did [Chicago] become an Alpha World City, in the same league as Paris, Mumbai, Shanghai, Frankfort, and Sydney, while Cleveland became the Mistake on the Lake, and Detroit become *the* destination for European art photographers documenting urban decay?"

It's a question with many complex answers. But one of those answers—long overlooked, ignored, disregarded—is the elevated Loop and the way that its rectangle of tracks, its "golden circle," its "magic circle," has anchored Chicago's downtown and, indeed, the entire city. The elevated Loop, the most important structure in the history of Chicago.

In its loud, gritty, ugly-duckling way, the elevated Loop has functioned as the transportation connection of the highest importance. It's not as rusty nor as loud as it used to be, but it still gets tens of thousands of people each day where they want to go. But even more, this rectangle of elevated tracks continues to root the center of Chicago—and the center of the metropolitan area—in this spot on Earth. To root Chicagoans—that vast mob of cultures, faiths, classes, races, attractions, incomes, dispositions, preoccupations, enthusiasms, ideologies, ages, genders, abilities, biases, arts, cuisines—together in this place they call home.

END

Acknowledgments

Notes

Bibliography

Index

⬅ Acknowledgments

This book would never have seen the light of day without the help, support, and love of my wife, Cathy Shiel-Reardon; our children, David and Sarah; our daughter-in-law, Tara Ruccolo Reardon; our granddaughter, Emmaline Patrick; and our friend John Fallon. Also, Julie Coplon and Joan Servatius.

After four decades of research and writing as a newspaper reporter, I moved across the road to the field of history with the encouragement and assistance of many scholars. At the start, Ann Durkin Keating, coeditor of *The Encyclopedia of Chicago* and author of several important books of Chicago history, met me for coffee and heartily cheered me on as I made my first tentative efforts at developing a book about the city's past. Early in my research, geographer Michael Conzen talked with me in his University of Chicago office and gave me important insights about the physical place that is Chicago. Tim Samuelson, the city's cultural historian, was a great source of inspiration to me when I was a *Chicago Tribune* reporter and when I began my work that has resulted in this book. Other scholars have been kind to me in many ways, including Gerald Danzer, Perry Duis, Michael Ebner, Ellen Skerrett, and Charles Fanning.

Bruce G. Moffat, the author of the bible of Chicago's elevated history, *The "L": The Development of Chicago's Rapid Transit System, 1888–1932*, showed me great kindness in interviews and in sharing with me photographs from his extensive collection. He was also gracious enough to read several draft chapters of this book and make apt suggestions. Similarly, Greg Borzo, the author of the detailed and sprightly *Chicago Cable Cars*, clarified for me in interviews and through emails many of the arcane aspects of the city's cable operations and closely read several draft chapters. In addition, Chicago bridge historian Patrick T. McBriarty read a section of the manuscript and helped me better understand the breakthrough nature of John Alexander Low Waddell's vertical lift bridge. LeRoy Blommaert allowed me to photograph and use an interesting little pamphlet from 1898, *The Union Elevated Loop in Chicago*, issued by the Lake Shore & Michigan Southern Railway.

In writing *The Loop*, I stood on the shoulders of great work by earlier historians of Chicago and of American cities, such as Harold M. Mayer, Richard C. Wade, Robert M. Fogelson, Neal Samors, John Franch, Ross Miller, and the editors and writers of the *Encyclopedia of Chicago*. In particular, because of the somewhat quirky nature of my book, drawing insights as it does from a wide array of fields, I want to give a shout-out to seven off-the-beaten-path books that were of great help: *Political Influence*, by Edward C. Banfield; *Building Lives*, by Neil Harris; *Liberal Dreams and Nature's Limits*, by James T. Lemon; *Industrial Archeology*, by Theodore Anton Sande; *Images of the American City*, by Anselm L. Strauss; *Form Follows Finance*, by Carol Willis; and *Brooklyn Bridge*, by Alan Trachtenberg.

Little did I know during the two decades in which I played basketball weekly with Jim Harper that he would turn out to be a key source for this book. As the chief engineer of the Chicago Transit Authority (CTA), he was able to explain to me John Alexander Low Waddell's design of the elevated Loop and communicate to me his admiration for Waddell, whose work continues to serve the city more than 120 years after the elevated Loop's construction. Another Waddell admirer, CTA engineer Joel Villanueva, gave me a street-level tour of the structure and answered dozens of my questions. Also supportive was Graham Garfield, the CTA's general manager of customer information.

Another longtime friend, Steve Kagan, went above and beyond the call of duty to help me with some great photographs of the present-day elevated Loop, and Dennis McClendon, my former colleague at the Burnham Plan Centennial, produced wonderfully clear and instructive maps for this book.

At important points during my twelve years of research, many people helped me, and I want to thank them: Melanie Bishop, Michael Dorf, Rita Dragonette, Tony Dudek, Robert M. Fogelson, Terry Gregory, Anne Haaker, Terry Holzheimer, Mark Jacob, Meg Kindelin, Thomas Leslie, Sylvia Lewis, Rob Parel, Kevin Roderick, Martin Tangora, Sam Bass Warner Jr., and Carroll William Westfall. My former *Tribune* colleague Rick Kogan steered me to a key quote from Mike Royko at an important moment in the writing of this book. And I thank everyone else who helped me.

As I mention in the text, the Chicago Public Library made available to me, as a library cardholder, the digital archive of virtually the entire run of the *Chicago Tribune*, which has been so essential to my analysis of the story of the elevated Loop. And I am especially grateful to the ever-helpful, ever-pleasant librarians at the Rogers Park branch library, particularly Emma Bradosty, Lyn Garrick-Weil, and branch manager Jacqueline Hui.

I also must acknowledge how much I owe, as a student of Chicago history and as a writer, to the *Chicago Tribune*, where I worked for thirty-two years and where I was paid to become an expert on the city.

Writing is a lonely occupation, so it has been indispensable for me to have a community of writers with whom to meet regularly and discuss our work—Thomas Pace, Jim Strickler, Patty Cloud, Rev. Dominic Grassi, Marjorie Skelly, and John Camper. Thanks for many helpful insights, much encouragement, and kindly hand-holding.

And it's been such a joy to have found Southern Illinois University Press, a publisher with a strong dedicated staff and a zest for fashioning a book into the best it can be. My thanks go to Joyce Bond, Linda Jorgensen Buhman, Jennifer Egan, Amy Etcheson, Chelsey Harris, Wayne Larsen, and everyone else at SIU Press for their kind treatment and savvy professionalism, and especially to Sylvia Frank Rodrigue, who took a chance on this idea of mine and helped immensely in bringing it to fruition.

Finally, I would like to say that I have learned much from working with and reading the work of so many great writers and historians. For me, the one who has been a constant inspiration as a researcher and a writer and who has become a friend is Robert A. Caro, and I can't thank him enough.

My thanks to Connie Fletcher and *Chicago* magazine for permission to quote from her 1977 article "The Loop El: Love It or Lose It" and to the publishers for permission to quote from these works: Eric Bronsky and Neal Samors, *Downtown Chicago in Transition* (Chicago: Chicago's Book Press, 2007); and Neal Samors and Michael Williams, *Chicago in the Fifties: Remembering Life in the Loop and the Neighborhoods* (Chicago: Chicago's Neighborhoods, 2005).

Notes

The abbreviation *CT* refers to the *Chicago Tribune* and IHSAC to the Illinois Historic Sites Advisory Council.

Introduction

1 "most astute Chicago friends": Liebling, *Second City*, 22.
1 "Roebling's claims": Trachtenberg, *Brooklyn Bridge*, 79
1 National Register: "NP Gallery," National Park Service, November 27, 1998, https://npgallery.nps.gov/AssetDetail/NRIS/98001351.
1 official Chicago landmarks: City of Chicago, "Chicago Landmarks," accessed April 29, 2020, https://webapps1.chicago.gov/landmarksweb /web/home.htm.
2 "vaulting the sea": Hart Crane, *The Bridge.*
2 "Coming into existence": Trachtenberg, *Brooklyn Bridge*, ix.
3 "symbolize and enhance": Trachtenberg, *Brooklyn Bridge*, ix.
5 "that grim rectangle": Liebling, *Second City*, 22.
5 "The rise of property": Trachtenberg, *Brooklyn Bridge*, 38.
5 "indirectly promoted": Trachtenberg, *Brooklyn Bridge*, 129.
5 "magic circle": "In Real Estate Circles," *Chicago Tribune* (hereafter *CT*), August 25, 1901, 43. See also "Rigid Growth outside Loop," *CT*, September 24, 1911, H13.
5 "golden circle": "The New 'Union' Loop," display ad, *CT*, October 15, 1897, 12. See also "Oppose Longer Loop Platforms," *CT*, August 16, 1905, 3.
6 "fitting symbol": Ron Grossman, "'L' rides high above the madding city crowds," *CT*, March 11, 1997, 2-metro.
7 "schizophrenic": See Ross Miller, *Apocalypse*, 16, and Strauss, *Images*, 41.
8 "milch cow": "Yerkes and the Newspapers," *CT*, January 14, 1897, 6.
8 The digital archive of the *Tribune*: After working as a reporter at the *Tribune* for thirty-two years, I am very familiar with the wealth of stories in its digital archive. I am also aware that the *Tribune* in those years (as in the years when I worked at the paper) had its own eccentricities and bias, all of which I took into account in using the archive. Whenever possible, I brought in voices from other papers, books, and documents.
9 "most distinctive of all man-made Chicago landmarks": Carl Smith, *American Literary Imagination*, 103.
9 "most distinctive trademarks": Mayer and Wade, *Metropolis*, 210.
9 "It's every man": Algren, *Chicago*, 23.
9 "While we shall leave": Algren, *Chicago*, 77. The name of this tribe has been spelled several ways by various writers and scholars.

1. The Loop, New Year's Eve 1911

10   The stately seven-ton bronze clocks: The details of the 1911 New Year's Eve celebration in the Loop are from "Sane New Year's Chill Winds Drive Gay Crowd Within," *CT*, January 1, 1912, 1; "'Sane' Celebrators See Art at New Year's Eve Fete," *CT*, January 1, 1912, 4; "New Year Gayety Lasts All Night," *CT*, January 2, 1912, 3.

10   Their hooves sound sharply: "See Larger Shopping Area," *CT*, December 16, 1906, 10; "Work on Tracks Meets No Delay," *CT*, September 22, 1908, 3; "Self-Interest versus Civic Pride," *CT*, June 28, 1909, 1; "Chicago Active in Improvement," *CT*, December 7, 1910, A6. Images of State Street for 1909 through 1913 clearly show asphalt along the curbs and, in the middle, creosote blocks and trolley rails.

10   "My, but it's quiet": "Sane New Year's Chill Winds Drive Gay Crowd Within," *CT*, January 1, 1912, 1

10   Just yesterday: "New Year's Fight Taken to Deneen," *CT*, December 31, 1911, 2; "Harrison: 'Be Gay, but Not Too Gay,'" *CT*, December 25, 1911, 4.

11   fourth most populous city: *World Almanac 1912*, 610.

11   When, in 1830: Thompson, "Thompson's Plat of 1830."

11   "almost a baby city": Noguchi, *Story*, 91–93.

11   The proper name "Loop": This section on the evolution of the word "loop" in reference to downtown is based in large part on a painstaking study of *Chicago Tribune* stories from 1882 through 1912. Even when employed as a proper name for either the elevated structure or downtown, "Loop" was often not capitalized during the early decades of the twentieth century. Indeed, the *Chicago Tribune* did not give it a capital "L" on a regular basis until the 1950s. Many others, however, had started to do so much earlier. To avoid confusion, I capitalize it when it is a proper name for the rectangle of elevated tracks or the downtown area, except in quoted material that has it lowercased.

11   2.1-mile-long rectangle: Elevated Railway Employees, *The Story*, 4.

11   "golden circle": "The New 'Union' Loop," display ad, *CT*, October 15, 1897, 12.

11   Later, a critic: Liebling, *Chicago*, 7–8.

12   quarter of a square mile of land: The two north-south legs of the rectangle between Lake Street and Van Buren Avenue are 3,280 feet in length. The east-west legs between Wabash Avenue and Wells Street are 2,133 feet long. The area they enclose covers just under 7 million square feet, or 0.25 square miles.

12   thirty-nine blocks: Chicago-L.org, "Metropolitan West Side Elevated R. R.," 1898, accessed July 3, 2018, http://www.chicago-l.org/maps/route/maps/1898met-downtown.jpg.

12   Just a year earlier: "Congested Loop Immensely Rich," *CT*, November 30, 1910, A9.

13   "down-town": This is the spelling the *Tribune* used prior to 1900. After that, it was "downtown."

13   1.58 square miles: WildOnions.org, http://www.wildonions.org/Chicago Resource/Loop-Information.htm, accessed April 29, 2014, adapted from the U.S. Census 2000.

13   "Vendors did a poor business": "Sane New Year's Chill Winds Drive Gay Crowd Within," *CT*, January 1, 1912, 1.

14   At a time: Willis, *Form*, 9. The paragraphs in my text comparing New York and Chicago skyscrapers rely heavily on Willis's groundbreaking book.

14   New York's celebration: "1912 Reaches Town in a Robe of Mist," *New York Times*, January 1, 1912, 1.

15   "All about you they rise": Steevens, *Land*, 396.

15   "The gorges and canyons": Archer, *America*, 90.

16   "compare with Chicago": Archer, *America*, 90.

16   Initially, American cities: Merchant, *Environmental*, 120.

16   "a huge smoke-cloud": Garland, *Son*, 268.

16   "Its air is dirt": Kipling, *Sea*, 230.

16   "O Lord": Noguchi, *Story*, 91–93.

16   "Chicago Is Enveloped": "Chicago Is Enveloped in Smoke," *CT*, December 2, 1898, 3.

16   Early in 1912: "Girls Too Plump for Gowns," *CT*, January 10, 1912, 3.

17   Throughout the Loop: Pacyga, *Biography*, 106.

17   "Our average downtown sunset": Charles W. Anderson, "Smoke Grimed Chicago," *CT*, August 4, 1911, 8.

17   For more than half a century: Platt, *Electric*, 25, 91 and 147.

17   gaslights: Flammable coal gas was used in streetlights that were ignited by lamplighters. In an arc light, a spark or "arc" of electric current would be run between two carbon rods, providing illumination. Ultimately, these technologies were replaced by the electric light bulb, invented by Thomas A. Edison in 1880. See Platt, "Gas and Electricity."

17   night flights: The first night flight in the United States was made in June 1910 by Charles W. Hamilton at Camp Dickinson, Knoxville, Tennessee. "The History of Flight from Around the World: 1910s," American Institute of Aeronautics and Astronautics, accessed July 3, 2018, https://www. aiaa.org/about/History-and-Heritage/History-of-Flight-Around-the-World.

18   some six hundred homeless: "Sane New Year's Chill Winds Drive Gay Crowd Within," *CT*, January 1, 1912, 1. See also "Jobless Line Up for Coffee," *CT*, December 13, 1911, 2; "Banker Feeds Street Waifs," *CT*, January 1, 1908, 1.

18   "Congested Loop": "Congested Loop Immensely Rich," *CT*, November 30, 1910, A9.

18 "little attempt to do good": "Banker Feeds Street Waifs," *CT*, January 1, 1908, 1.

18 "carrying the banner": "Jobless Line Up for Coffee," *CT*, December 13, 1911, 2.

18 "a million dollar celebration": "New Year Gayety Lasts All Night," *CT*, January 2, 1912, 3.

19 "the fun spirit": "Sane New Year's Chill Winds Drive Gay Crowd Within," *CT*, January 1, 1912, 1.

19 "fair young things": "New Year Gayety Lasts All Night," *CT* January 2, 1912, 3.

2. Academic Fashion

23 sixth in population: Lewis, *Encounter*, 1.

23 unsettling new world: For instance, Lewis quotes English journalist George Warrington Steevens: "The truth is that nobody in this rushing, struggling tumult has any time to look after what we have long ago come to think the bare decencies of civilisation." Lewis, *Encounter*, 14, 130.

23 "foreign visitors": Lewis, *Encounter*, 139.

23 "It was exceptional": Lewis, *Encounter*, 3–4.

23 Sigfried Giedion: Lewis, *Encounter*, 125, citing Giedion, *Space*, 10.

24 Lewis makes extensive use: Lewis, *Encounter*, 136–38, citing "Day on State Street," *CT*, May 6, 1888, 25.

25 Perhaps the most extreme: Bennett, *Forced*.

25 "It was from these cable car loops": Hilton, *Railways*, 2.

25 "In Chicago most of the public transit systems": Duis, "Shaping," 6.

25 "The initial cable car lines": Spinney, *Shoulders*, 150.

26 "The Loop is the popular name": Danzer, "The Loop."

26 "In turn, as growing numbers": Junger, *Becoming*, 94–95.

26 "These surface lines": Cudahy, *Destination*, 7.

27 "How did the Loop": unknown Chicago newspaper, April 19, 1940, "How Did Loop . . . That's Right . . . ," in the files of the *Chicago Tribune* but apparently not from that newspaper.

27 As the source: Windsor, *Souvenir*. The Chicago City Railway Co. is described by cable car historian Greg Borzo as "the largest and most important cable car system ever in the United States and possibly the world." See Borzo, *Cable Cars*, 75. Later, in 1902, Windsor founded and edited *Popular Mechanics* magazine.

27 "By Christmas": Donald L. Miller, *Century*, 266.

27 "Rationalizers and Reformers": Weber, "Rationalizers."

28 "It also created": Mayer and Wade, *Growth*, 138.

28 "The loop": White, "Chicago," 729.

29 "To find the loop": White, "Chicago," 730.

3. Silence

30 Two paragraphs before: Dreiser, *Dawn*, 530, quoted in Donald L. Miller, *Century*, 265.

30 "in the business heart of Chicago": Dreiser, *Dawn*, 574.

31 "They arose": Dreiser, *Sister*, 60–61.

31 "I wud rigidly": *Chicago Evening Post*, March 27, 1897, in Dunne, *Irish*, edited by Fanning, 196, 246. Thanks to Charles Fanning for his help.

31 "condensation of the business activity": Ade, "After the Sky-Scrapers, What?" in *Stories*, 104–8.

31 "Between the former site": Fuller, *Cliff-Dwellers*, 1.

32 "An overhanging pall": *The Times*, London, October 24, 1887, reproduced in Pierce, *Others*, 230.

32 "Stand with me here": King, "World's Fair," 59–63.

33 "Chicago will be": Ralph, "Exhibit," 425.

33 Nine years later: Hilton, *Railways*, 2 and back cover

34 Darrow and Masters as law partners: See Tietjen, "Darrow," 411–25; Russell, *Masters*.

34 "During his period of prosperity": Darrow, *Life*, chap. 13.

34 "the 'Loop' area": Lewis, *Encounter*, 125, citing Giedion, *Space*, 10.

35 "the city of the Loop district": Masters, *Across*, 141, 145.

35 "This is me": Russell, *Masters*, 73.

35 "fops": Masters, *Spoon*, 173.

35 "Down in the loop": Edgar Lee Masters, "The Loop," originally in *New Republic*, January 1, 1916, 226, and included in *Songs*, 32–39.

4. Lots of Loops

36 "in some respects": "Street-Car Travel," *CT*, December 18, 1880, 7.

36 "Under this arrangement"—"The New Cable Street-Railway," *CT*, December 29, 1880, 4. The editorial refers to the Chicago City Railway Company by another name that was used occasionally, the South Side Street Railway Company.

37 "Chicago Cable Havana": "Chicago Cable," *CT*, January 1, 1885, 7. Ads for the cigar ran in the *Tribune* from October 18, 1884, through June 23, 1891, when Chicago Cable cigars were among 350,000 being sold in a fire salvage sale.

37 the city's cable-car system: Borzo, *Cable Cars*, 19–20. This book was especially helpful to me in writing this chapter and the book as a whole. In addition, Greg Borzo graciously answered my many questions about cable cars and Chicago's elevated system, the subject of another of his books, *Chicago "L."*

37 503,185 residents: Chicago population and the list of top cities are from the U.S. Bureau of the Census, "Table 11. Population of the 100 Largest

Urban Places: 1880," June 15, 1998, https://www.census.gov/population /www/documentation/twps0027/tab11.txt. Brooklyn was a separate city until 1898, when it was merged into New York City.

37   Abraham Brower: Borzo, *Cable Cars*, 57. Brower's first name is sometimes given as Abram.

37   It was home: Population figures are from Pierce, *History*, 44.

37   "The interior of the village": Latrobe, *The Rambler*, 201–16, excerpted in Pierce, *Others*, 60.

38   By 1850: Population figures are from Skogan, *Chicago*, 18.

38   the horsecar: This section on the horsecar is based on Borzo, *Cable Cars*, 57–67, and Rowsome, Jr., *Trolley*, 17–34. Comments by Greg Borzo on an earlier draft improved this section.

38   "organic city": Steinberg, *Down to Earth*, 159.

38   "In the passenger compartment": Rowsome, *Trolley*, 19.

39   sixty-six hundred horses: David M. Young, "Street Railways." The horse urine also corroded the metal horsecar tracks.

39   According to one estimate: Melosi, "'Out of Sight,'" 332.

39   "Such sights": Merchant, *Environmental*, 122.

39   "Worse still": Steinberg, *Down to Earth*, 162.

39   horses were used: As late as 1900, Chicago had a horse population of about seventy-four thousand, or one for every 22.9 residents. In 1914, the figure was even higher: eighty-two thousand. The horsecar companies remained a significant part of Chicago's public transportation system for many years, operating more than 150 miles of tracks in 1890. But by 1900, they were reduced to just a few lines. By 1906, the only horses in use were those pulling cable cars during the late night and early morning hours to provide time for maintenance of the cable machinery. And they were phased out when, by the end of that year, the cable cars themselves were replaced by trolleys. See McShane and Tarr, *Horse*, 16; Merchant, *Environmental*, 122; Borzo, *Cable Cars*, 66; "Surprised to See Horse Cars," *CT*, December 9, 1900, 59; "The Last Horse Car," *CT*, October 14, 1906, B4.

39   "Being freed": "Street-Car Travel," *CT*, December 18, 1880, 7.

39   "The value": John Anderson Miller, *Fares*, 45.

39   "system destined": "The Cable Scheme," *CT*, June 26, 1881, 10.

40   An ordinance: "The Council," *CT*, December 28, 1880, 12; "The Council," *CT*, January 18, 1881, 9.

40   Work delayed: "The Cable Road," *CT*, May 13, 1881, 8.

40   Once that was done: Windsor, *Souvenir*.

40   "Day after day": Borzo, *Cable Cars*, 83.

40   Meanwhile, the city: "Street Railways," *CT*, May 26, 1881, 8.

40   State Street south of downtown: Hilton, *Railways*, 4; Carey, "Prairie Avenue."

40   "utterly demoralized": "State Street between Polk and Twenty-Second St. Is Absolutely Useless," *CT*, September 25, 1881, 8.

40   delegation: "City Council," *CT*, July 26, 1881, 8.
40   Within a week: "Intramural Travel," *CT*, August 3, 1881, 6; "Cable Railway," *CT*, October 16, 1881, 20; "The Cable Street-Railway," *CT*, November 6, 1881, 4; "The Cable Road," *CT*, January 14, 1882, 8.
41   "I have seen": "Highly Successful," *CT*, January 29, 1882, 5. Unless otherwise indicated, all descriptions of the inauguration ceremony are based on or quoted from this seven-thousand-word story that took up more than half of a page in the *Tribune*, a huge amount of space for the paper to devote to the account.
41   "That indomitable perseverance": Bross, *History*, 98.
41   "There has not been": Bross, *History*, 100.
41   "repeated, embroidered": Ross Miller, *Apocalypse*, 29.
42   "there is no limit": "Highly Successful," *CT*, January 29, 1882, 5.
42   temperature: "The Weather," *CT*, January 29, 1882, 3.
42   fifty thousand Chicagoans: Another estimate was three hundred thousand, which seems greatly inflated since that would have required three of every five Chicagoans to be in attendance.
42   red grip car: Borzo, *Cable Cars*, 84.
42   small boys: See Hilton, *Railways*, 41; John Anderson Miller, *Fares*, 47–48; Rowsome, *Trolley*, 61–62.
43   Reversing direction: An essential source for me for this discussion of loops and turntables—and, indeed, for cable cars in general—was Borzo, *Cable Cars*, particularly 84–85. Another key source was Hilton, *Cable Car*. Also important were comments on an early draft from Roy G. Benedict, who has written widely about early Chicago public transportation and holds the extensive unpublished research of the late transit researcher James J. Buckley. In addition, my understanding of cable systems was greatly enhanced by conversations with Borzo, Benedict, and Robert Callwell, coauthor with Rice of *Cables and Grips*. I conducted interviews with Benedict on August 18, 2014, and Callwell on August 25, 2014. I spoke with and communicated with Borzo several times.
44   "downtown belt": "Cable Cars," *CT*, January 28, 1882, 8; "The Cable Car Road, the Washington Boulevard, and Other Thoroughfare Matters," *CT*, January 1, 1882, 7; "The Cable Road," *CT*, February 19, 1882, 8. In his 1887 book about cable systems, J. Bucknall Smith also referred to this loop as a "belt line." Smith, *Treatise*, 84. In 1885, W. W. Hanscom described this cable as going around "a square," but that word never caught on. Hanscom, *Archaeology*, 117.
44   "The Grip-Cars": "Turned the Corner," *CT*, February 24, 1882, 3.
44   "most spectacular": Hilton, *Cable Car*, 239.
44   a new system: Borzo, *Cable Cars*, 36–37; Hilton, *Railways*, 7, 10. Comments by Greg Borzo on an earlier draft improved this section.
44   one horsecar company: Roy G. Benedict passed along this information to me in a letter, based on the data collected by James J. Buckley.

45   this early horsecar loop: This explanation was suggested by Roy G. Benedict.

45   balloon loop: See Fairchild, *Street Railways*, 90–93. A balloon loop is also called a balloon track or a reversing loop.

45   Chicago's loop innovation: Hilton, *Cable Car*; various articles by Joe Thompson, *Cable Car Home Page*, last updated February 20, 2020, http://www.cable-car-guy.com/html/ccmain.html.

45   "a most bold undertaking": Smith, *Treatise*, 82.

45   "Transit cars": Borzo, *Cable Cars*, 22.

46   "the horse car": Weber, "Rationalizers," 84.

46   elbow room: Based on Sanborn Map Company fire insurance maps for Chicago for 1894–97, particularly those for the newly developed areas of the South Side, showing many lots with generally small front yards, much larger back yards, and occasionally a narrow side yard. By contrast, many lots in the older parts of the city have no front or side yard and only a small back yard.

46   "the increase in value": "Cable-Car System," *CT*, January 1, 1884, 18.

46   "Within six months": Windsor, *Souvenir*.

47   "Improved transportation": Weber, "Rationalizers," 4.

47   Lots of Loops: This discussion of cable lines, loops, and the meanings of the word "loop" relies heavily on Borzo, *Cable Cars*, particularly his five color maps of the cable service downtown and in other sections of the city. Also very helpful have been my conversations and email exchanges with Borzo.

5. The Word "Loop"

50   as a synonym: *Rand, McNally & Co.'s Bird's-Eye*, 43. Also cited in Borzo, *Cable Cars*, 88.

50   a thick hemp rope: Borzo, *Cable Cars*, 28. The term is still used this way in San Francisco, where a present-day description of the cable car service gives tourists this advice: "Watch the sheaves that control the three continuous loops of cable, and peer down at the machines that turn them." See Malloy, "Cable Car Tour," and Gerrylynn K. Roberts, *American Cities*, 35.

50   Generally, the cable: Borzo, *Cable Cars*, 28–29.

50   "It was quickly found": "Jack Frost Grips the Cable," *CT*, March 10, 1888, 7.

51   "An Energetic Protest": "South Side Street Cars—An Energetic Protest against the Disregard of the Loop," *CT*, June 9, 1883, 8. See also "Street Railways," *CT*, July 8, 1883, 8.

51   "boodle Aldermen": "The Boodlers Elated," *CT*, February 13, 1887, 6. In urban America in the 1880s, "boodle" was a synonym for bribery. The "boodle Aldermen" mentioned by the *Tribune* were predecessors of the Gray Wolves faction that dominated the City Council during the 1890s and early twentieth century.

51   "The new power house": "Gleanings in Local Fields," *CT*, August 2, 1891, 3.

52   wide variety: In fact, the use of loops became so ubiquitous in transit operations that the word "loop" was also employed, at times, to describe something that in another place or at another time might simply have been called a circle. For example, a new half-mile cement bicycle track in Garfield Park was called a loop in a *Tribune* headline in 1896. And the street layout of the U.S. Army post Fort Sheridan in Lake County, Illinois, was described in an 1891 *Tribune* story as having three loops. See "Garfield Loop Neary [sic] Done," *CT*, July 25, 1896, 6; "Uncle Sam's Best Post," *CT*, June 28, 1891, 33.

52   "their terminal systems": "Street Railways," *CT*, July 8, 1883, 8.

52   first trolley line: Borzo, *Cable Cars*, 162. Inaugurated on October 2, 1890, the Calumet Electric Street Railway trolley line ran on Ninety-Third Street between Stony Island and South Chicago Avenues.

52   its route: "Electric System in Operation," *CT*, April 15, 1892, 1.

52   "Old Citizen": "Railroad Circle for Hyde Park," *CT*, March 31, 1885, 12. In 1885, the southern border of Chicago was Egan Avenue (now Pershing Road). The towns mentioned in the letter were all annexed to Chicago in 1889.

53   "Uncle Dan": Burchard and Bush-Brown, *Architecture*, 296.

53   "Burnham had a natural ability": Schaffer, *Burnham*, 63.

53   "As a result": "Effect of the Change," *CT*, June 28, 1891, 3.

53   "A few weeks ago": "Chief Gottlieb Resigns," *CT*, August 12, 1891, 8.

53   key issue: The other was a dispute over the technical matter of how strong the building timbers should be.

54   "No Loop": "No Loop on the Fair Grounds," *CT*, August 22, 1891, 12. See map and photo of train lines dead-ending at Terminal Station in Bolotin and Laing, *Columbian*, 49, 144–45.

54   "At the first glance": "The Underground Loop," *CT*, July 7, 1895, 12.

54   Sidewalk loop ideas: See "To Try the Movable Sidewalks," *CT*, September 12, 1891, 12; Earl Shepard Johnson, "The Natural History," 385; "An Elevated Loop Project," *CT*, October 22, 1893, 30; "For Sidewalk Loop," *CT*, December 23, 1893, 6.

54   "aerial bicycle highway": "To Pedal Up in the Air," *CT*, June 7, 1897, 4.

6. The Last Cable Car

55   Clement: Old Tippecanoe Club of Chicago, 91–99; "Stephen H. Clement," *CT*, May 7, 1897, 2; "Was in Ellsworth's Zouaves," *New York Times*, May 8, 1897, 11.

55   special meeting: "Must Have Relief," *CT*, December 6, 1891, 1.

55   Halley: "Unique Souvenir of Father Mathew;" *CT*, October 7, 1894, 35; "Lawyer and Editor Fight in Austin," *CT*, August 15, 1897, 12; *Geo. P.*

Rowell, 38; *Rowell's*, 139–40; Halley, *Centennial*; Halley, *Halley's Pictorial*; Murray, *Journal*, 157; Schneirov, *Labor*.

56   riders complained: Borzo, *Cable Cars*, 20.

56   "Since trains": Borzo, *Cable Cars*, 44.

56   Ever since the surface loops: "The Council and the Loops," *CT*, March 24, 1904, 6. The "Alexander" reference is to Alexander the Great, who, according to the ancient legend, was confronted with an intricate knot tying down the chariot of Gordius, the ancient founder of Gordium, the capital of Phrygia, and solved the puzzle by simply cutting through the Gordian knot with his sword.

56   Cable train accidents: Borzo, *Cable Cars*, 45. The *Hyde Park Herald* story, quoted by Borzo, was published December 14, 1888.

57   "Thousands": "Thousands Have to Walk," *CT*, July 28, 1888, 1.

57   front-page headlines: "Thrown from a Cable Train," *CT*, November 24, 1893, 8; "Cable Wreck Hurts Nine," *CT*, October 27, 1900, 1; "Car Crash Hurts Women," *CT*, September 22, 1901, 1.

57   William Burtrass: "Cable Car Accidents," *CT*, July 1, 1888, 9; "Fatally Injured by a Cable Car," *CT*, July 2, 1888, 5.

57   couple tons: Hilton, *Cable Car*, 173, reports the weight of the grip car as about five thousand pounds. While my survey of the extensive literature on cable cars couldn't find the weight of the trailer cars, Borzo, *Cable Cars*, 64, indicates that an empty horsecar weighed about four thousand pounds. It is reasonable to assume the cable car trailers were similar.

57   Maria Stanton: "Helpless before Danger, Woman Is Killed by Cars," *CT*, March 10, 1903, 16; "Several Meet Sudden Death," *CT*, March 11, 1903, 2; "Deaths," *CT*, March 12, 1903, 9. The victim was identified variously as Mary and Maria. I've used the latter name because that was the one in the latest of the three stories.

58   If the stranger's first impression: Stead, *If Christ*, 187–94.

58   "Every now and then": Grandin, *Parisienne*, 29–30.

58   fastest a cable car could go: Borzo, *Cable Cars*, 113; Hilton, *Railways*, 11, 25, 33.

58   "Railroad companies": Lewis, *Encounter*, 72.

58   1887 investigation: Lewis, *Encounter*, 72.

58   annual average of 340 people: Stead, *If Christ*, 194.

59   "The intricate cogs": Lewis, *Encounter*, 72–73. Upton Sinclair's 1906 novel, *The Jungle*, is perhaps the most vivid description from that age of the way machines, profit, and processes ground up, sometimes literally, individual human beings.

59   "Mad Ride": "Mad Ride on a Grip," *CT*, April 15, 1893, 1; "Gripman Elliott Tells of His Ride," *CT*, April 15, 1893, 1.

60   Two similar incidents: The incident ten days earlier involved a runaway North Side train that smashed into several carts and wagons before coming to a halt when the grip broke from its fastenings. Such occurrences

were apparently so routine that the *Tribune* didn't do a story at the time. On the previous December 3, a kink in the cable on the West Madison Street line led to a runaway grip car and the derailment of seven trains. Over a dozen people suffered minor injuries. See "Mad Ride on a Grip," *CT*, April 15, 1893, 1; "Freak of a Cable," *CT*, December 4, 1892, 1.

60   "The only way": Borzo, *Cable Cars*, 46.

61   "a thorough-going Sancho Panza": Hilton, *Railways*, 40.

61   Cable systems in New York and San Francisco: See Borzo, *Cable Cars*, 72–74.

61   four hundred million a year: Borzo, *Cable Cars*, 20.

61   a parallel transportation revolution: See RailServe.com, *World Railroad Records & Firsts*, accessed July 11, 2018, http://www.railserve.com/stats _records/railroad_firsts.html.

61   Calumet Electric Street Railway: "The Calumet Electric Road Opens," *CT*, October 5, 1890, 10.

61   "The word 'trolley'": Weber, "Rationalizers," 103.

62   *Tribune* headlines: "Insurance Affairs: Menace Is Seen in Overhead Trolley Wires," *CT*, June 2, 1895, 13; "Death in the Wire: Why Firemen Oppose the Electric Trolley System," *CT*, November 15, 1895, 2; "Death in the Air: Wires Break and Cross the Live Trolley Feeders," *CT*, November 26, 1895, 1; "Where Trolley Wire Danger Is: Experts Make Signed Statements on the Terrors of Monday Night," *CT*, November 27, 1895, 1; "Remove the Deadly Trolley Wires," *CT*, November 28, 1895, 12.

62   the death of a horse: "Live Trolley Wire Kills a Horse," *CT*, November 10, 1895, 1.

62   the current: Weber, "Rationalizers," 103.

62   first recorded electrocution death: *Street Railway Review* 4, June 15, 1894, 325.

63   "It is also impossible": "Traction This Afternoon," *CT*, October 1, 1904, 8.

63   "The public has shown": "Urgent Traction Questions," *CT*, August 10, 1905, 6.

63   "State street should carry": "Poor Relation on State Street," *CT*, December 9, 1905, 8.

63   two ordinances: "Cables to Stop; Tunnels to Sink," *CT*, June 12, 1906, 1.

63   "The people of Chicago": "The Cables Are to Go," *CT*, June 13, 1906, 8.

63   The first to cease operation: "Shouts 'So Long' to Cable Cars," *CT*, July 22, 1906, 3.

63   even more rambunctious: "Hoodlums Wreck Two Cable Cars," *CT*, August 19, 1906, 1.

64   A similar crowd: "Cables Quit Ahead of Time," *CT*, October 21, 1906, 1; "Man Killed Trying to Get Souvenir from Last Cable," *CT*, October 22, 1906, 2.

65   "Thousands": "Thousands Have to Walk," *CT*, July 28, 1888, 1.

65   "A Cable Road Collision": "A Cable Road Collision," *CT*, July 2, 1888, 1.

65   "Many Had to Walk": "Many Had to Walk," *CT*, November 29, 1888, 1.

65   Julius Goldzier: "Liquor Dealers," *CT*, September 20, 1882, 6; "Better Aldermen," *CT*, April 2, 1890, 1; "Julius Goldzier, Former Member of Congress, Dies," *CT*, January 21, 1925, 12; See also *Biographical Directory of the United States Congress*, s.v. "Goldzier, Julius," accessed July 3, 2018, http://bioguide.congress.gov/scripts/biodisplay.pl?index=G000269; "Jewish Politicians in Illinois," Political Graveyard, last updated August 19, 2019, http://politicalgraveyard.com/geo/IL/jewish.html.

7. Dreaming of a "Union Loop"

77   "For a few weeks": Thomas, *London's First Railway*, 48.

77   densely crammed: Brandon, *Victorian Railway*.

77   vast slums: These slums were described in detail not many years later by German social scientist and Marxism cofounder Friedrich Engels in *The Condition of the Working Class in England* (1845).

77   "through the most horrible": quoted in Thomas, *London's First Railway*, 30.

78   "They appreciated": Caton, *Last of the Illinois*, 32. This account of the funeral march of eight hundred warriors in the summer of 1835 is based on Caton, 30–36. For street names, I relied on the map in Andreas, *History of Chicago*, vol. 1, 112.

78   Battle of Fort Dearborn: Throughout most of Chicago's history, this battle, which occurred on August 15, 1812, on the Lake Michigan shore near what is now Eighteenth Street, has been known as the Fort Dearborn Massacre. However, Ann Durkin Keating argues persuasively in *Rising Up from Indian Country* that the fighting that day shouldn't be seen as an unprovoked attack by some 500 Potawatomi and their allies on 110 men, women, and children who had marched out of Fort Dearborn at the mouth of the Chicago River that morning, heading for Fort Wayne. Rather, she argues, it was a clash of two forces in two simultaneous wars—one waged by a pan-Indian confederacy against forts on the outskirts of U.S. territory in an effort to push back the tide of settlers invading their land, and the other the American-declared War of 1812 against Great Britain.

78   more than a dozen: Edmunds, *The Potawatomis*, 235. The name of this tribe is spelled several ways, as is evident in the titles of the books by Caton and Edmunds.

78   new Fort Dearborn: The original Fort Dearborn, built in 1803, was burned to the ground by Indians the day after the Battle of Fort Dearborn. In 1816, a replacement was built on the same site.

78   twenty-three-year-old immigrant: *The Third Branch: A Chronicle of the Illinois Supreme Court*, s.v. "John Dean Caton: Previous Illinois Supreme Court Justice," accessed July 3, 2018, http://www.illinoiscourts.gov/supremecourt/JusticeArchive/Bio_Caton.asp.

79   "the culmination": "Highly Successful," *CT*, January 29, 1882, 5.

79   Manhattan: The first elevated train line in New York was the New York West Side and Yonkers Patent Railway, erected on Greenwich Street along the western edge of the island and powered by a cable system similar to those that eventually would be used at street level in San Francisco, Chicago, and other cities. Service began in July 1868 but was discontinued in 1870 as a result of constant breakdowns. A year later, the line was reopened as the Ninth Avenue El, employing steam engines to pull its cars. Other early elevated lines in the United States were the Manhattan Railway (organized in 1875) and the Boston Elevated Railway (1887).

79   "all necessity": "The Cable Street-Railway," *CT*, November 6, 1881, 4.

80   In early 1869: See Bullard, *Illinois Rail Transit*, 47, 54–55.

80   One plan: "Elevated Railway," *CT*, January 21, 1874, 2.

80   Another, from J. M. Hannahs: "Rapid City Transit," *CT*, June 9, 1877, 8. See also *Album of Genealogy and Biography, Cook County, Illinois* (Chicago: Calumet Book and Engraving, 1897), s.v. "James M. Hannahs," 85–86; *WikiTree*, s.v., "James H. Hannah," last updated March 27, 2019, http://www.wikitree.com/wiki/Hannah-542.

80   "tens of thousands": "The City Transit Question," *CT*, May 9, 1875, 2. For Warren, see "Hudson-Mohawk Genealogical and Family Memoirs: Warren," *Schenectady Digital History Archive*, last updated March 30, 2015, http://www.schenectadyhistory.org/families/hmgfm/warren-1.html.

81   "The constant jarring": "Elevated-Railway Speculators in Chicago," *CT*, July 13, 1879, 4.

81   three elevated lines: An important source for the details on these lines, as well as much else in this chapter, has been Moffat, *The "L."*

81   Polly "L": It's not clear how the Metropolitan West Side Elevated Railroad Company came to be called the Polly "L." It may simply have been a function of the tendency of people to shorten names in everyday conversation—from "Metropolitan" to "'Politan" to "Polly." In 1922, a regional business magazine said the nickname came from traders on the Chicago Stock Exchange. See "Chicago Elevated Bonds Rise on Merger Plan," *Commercial West*, May 13, 1922, 12.

82   "There is to be no terminus": "An Electrical 'L' Road," *CT*, January 22, 1888, 15.

84   In February 1893: "To Build 'L' Loops," *CT*, February 15, 1893, 3. On the same day the *Tribune* wrote about this multiple-loop plan, the newspaper had a second article about a proposal that had been submitted to the Central Elevated Company to build a double-decker loop downtown: "One Track above Another," *CT*, February 15, 1893, 3.

84   "One loop": "To Build 'L' Loops," *CT*, December 14, 1893, 2.

84   Alley "L" loop: "The Alley 'L' Terminal Loop," *CT*, August 16, 1891, 13. See also "Smooth for Alley L," *CT*, January 18, 1894, 4; "Loop for Alley 'L,'" *CT*, October 31, 1894, 12.

84   "the principal streets": "Would Have Four 'L' Loops," *CT*, February 17, 1895, 31.

84   "I am not": "L. Z. Leiter Likes the Loop Project," *CT*, May 25, 1894, 12.

84   this loop: See, for instance, "For a Joint Down-Town Loop," *CT*, May 7, 1894, 8; "New Issue in Sight," *CT*, May 30, 1894, 4; "To Plan a Union Loop," *CT*, June 24, 1894, 13.

85   preferred term: "Union" had been used in a variety of ways earlier. In September 1892, a *Tribune* story mentioned "a traffic union" of the three elevated lines then in operation. In June 1893, a story in the newspaper about the proposed loop was headlined "Union of All Lines." The first time the word "union" was used in a proper name was in November of that year, when the Union Elevated Railroad Co. was established. See "'L' Roads Terminal," *CT*, September 22, 1892, 2; "Union of All Lines," *CT*, June 23, 1894, 9; "Sure of an L Loop," *CT*, November 23, 1894, 1.

85   In 1892: This structure, now known as the Chicago Cultural Center, was opened on October 9, 1897, the Twenty-Sixth anniversary of the Great Chicago Fire. Six days earlier, the Union Loop had gone into operation. See Seeger, *The People's Palace*; "Vow Pile to Books," *CT*, October 10, 1897, 4.

85   "was deemed": City of Chicago, "Quincy Elevated Station," 10.

85   weren't in agreement: "Views Differ Regarding the L Loop," *CT*, February 10, 1893, 3.

86   The idea of an alley route: The unsuitability of downtown alleys for an elevated loop can be seen in the map that accompanies "The Chicago Union Elevated Loop," 603.

86   "Floating population": Stead, *If Christ*, 161–62.

87   most significant expense: See Weber, "Rationalizers," 261–62,

87   such payments were illegal: "Legal War on Loop," *CT*, October 31, 1895, 1. Justice Benjamin D. Magruder, a Chicagoan, wrote, "The question arises whether the consent of a property-owner . . . can be purchased for money. . . . We do not think it was the intention of the Legislature . . . to make the consent of the abutting property-owner in such cases a purchasable article."

87   Adams Law: My description of the Adams Law and its consequences relies heavily on Cudahy, *Destination*, 19–21. Also important was Weber, "Rationalizers," 255–62,

88   Victor Lawson: Franch, "Opposite Sides," 48.

88   Citizen groups: Cudahy, *Destination*, 20.

88   a long public letter: "Anxious to Give Aid," *CT*, December 30, 1891, 8.

88   "The city is not ready": *Chicago Globe*, May 4, 1893, quoted in Franch, *Robber Baron*, 182.

8. Willing the Union Loop into Existence

89   Northwestern Elevated: "Another 'L' Road Incorporates," *CT*, October 31, 1893, 9.

89   "in his individual capacity": "Yerkes Admits Interest in the 'L,'" *CT*, February 17, 1894, 3.

90   "inclined to put": "Bonds Not Awarded," *CT*, July 12, 1894, 4.

90   "who debauches Councils": "Yerkes and the Newspapers," *CT*, January 13, 1897, 6.

90   gymnasium: "Yerkes and His Gloves: Cable Magnate Polishes Off a Guest in His Michigan Avenue Gymnasium," *CT*, December 23, 1894, 23.

90   "Dumbbells": Franch, *Robber Baron*, 201.

91   "corpulent plunderer": Andrews, *Battle*, 176.

91   "five-star": Chicago transportation writer F. K. Plous, quoted in Sherwood, *Yerkes*, 9.

91   "brought the 20th century": Martin, *Underground*, 128.

91   extensive collection: See Liedtke, "Dutch Paintings," 37–38; "The Fine Arts," *CT*, July 17, 1892, 36. At least a dozen artworks purchased by Yerkes can be found in American museums: *Bacchante and Infant Faun*, bronze sculpture by Frederick William MacMonnies (1901), Museum of Fine Arts, Boston; *Cupid and Psyche*, marble sculpture by Auguste Rodin (about 1893), Metropolitan Museum of Art, New York; *Diana*, bronze sculpture by Jean-Antoine Houdon (1782), Huntington Library, San Mateo, CA; *Orpheus and Eurypides*, marble sculpture by Auguste Rodin (1893), Metropolitan Museum of Art, New York; *Philemon and Baucis*, painting by Rembrandt van Rijn (1658), National Gallery of Art, Washington, DC; *Portrait of Joris de Caullery*, painting by Rembrandt van Rijn (1632), Fine Arts Museums of San Francisco; *Portrait of a Woman*, painting by Frans Hals (1635), Frick Collection; *Pygmalion and Galatea*, painting by Jean-Leon Gerome (1890), Metropolitan Museum of Art, New York; *Rockets and Blue Lights (Close at Hand) to Warn Steamboats of Shoal Water*, painting by J. M. W. Turner (1840), Clark Art Institute, Williamstown, MA; *Spring*, painting by Lawrence Alda-Tadema (1894), J. Paul Getty Museum, Malibu, CA; *Valley of Tiffauge*, painting by Theodore Rousseau (1837–44), Cincinnati Art Museum; and *View up the Grand Canal toward the Rialto*, painting by Francesco Guardi (about 1785), Minneapolis Institute of Arts.

92   Grant's political directive: Franch, *Robber Baron*, 70–77.

92   "Mara's bright robes": Towner, *Elegant Auctioneers*, 197.

93   "sacking of the Yerkes palace": Towner, *Elegant Auctioneers*, 237.

93   a Caesar, a "seizer": "Cry Out in Protest," *CT*, March 21, 1897, 1.

93   "master of the arts": Lerner and Holter, "Yerkes," 610.

93   "Goliath of graft": Poole, *Giants*, 254.

93   Harold L. Ickes: Ickes, *Autobiography*, 111.

93   "An' why shud I cillybrate": Finley Peter Dunne, "Memories of the Chicago Fire," quoted in Schaaf, *Mr. Dooley's*, 334. It's worth noting that this comic rant was published in the *Chicago Evening Post* on October 9, 1897, less than a week after the Union Loop went into operation.

93 "Yerkes Has the Key": "Yerkes Has the Key," *CT*, May 26, 1894, 1. See also Moffat, *The "L,"* 187–88, particularly the map and illustration.

94 an alternate plan: See map in Moffat, *The "L,"* 58.

94 At 7 p.m. on June 7: Moffat, *The "L,"* 188. See also "Yerkes' Line Cut Out," *CT*, June 8, 1894, 1.

94 "to fill the souls": "Yerkes' Line Cut Out," *CT*, June 8, 1894, 1.

94 "Trains on the proposed": *Chicago Herald*, June 8, 1894, 1, quoted in Franch, *Robber Baron*, 185.

94 "The purchasers": "Lake Street Sold," *CT*, July 4, 1894, 4. This was confirmed later in the month by Yerkes's top aide. See "It May Connect with the Alley L," *CT*, July 29, 1894, 8.

95 "Where Reform": "Where Reform Is Necessary," *CT*, July 29, 1894, 16.

95 "There is always": "Lake Street L Extended to Wabash," *CT*, July 29, 1894, 12.

95 Waddell: "Union Elevated Railroad," 1994 addendum, 10. Waddell had apparently begun work for the Northwestern at least as early as May 1894. See "Favor Northwestern 'L' Bridge," *CT*, May 10, 1894, 4; "Served by a Noted Engineer," *CT*, August 5, 1894, 10.

95 "first step": "It May Connect with the Alley L," *CT*, July 29, 1894, 8. The comments by Yerkes's lieutenant DeLancey H. Louderback quoted in this article, as well as the newspaper coverage from this point on, contradict the assertion by transportation historian Brian J. Cudahy that Yerkes sought to keep secret his plans for a union loop. See Cudahy, "Early Elevated Lines," 200; Cudahy, *Destination*, 20.

9. The Birth of the Union Loop

96 "The Gordian knot": "Sure of an L Loop," *CT*, November 23, 1894, 1.

96 series of *Tribune* stories: "Loop Is Now Assured," *CT*, December 2, 1894, 12; "Hitch in Loop Plan," *CT*, December 6, 1894, 4; "Loop Will Be Built," *CT*, December 28, 1894, 1.

97 "The loop agreement": "L's Agree on a Loop," *CT*, December 19, 1894, 8.

97 Union Loop: The evolution in the use of the "union loop" and "Union Loop" terms can be seen in the *Tribune* coverage between December 1894 and November 1895. See, for instance, "Break and Recover," *CT*, December 27, 1894, 4; "Some Good Points," *CT*, March 11, 1895, 9; "Terms of the Loop Agreement," *CT*, March 17, 1895, 31; "Object to the Loop," *CT*, May 25, 1895, 11; "Yerkes Will Not Yield in the Least," *CT*, August 20, 1895, 2; "Holbrook Names His Supporters," *CT*, September 5, 1895, 12; "L. Z. Leiter Discusses Union Loop," *CT*, November 10, 1895, 3.

97 "parallelogram": Examples of *Tribune* stories that called the loop a parallelogram are "'L' Roads' Terminal," *CT*, September 22, 1892, 2; "L. Z. Leiter Likes the Loop Project," *CT*, May 25, 1895, 12, the source of the Leiter quote; "Cash for the Loop," *CT*, October 16, 1895, 8, the source of the quote about "the Loop company's plan." As far as can be

determined, no one suggested calling the completed structure the Union Parallelogram.

97   "quadrilateral": "The Underground Loop," *CT*, July 7, 1895, 12.

97   "rectangle": "Rail Terminals Big Obstacle of Traction Service," *CT*, December 5, 1913, 13.

98   "a scramble": "Bid for a Loop Line," *CT*, December 4, 1894, 1.

98   Fifth Avenue: "Work of Last Year," *CT*, January 8, 1895, 4. See also Moffat, *The "L,"* 170; Weber, "Rationalizers," 255–56,

98   paid $50: Franch, *Robber Baron*, 188.

98   "Public acceptance": Moffat, *The "L,"* 69.

99   "in their determination": "Cannot Get His Loop," *CT*, May 1, 1895, 8.

99   "The property-owners": "Yerkes in the City," *CT*, April 16, 1895, 8.

99   "You may talk": "Yerkes Makes Reply to Leiter," *CT*, November 19, 1895, 6.

100   "a crew of 150 men": This episode about the construction on Wabash Street is based on "Race with the Law," *CT*, October 27, 1895, 1; "Drive Work on Loop," *CT*, October 28, 1895, 5; "Partial Check on Loop," *CT*, October 29, 1895, 7; "Loop Causes a Tangle," *CT*, November 1, 1895, 14; "Rush Loop Construction All Day," *CT*, November 4, 1895, 1; "Decides for the Loop," *CT*, November 15, 1895, 2.

100   The payments Yerkes made: Weber, "Rationalizers," 260–62,

101   the price: "Cash for Consents," *CT*, November 2, 1895, 1.

101   rumors: "Negotiations on the Loop Question," *CT*, September 25, 1895, 9.

101   Van Buren Street: Today Van Buren is two blocks north of Harrison. That is because in the 1950s, Congress Parkway (now Ida B. Wells Drive), previously a two-block-long street, was extended west to link with the new federal superhighway, initially called the Congress Expressway and presently known as the Eisenhower Expressway.

101   "We wish": "Make War on the Loop," *CT*, October 23, 1895, 1.

101   "Take Off": "Take Off the Mask," *CT*, October 24, 1895, 9.

101   Behind the scenes: In addition to the *Chicago Tribune*, important sources for the controversy over the switch from Harrison Street to Van Buren Street are Moffat, *The "L,"* 171–73; Franch, *Robber Baron*, 188–90

102   "Loops": "Yerkes Makes Reply to Leiter," *CT*, November 10, 1895, 6.

102   Levi Leiter: See "Dry Goods: Grand Opening Last Night of Field, Leiter and Company," *CT*, October 13, 1868, 4; "Death Comes to Levi Z. Leiter," *CT*, June 10, 1904, 5; "'Crash in Leiter Deal,'" *CT*, June 14, 1898, 1; "Leiter Sells His Land," *CT*, July 14, 1898, 10; "Lets His Property Go," *CT*, July 23, 1898, 3. See also "Marshall Field's," October 23, 2016, http://www.pdxhistory.com/html/marshall_fields.html; Wilson, "Field (Marshall) & Co."; Wilson, "Farwell (John V.) & Co.".

102   Yerkes ally: See "In Council of War," *CT*, September 6, 1895, 3; Weber, "Rationalizers," 257–58.

102   Siegel-Cooper Building: The sole tenant of the Leiter building for its first twenty-seven years was the Siegel, Cooper & Co. department store.

102   "height of folly": "Folly in the Plan," *CT*, November 9, 1895, 1.

102   "There is no question": "Yerkes Makes Reply to Leiter," *CT*, November 10, 1895, 6.

103   "falsehood": "Yerkes Writes in Gall," *CT*, November 22, 1895, 1.

103   "So Louderback": "Likens Louderback to Satan," *CT*, November 23, 1895, 9.

103   Jackson Street: "Loop in Jackson Street," *CT*, December 1, 1895, 3; "For Franchise in Jackson Street," *CT*, December 3, 1895, 3.

103   Congress Street: "Will Stick to Van Buren Street," *CT*, December 10, 1895, 3.

104   a list published: "Oppose the Union Loop," *CT*, November 6, 1895, 9. The representatives of the two largest sections of frontage were Owen F. Aldis, an important and innovative downtown real estate developer (266 feet), and Leiter (188.68 feet). Leiter was an owner, but Aldis was an agent for owners. Among those enlisted in the antiloop effort was Roman Catholic archbishop Patrick Augustine Feehan (100 feet).

104   "The south line": "Loop Is on Van Buren," *CT*, March 13, 1896, 1.

104   nimble tour de force: See Moffat, *The "L,"* 173; Franch, *Robber Baron*, 189–90; Weber, "Rationalizers," 258–59.

105   "novel weapon": "Loop Is on Van Buren," *CT*, March 13, 1896, 1.

105   "The first thing": "Loop Is on Van Buren," *CT*, March 13, 1896, 1.

105   "As everyone knows": "Will Not Pay the City," *CT*, April 28, 1896, 6.

106   "I am no soothsayer": "May Run on Three Legs," *CT*, May 12, 1896, 8. Yerkes was certainly overoptimistic about when the nonloop Union Loop might be able to begin operations. As it turned out, trains didn't start to operate on the Wabash Avenue section until November.

106   "There is such a public demand": "The Loop Question at Last Settled," *CT*, July 8, 1896, 12.

107   Instead, they wanted to lynch him: My description of the talk of hanging Yerkes and his allies, along with my account of the tumultuous two City Council meetings at which his power over the city's political and business leaders was broken, relies heavily on the coverage of the *Chicago Tribune*, as well as on Franch, *Robber Baron*; Harrison, *Stormy*; Wendt and Kogan, *Bosses*; Weber, "Rationalizers."

107   "eternal monopoly": Dedmon, *Fabulous Chicago*, 260.

107   "That proud and haughty bandit": "Harlan Arraigns the Directors," *CT*, April 19, 1897, 2.

107   "Hang 'em": Andrews, *Battle*, 184.

107   "noose badge": "Franchise Fight in Chicago," *Street Railway Review*, December 1898, 908.

107   "WANTED: 10,000": *Chicago Chronicle*, December 8, 1898, 1, quoted in Franch, *Robber Baron*, 259, and also mentioned in "Street Railway Franchises," *Electrical Engineer*, January 6, 1899, 3–4, and "Threaten to Lynch Councilmen," *San Jose Evening News*, December 8, 1898, 5.

107   "Trained in the public utility": Harrison, *Storm*, 111.
108   divested himself: See Franch, *Robber Baron*, 268–70; Moffat, *The "L,"* 99.
108   "a fighter": Harrison, *Stormy*, 168, 206.
108   "In a purely": Jackson, *Crabgrass*, 110.
109   Modern-day London: This account of the visit by Yerkes to Hampstead Heath on August 3, 1900, is based on Franch, *Robber Baron*, 284–85, as well as on my own visit to the site in September 2017. See also Wolmar, *Subterranean Railway*, 168–69; Jackson and Croome, *Rails*, 65–66; Garrison and Levinson, *Transportation Experience*, 128–29; Edwards and Pigram, *Suburbs*, 10; "Charles Yerkes, Conquistador."
109   While the taxi maneuvered: The description of London streets at this time is based on two videos. "The Lost Film Footage of 1904 London" is a one-minute snippet of a movie that "was shot in London, 1904 as a 'travelogue' for Australians curious about life in what was 'one of the most exciting cities anywhere,'" accessed on April 27, 2020, at https://www.youtube.com/watch?v=nYLyvrqIKRE. "Amazing Footage of England in the Edwardian Era" is five minutes long and shows England in the early 1900s, accessed on July 9, 2018, at http://www.vintag.es/2015/08/amazing-footage-of-england-in-edwardian.html.
109   "one might hear": Schneer, *London*, 8.
109   "he had never": Letter from Henry C. Davis to his boss New York broker, Arthur Housman, in *Housman et al. v. Owsley*, referee's opinion, 33, Theodore Dreiser Papers, Box 271, Folder 10390, Van Pelt Library, University of Pennsylvania, Philadelphia, quoted in Franch, *Robber Baron*, 285.
110   "a panorama": Letter from Henry C. Davis to his boss New York broker, Arthur Housman, in *Housman et al. v. Owsley*, plaintiff's brief, 17, quoted in Franch, *Robber Baron*, 285.
110   Yerkes in London: For detailed accounts of the London subway system and Yerkes's accomplishments there, see Franch, *Robber Baron*, 278–310; Halliday, *Underground*, 62–83; Jackson and Croome, *Rails*, 70–105; Martin, *Underground Overground*, 126–50; Passingham, *Romance*, 61–63; Sherwood, *Yerkes*; Wolmar, *Subterranean Railway*, 163–95.
111   "the Moleonnaire": *Punch*, December 10, 1902, 397, quoted in Franch, *Robber Baron*, 298.
111   "Dictator of London Transit": *Town Topics*, December 30, 1902, 74, quoted in Franch, *Robber Baron*, 298.
111   "magnificent organism": Wolmar, *Subterranean Railway*, 5–6.
112   "We owe much": *Westminster Gazette*, quoted in *New York World*, December 31, 1905, 2, as quoted in Franch, *Robber Baron*, 320.
112   "a fresh and virile influence": Passingham, *Romance*, 61.
112   "one of the most rugged": Gray, *London*, 299.
112   "brought the 20th century": Martin, *Underground Overground*, 128.
112   "a financial adventurer": Bobrick, *Labyrinths*, 112.
112   "an irrepressible predator": Sherwood, *Yerkes*, 26.

112　"the prototype of the money-grabbing tycoon": D'Eramo, *Pig*, 103.

112　"the precursor of the gangsters": Johnson and Sautter, *Wicked*, 6.

112　"the most unpopular man": "Charles T. Yerkes," *CT*, December 31, 1905, B4.

10. The Rectangular Bridge and the Builder

115　A pamphlet: Lake Shore & Michigan Southern Railway, *The Union Elevated Loop*, 3. This is also the source of the number of trains and passengers per day.

115　bridge-building company: "Union Elevated Railroad," *Historic American Engineering Record*, 10. It's worth noting that six years after its construction, the Union Loop was described as "a knot of steel bridgework tied around the heart of the city." "Downtown Parades," *CT*, September 13, 1903, 16.

115　J. A. L. Waddell: No book-length biography of John Alexander Low Waddell has been published. This biographical sketch is based on numerous sources, the best of which was Harrington, "Biographical Notes." Other important sources were Finch, "Waddell," 685–86; Brown, *Diversity*, ii–14; Weingardt, "Waddell," 61–64; Millstein, "Historical Perspective"; Nyman, "Contributions"; American Society of Civil Engineers, s.v. "John A. L. Waddell," accessed July 3, 2018, http://www.asce.org/templates /person-bio-detail.aspx?id=11229; Parker, *Who's Who and Why*, s.v. "John Alexander Low Waddell," 2:828–29.

116　"became the seminal text": Weingardt, "Waddell," 62.

116　John Lyle Harrington: Waddell, *Principal Professional Papers*, 3–4.

116　Waddell's introduction: Waddell, *Bridges for Japan*, 1–11.

117　"Into the merits of the case": Harrington, "Biographical Notes," 4.

117　"a robust constitution": Finch, "Waddell," 686.

117　"quite stately": Nyman, "Contributions," 4.

117　amusement of some of his colleagues: Finch, "Waddell," 686.

117　"not known for his humility": Brown, *Diversity*, 13.

118　a rare account: Waddell is mentioned in McBrien, *Pocket Guide*, 102.

118　"one of the leading bridge engineers": "John A. L. Waddell: A Bridge Engineer," *New York Times*, March 3, 1938, 21.

118　inventor of the modern vertical lift bridge: "Dr. John A. L. Waddell," *CT*, March 4, 1938, 14.

119　"genius in the art of bridge building": "John Alexander Low Waddell," *Civil Engineering* 7, January, 1937, 77, quoted in Millstein, "Historical Perspective."

119　"the father of twentieth century bridge design in America": Brown, *Diversity*, 1.

119　"an inspiration": Nyman, "Contributions," 2.

119　"developed his lifelong love": Weingardt, "Waddell," 62.

120　$50 million worth of projects: Motter, *The International Who's Who*, 1056.

120　his son Everett: Millstein, "Historical Perspective."

120   built bridges from one end: No list of Waddell's projects exists. Help-
       ful lists of some of the most important are provided in Wikipedia, s.v.
       "John Alexander Low Waddell," last modified February 5, 2020, http://
       en.wikipedia.org/wiki/John_Alexander_Low_Waddell, and s.v. "Waddell
       & Harrington," last modified July 18, 2019, http://en.wikipedia.org/wiki
       /Waddell_%26_Harrington.
121   "He is acquainted": Harrington, "Biographical Notes," 10.
121   "intensely practical": *Forest and Stream*, July 26, 1903, 1.
121   more than a quarter century beyond: Data from "Life Expectancy by
       age, 1850–2011," Department of Health and Human Services, National
       Center for Health Statistics, Centers for Disease Control and Prevention,
       National Vital Statistics Reports, last updated February 11, 2017, http://
       www.infoplease.com/ipa/A0005140.html.
121   "By this time": Waddell, "To the Graduating Class," 201–11.
122   "the red bridge": Fanning, *Finley Peter Dunne*, 76. For more about the
       bridge's history, see "Halsted Street South Branch Bridge," Historic
       Bridges.org, April 29, 2020, https://historicbridges.org/bridges/browser
       /?bridgebrowser=illinois/halsted/.
122   "No other city": McBriarty, *Chicago River Bridges*, 31.
122   "great obstruction": "Dispute over the Bridge Plans," *CT*, July 20, 1892
122   "freak": "Sees Need of River," *CT*, July 21, 1897, 1.
122   Mayor Fred A. Busse: "Seven Wonders of Chicago: Thousands of People
       Journey from Europe and All over America to See Them," *CT*, March 22,
       1908, F4.
122   refined the design: Nyman, "Contributions," 2
123   Labor Day: Labor Day became a national holiday in 1894.
123   test run: The description of the test of the Union Loop is based on "First
       Trip on Loop," *CT*, September 7, 1897, 12, as well as Moffat, *The "L,"* 174;
       Cudahy, *Destination*, 27.
123   "The impression": "First Trip on Loop," *CT*, September 7, 1897, 12.
123   culmination of two years: See "Union Loop Is Begun," *CT*, September 1,
       1895, 1; "Begin Work on the 'L' Loop," *CT*, March 30, 1896, 1; "Build-
       ing Loop in Fifth Avenue," CT, April 6, 1896, 5; "Permit for Van Buren
       Street Loop," *CT*, November 25, 1896, 2; "Union Loop Now Linked," *CT*,
       January 31, 1897.
123   using plans drawn up: I owe a great debt to James Harper, the chief
       engineer for infrastructure for the Chicago Transit Authority (CTA), and
       CTA engineer Joel Villanueva for their insights and assistance during my
       research on Waddell's design of the elevated structure. They patiently ex-
       plained to me how Waddell's design worked. Also very helpful at the CTA
       were transportation scholar Bruce Moffat and Graham Garfield, editor of
       the Chicago-L.org website.
125   When finished: See "Union Elevated Railroad," *Historic American Engi-
       neering Record*, 2–4.

125   two steel columns: Although steel wire had been employed in the construction of the Brooklyn Bridge in 1883, the use of steel in construction was still new enough that in reporting on the elevated Loop, the *Tribune* erroneously at times described the metal as iron. See, for instance, "Work on the Elevated Roads," *CT*, January 6, 1896, 10; "Permit for Van Buren Street Loop," *CT*, November 25, 1896, 2.

125   rivets: Harper explains that it is no longer possible to use rivets when repairs are made to the elevated Loop. "Riveting is a dying art, and we would be hard-pressed to find a contractor that could perform this work any longer. We now specify high-strength bolts for all our structural repairs and new construction." Author interview with James Harper, November 20, 2015. For a view of the riveting process, see these videos: "Skyscrapers of New York 1906 (Part 1)," "Rosie, Pass the Rivets aka Ship Building," and "A Riveting Squad at Work at John Brown's Shipyard, Glasgow in 1949."

125   "A lot of small pieces": Fletcher, "The Loop El," 194.

126   "The Union Loop": Sande, *Industrial Archeology*, 109.

126   "I walked": Sandburg, *Strangers*, 379. Sandburg writes that he was eighteen at the time of this first visit to Chicago, but that would have been in 1896, before the Union Loop was completed. Either he was wrong about his age, or he was misremembering when he first heard and saw the Loop el trains overhead.

126   "In the Loop": Author interview with James Harper, November 20, 2015.

127   fourteen-thousand-word paper: Waddell, *Principal Professional Papers*. The quotations from this paper in the following paragraphs can be found on pages 591, 594, 595, 601, 633, 634, 727, 729.

11. Inside and outside the Loop

130   "dangerous procession": Noguchi, *Story*, 85–102.

130   "brutal, immense": Albert Fleury, "Picturesque Chicago," 280–81.

130   "the southbound El": Algren, *Neon Wilderness*, 246.

130   "The entire elevated": Quoted in Fletcher, "The Loop El," 198.

131   Colonel Richard Price Morgan: "Father of Elevated Roads Denounces the Chicago Union Loop Nuisance," *CT*, September 12, 1897, 45.

131   "Noises, ugly sights": Burnham and Bennett, *Plan of Chicago*, 74.

131   In January 1884: "Cable Car System," *CT*, January 1, 1884, 18.

132   "The scheme": "Peace and New Loops," *CT*, June 20, 1891, 1.

132   ad hoc group: For the meeting and Brady's comments, see "West Side Up in Arms," *CT*, October 30, 1895, 8.

133   "Many capitalists": "Real Estate Review of the Year 1895," *CT*, December 29, 1895, 28.

133   "Down-town real estate": "Effect of 'L' Loop," *CT*, March 15, 1896, 39.

133   "not anxious to sell": "Real Estate Review," *CT*, August 23, 1896, 31.

133   "It is an entirely safe statement": "In Real Estate Circles," *CT*, August 25, 1901, 43.

133   Siegel, Cooper & Co.: See "Chicago Real Estate," *CT*, November 13, 1898, 38; "Chicago Real Estate," *CT*, December 11, 1898, 38; "Big Bids for Land in Loop," *CT*, December 22, 1907, 2.

134   "small advance": "Big Bids for Land in Loop," *CT*, December 22, 1907, 2.

134   went under: "Siegel-Cooper Sell Business to Boston Store," *CT*, May 1, 1918, 17.

134   Sears, Roebuck: Wilson, "Sears, Roebuck & Co."

134   "A steel girdle": Mayer and Wade, *Growth*, 214.

134   "one of the most densely packed": Donald L. Miller, *Century*, 266.

134   "is the heart of Chicago": Zorbaugh, *Gold Coast*, 1.

134   in 1892: The data for the property values in Chicago in 1892 and 1910 are from Hoyt, *One Hundred Years*, 337, table 43.

135   "otherwise extreme": Hoyt, *One Hundred Years*, 183.

135   "nothing in the world": *Economist*, quoted in Hoyt, *One Hundred Years*, 211.

135   "If the land values": Hoyt, *One Hundred Years*, 297.

135   George E. Hooker: Hooker, "Congestion," 42–57.

136   "Retail shopping": Conzen, "Changing Character," 226.

136   The skyscraper wasn't: Donald L. Miller, *Century*, 307.

136   "The great value": "Skyscrapers Treble Space," *CT*, February 23, 1902, 41.

136   "When it was found": Hooker, "Congestion," 46–47.

136   eighty-seven buildings: This information is based on my analysis of the list of tall buildings erected between 1871 and 1934 in the appendix of Leslie, *Skyscrapers*, 185–91. In an email exchange in 2013, Leslie estimated that this list probably captured about 90 percent of all tall structures for this time period, certainly all the important ones. He noted that he came across the names of some structures in contemporary newspapers for which he couldn't find additional information.

137   maximum height: Leslie, *Chicago Skyscrapers*, 100, 146.

137   "two objections": Leslie, *Chicago Skyscrapers*, 100.

137   Alderman William Mavor: "The Height of Offices," *CT*, June 16, 1901, 29.

137   "the City responded": Leslie, *Chicago Skyscrapers*, 100.

137   Between 1895 and 1915: This information is based on my analysis of the detailed color-coded map "Office Buildings Erected in Certain Year Periods, Demolitions, and Stories Added, 1880–1895," Johnson, "Natural History," 532, figure 107.

137   Yet if some saw: Hoyt, *One Hundred Years*, 183.

137   "It is a notorious fact": Julian Street, *Abroad*, 185.

137   "Without any good": "Rigid Growth outside Loop," *CT*, September 24, 1911, H13.

138   Johnson's figures: My analysis of figure 107 in Johnson, "Natural History," 532.
138   "designed to afford": Hungerford, *Personality*, 205–6.
138   Frederick S. Oliver: Oliver, "Union Loop Should Go to Harrison St.," *CT*, August 25, 1901, 43.
138   Alderman James Patterson: "Locating a Trolley Loop," *CT*, January 29, 1902, 3; "'L' Extension Is Up to Council," *CT*, February 2, 1902, 8.
138   Real estate dealers: "New 'L' Loop Finds Favor," *CT*, February 3, 1902, 11. Biographical details of the real estate dealers are from "W. D. Kerfoot, Pioneer Realty Dealer, Is Dead," *CT*, January 6, 1918, 9; "Dies at His Door after Struggle through Storm: W. A. Merigold, Real Estate Man, Victim of Fight with Snow, *CT*, January 13, 1918, 1; "Pioneer [Donnersberger] Dies," *CT*, July 26, 1929, 15.
139   one of several ideas: "Mayor Opposes New Loop," *CT*, June 1, 1902, 36.
139   A committee of the owners: "Setback for Loop Plans," *CT*, October 29, 1902, 13.
140   "much-ballyhooed *Plan*": The following discussion of the *Plan* is based on Burnham and Bennett, *Plan of Chicago*, as well as Reardon, "Man Who Envisioned," "Burnham Plan," Review of *The Plan*.
140   single most important: Carl Smith, *Plan of Chicago*, 151–67.
140   "As carefully thought out": Carl Smith, *Plan of Chicago*, 87.
140   "Janin's hushed": Carl Smith, *Plan of Chicago*, 91.
141   "maintain the Loop's": Lemon, *Liberal Dreams*, 167–69.
142   elevated loop expansion: Moody, *Wacker's Manual*, 1911, 102, 136.
142   1915 reprint: Moody, *Wacker's Manual*, 1915 reprint, 102, 136.
142   revised edition: Moody, *Wacker's Manual*, 1916 revised edition.

12. The Name "Loop"

153   The Name "Loop": This chapter benefited greatly from conversations with my writing colleague Thomas Pace.
153   newly built Italian villa: The move to California took a tragic turn for the couple when, on April 1, 1918, Rose Chatfield-Taylor came down with double pneumonia after surgery for gallstones and appendicitis. She died four days later. See "Mrs. Chatfield-Taylor Is Dead in California," *CT*, April 6, 1918, 1.
154   capitalization: See, for instance, "Martins Mass Here to Start Flight South," *CT*, August 14, 1949, 35, which begins, "Almost anywhere in Chicago, even near the Loop, one can look up," and " M'Arthur's Plane Flies over Chicago's Loop at 19,000 Feet," *CT*, April 19, 1951, 1, which begins, "Gen. MacArthur flew over Chicago's loop at 19,000 feet."
155   "transact business": Chatfield-Taylor, *Chicago*, 25–26.
155   Hemingway: Hemingway, "A Very Short Story." See also Donaldson, "'A Very Short Story' as Therapy"; Philip Young, *Hemingway*, 89.

156 Gompers school: "Labor Leaders Dedicate New Gompers School," *CT*, July 17, 1927, 16; Hutson, "Roseland Elementary School"; Cox et al., "CPS Closings."

156 Population and annexations: See "Population & Annexation," *Chicagology*, accessed November 24, 2018, https://chicagology.com/population/comment-page-1/; Bobeda and Edes, "Gulp!"

156 Edward Brennan: Patrick T. Reardon, "A Form of Mapquest Back in the Day, *CT*, August 25, 2013, 18.

157 *The Kiss:* See Le Normand-Romain, *Rodin*, 37; Butler, *Rodin*, 229.

157 "I call it": "Anish Kapoor, 'Cloud Gate' Artist: 'I Call It "The Bean," Too,'" *Chicago Sun-Times*, October 13, 2017.

157 "In the case of office buildings": Harris, *Building Lives*, 56.

158 "what is now": Harris, *Building Lives*, 90.

158 "The image really": Alexiou, *Flatiron*, 59.

158 "To call": Quoted in Alexiou, *Flatiron*, 107.

159 "BUTTERICK announces": "BUTTERICK announces . . . ," advertisement, *CT*, January 10, 1907, 11.

159 a similar advertisement: "BUTTERICK announces . . . ," advertisement, *CT*, January 22, 1907, 18; italics added.

159 The final ad: "BUTTERICK announces . . . ," advertisement, *CT*, February 11, 1907, 9; italics added.

160 immediate hit: Moffat, *The "L,"* 175, reports that completion of the Union Loop "resulted in significant ridership gains for the companies. The Metropolitan, for example, saw its average workday traffic jump from 40,000 to 60,000, an increase of 50%."

162 such skyscrapers: The Monadnock Block, at the southwest corner of Dearborn Street and Jackson Boulevard, was completed in 1893, while the Marquette Building, at the northwest corner of Dearborn and Adams Streets, and the Reliance Building, at the southwest corner of State and Madison Streets, date from 1895.

163 "Picture to yourself": "Chicago Cleared of Street Car Lines and Made a City of Boulevards and Motorcycles," *CT*, December 12, 1897, 25.

163 "the Only One on the Loop": "Bird's-Eye View of Chicago," *CT*, October 15, 1897, 12.

163 "Stairs from the Loop": "James Wilde Jr. & Co.," *CT*, March 5, 1898, 5.

163 "The Store": "The Store of the Wage Earner," *CT*, April 29, 1906, 8.

163 "lying within": "Adds Millions in Loop," *CT*, September 10, 1899, 14.

163 "within the loop": See, for instance, "Chicago Real Estate," *CT*, January 9, 1898, 34; "Oppose a Higher Tax," *CT*, August 27, 1899, 12; "Plan New Variety Theater," *CT*, February 27, 1901, 7; "War on Street Florists," *CT*, April 20, 1901, 1; "Raise Sky Scraper Limit," *CT*, June 11, 1901, 8.

163 first use: "See-Saw of Chicago Real Estate Values," *CT*, December 19, 1897, 25.

163   "into the union loop district": "You May Tell the Time of Day by Study-
       ing Faces on the Suburban Trains," *CT*, October 23, 1898, 38.

163   three articles: "Issue on Land Values," *CT*, August 11, 1899, 5; "To have
       expert advice," *CT*, September 12, 1899, 4; "Cash for New Pawn Shop,"
       CT, September 27, 1899, 9.

164   "Once it was said": "See Perils in City in Loop's Congestion," *CT*, Janu-
       ary 17, 1904, 34.

164   "Chicago's Loop": "Chicago's Loop Is the Busiest Spot on Earth," *CT*,
       April 28, 1907, 12.

165   two stories: "Sane New Year's Chill Winds Drive Gay Crowd Within,"
       CT, January 1, 1912, 1; "Joy Unconfined in Levee Cafes," *CT*, January 1,
       1912, 4.

13. "My 'Other Neighborhood'"

169   J. Ogden Armour: The main sources for this discussion of Armour are
       "Business: Death of Armour," *Time*, August 29, 1927; "Operate on Ar-
       mour Girl," *CT*, October 13, 1902, 2; "Ogden Armour, Dead in London,
       to Be Buried Here," *CT*, August 17, 1927, 1; "Armour a Leader in Vast
       Growth of Meat Packing," *CT*, August 17, 1927, 5.

170   Edward Hungerford: Hungerford, *Personality*, 199–200.

170   "neutral land": Chatfield-Taylor, *Chicago*, 25–26.

171   "my 'other neighborhood'": Quoted in Samors and Williams, *Chicago in
       the Fifties*, 84.

171   "To a degree": Warner, *Urban Wilderness*, 110.

173   "defines": Fletcher, "The Loop El," 202.

173   "Jekyll-and-Hyde": Algren, *Chicago*, 66.

173   "Old Seesaw Chicago": Algren, *Chicago*, 83.

173   "forever keeps": Algren, *Chicago*, 23.

173   "last rival": "Commencement of Volume XI," *CT*, June 10, 1857, quoted
       in Liebling, *Chicago*, 43.

173   "People you meet": Liebling, *Chicago*, 107–8.

174   Robert Merriam: Quoted in Liebling, *Chicago*, 107.

174   "first-or-nothing psychology: Liebling, *Chicago*, 66.

174   continental divide: See Conzen, "Changing Character," 224.

175   "The fires": *Industrial Chicago*, 115. The punctuation in the quotation
       from the poem by John Greenleaf Whittier, "Chicago," written in 1871,
       is slightly inaccurate. See https://www.gutenberg.org/files/9586/9586
       -h/9586-h.htm for the full poem.

175   "an ingrained": Ross Miller, *Apocalypse*, 16.

176   "studied, loved": Lewis and Smith, *Chicago*, xi.

176   "schizoid spirit": Strauss, *Images*, 41.

176   "The World's Fair": "His Last Address," *CT*, October 29, 1893, 3.

177   political murder: Burke, "Lunatics."

177   Sauganash Hotel: Randall, *Building Construction*, 6.

177   greatest concentration: "History of Chicago," *Chicago Magazine*, June 15, 1857, 293–303.

177   Wolf Point Tavern: Danckers and Meredith, *Early History*, 365–66.

178   "premature platting": Conzen, "Themes," 41.

178   fifty-eight blocks: See Thompson, "Thompson's Plat."

178   "During all the years": Arthur Meeker, *Chicago*, 65–66.

178   "was a force for division": Binford, "Multicentered Chicago," 43.

178   wooden bridges: Kogan and Cromie, *Great Fire*, 9.

179   "two-story wooden": Mayer and Wade, *Metropolis*, 160.

179   "One must be": Chatfield-Taylor, *Chicago*, 49.

179   the slum: Zorbaugh, *Gold Coast*, 4.

180   "The popular belief": Conzen, "Themes," 41. This section on the many ways the Chicago grid is divided relies heavily on the work of Conzen.

180   "all suffer": Conzen, "Themes," 43.

180   "three giant wedges": Conzen, "Changing Character," 226.

181   "neighborhood-towns": Royko, *Boss*, 24. Thanks to Rick Kogan for helping me find these sentences.

181   "The city of Chicago": Liebling, *Chicago*, 95–96.

181   "I totally knew": Quoted in Bronsky and Samors, *Downtown Chicago*, 84.

181   "Go that way": Royko, *Boss*, 25.

182   "The pulsing heart": Walker, "Chicago," 197.

182   "exciting place": Quoted in Bronsky and Samors, *Downtown Chicago*, 84.

182   "So vital": Bronsky and Samors, *Downtown Chicago*, 44.

182   "The Loop was the mecca": Quoted in Samors and Williams, *Chicago in the Fifties*, 84.

182   "The Loop seemed to have room": Samors and Williams, *Chicago in the Fifties*, 73.

183   "it was still a special thing": Quoted in Samors and Williams, *Chicago in the Fifties*, 108.

183   "There is something": Quoted in Bronsky and Samors, *Downtown Chicago*, 188.

183   "The [Loop] district": Ebner, "Suburbs and Cities," 33.

183   "For being a big place": Quoted in Bronsky and Samors, *Downtown Chicago*, 182.

183   "People usually walk": Quoted in Bronsky and Samors, *Downtown Chicago*, 191.

183   State Street was: Thanks to Patrick G. Reardon for reminding me about the pecking order of the department stores.

184   "barbers, tailors": Huth, "Chicago's El," 6.

184   "Everybody's store": "A Word to the Public," CT, September 26, 1902, 8.

184   celebrity customers: Wendt and Kogan, *Give the Lady*, 227–28.

184   "They brought": Quoted in Kimbrough, *Charley's Door*, 19.

184   "Give the lady": Wendt and Kogan, *Give the Lady*, 276, 183.

184   Bob Dauber: Samors and Williams, *Chicago in the Fifties*, 108.

184   "Because my mother": Quoted in Bronsky and Samors, *Downtown Chicago*, 91.

185   "A seven-year-old kid": Quoted in Samors and Williams, *Old Chicago Neighborhood*, 116.

185   The story of David: This is a story of my family. David is my brother David Michael Reardon. See Reardon, "David Michael Reardon (1951–2015)."

185   Rutabaga Club: Patrick T. Reardon, "Just 4 Guys Doing a Day in the Loop," *CT*, January 29, 1992, Section 2, 1.

14. Wandering Downtowns

187   announcement: My account here is based on Clayton Kirkpatrick, "Outline Vast Civic Center!" *CT*, March 17, 1954, 1. My description of the Fort Dearborn Project in the opening pages of this chapter is rooted in Banfield, *Political Influence*, 126–58.

189   nearly identical in acreage: The Fort Dearborn Project would have covered an area of 151 acres, compared with the 161 acres of the land inside the elevated Loop rectangle.

189   American phenomenon: This section of the chapter relies heavily on Fogelson, *Downtown*.

189   Europeans: Fogelson, *Downtown*, 20–21. See also Towle, *American Society*, 281; "Shaping of Towns," 203–4.

189   "Except for shoppers": Fogelson, *Downtown*, 16–17.

189   Boston and Pittsburgh: Fogelson, *Downtown*, 13.

190   "Even minor moves": Fogelson, *Downtown*, 114.

190   "highly unstable": Fogelson, *Downtown*, 112–15.

190   "Downtown St. Louis": Fogelson, *Downtown*, 113.

191   "a tendency": Fogelson, *Downtown*, 181.

191   downtown wandered: The shifting of Chicago's business center can be seen in Mayer and Wade, *Metropolis*, 15, 18, 36, 54, 55. See also Wendt and Kogan, *Give the Lady*, 114–31.

192   Potter Palmer and his development of State Street: Mayer and Wade, *Metropolis*, 54–56; "Career of Potter Palmer," *CT*, May 5, 1902, 2; "Death of Potter Palmer," *New York Times*, May 5, 1902, 9.

192   Business moves after the fire: "Field, Leiter & Co.," *CT*, October 21, 1871, 1; "Carson, Pirie & Co," *CT*, October 24, 1871, 1; "John V. Farwell & Co.," *CT*, October 26, 1871, 1; "John V. Farwell & Co.," *CT*, November 19, 1871, 7; "Notice. Carson, Pirie & Co," *CT*, January 9, 1872; "Field, Leiter & Co.," *CT*, April 24, 1872, 2; Wendt and Kogan, *Give the Lady*, 114–23.

193   "If a store": Wendt and Kogan, *Give the Lady*, 120.

193   "the mighty, splendid Chicago": "New Chicago," *CT*, October 9, 1873, 2.

194   "city's principal magnet": Abrams, *Language*, 41.

194   "downtown of department stores": Frieden and Sagalyn, *Downtown, Inc.*, 11.

195   "Governmental policy": Gorsuch, "City's Functions," 12–13.

196   Omaha's downtown: Daly-Bednarek, *Changing Image*, 162, 200.

196   downtown Phoenix: Gober, *Metropolitan Phoenix*, 175.

196   "The decline of downtown": Whyte, *City*, 321.

196   "When a city heart": Jacobs, *Death and Life*, 165.

196   "You name it": Paul Gapp, "Slow, Devastating Illness Felled Cleveland," *CT*, December 24, 1978, 1.

196   "virulent case": Dorothy Collin, "Detroit's Self-Hatred: Symptoms Seem to Be Everywhere," *CT*, September 27, 1976, 1.

197   "into a fashionable boulevard": Ehrenhalt, *Great Inversion*, 187.

197   "largely because": Halpern, *Downtown USA*, 151.

197   "a wonderful dream": "Civic Center," *CT*, March 18, 1954, 12.

198   "an orderly retreat": Banfield, *Political Influence*, 131.

198   Aschman: Banfield, *Political Influence*, 132. Banfield asserts that the project fit well with Aschman's idea of a compressed Loop. However, especially in light of what happened in other downtowns, it's difficult to see how the new development north of the river wouldn't have sapped the Loop and weakened Chicago's economic center of gravity.

198   "Ten thousand lawyers": Banfield, *Political Influence*, 138.

198   "The future": Banfield, *Political Influence*, 142.

199   "The concentration of downtown": Jones, *Metropolis*, 76.

199   Lang study: Lang, *Edgeless Cities*, 55.

199   "Chicago captured": Lang, *Edgeless Cities*, 60.

199   "Manhattan is so strong": Lang, *Edgeless Cities*, 67.

199   "They took": Banfield, *Political Influence*, 149.

15. Raze the Loop

201   terrible accident on the Loop: Chicago-L.org, "The Loop Crash," accessed January 30, 2019, https://www.chicago-l.org/mishaps/loop.html.

201   Bilandic-Carter conversation: See William Griffin, "Bilandic, Percy Support a Subway," *CT*, February 6, 1977, 15; "Mayor to Confer with Carter about Federal Funds for Subway," *CT*, February 7, 1977, 1; Arthur Siddon, "Carter Vows Subway Aid," *CT*, February 8, 1977, 1.

201   "Those who want": Fletcher, "The Loop El," 193, 202.

201   "The Loop's elevated train": Harry Weese, "Let's Spare Chicago's Splendid 'L,'" *CT*, August 27, 1978, A5.

202   drumbeat of demolition: See "Compromise Sought for Survival of the El in Downtown Chicago," *New York Times*, December 19, 1978; John D. Moorhead, "Controversy Building Up on Future of Chicago L," *Christian Science Monitor*, published in the *Champaign-Urbana News-Gazette*, February 15, 1979.

202   "The Loop, perhaps": Arthur H. Rotstein, "Chicago's Famed 'Loop' May Be on the Way Out," Associated Press, published in the *Ludington Daily News*, March 13, 1979.

202   "I was surprised": Author interview with Harold Hirsch on October 22, 2013.

202   "cultural provocateur": Sharoff, "Harry Weese."

202   "to stop": See "Our History," *Landmarks Illinois*, accessed January 31, 2019, http://www.landmarks.org/landmarks-illinois-history/.

202   "extraordinary": Paul Gapp, "Landmark Unit Opposed to Saving of 'L' Structure," *CT*, December 6, 1978, E1 "Who Says the 'L' Is a Landmark?" *CT*, December 10, 1978, A4.

203   "Chicago has a great": "Chicago's Great Down-Town Nuisance—the Union Loop," *CT*, September 5, 1897, 33.

203   "an awful mistake": "Union Loop a Nuisance," *CT*, September 5, 1897, 28.

203   "It all comes down": "Father of Elevated Roads Denounces the Chicago Union Loop Nuisance," *CT*, September 12, 1897, 45.

203   "cancer": "Wabash Avenue's Bright Possibilities Turned to Mourning through the Invasion of the Union Loop," *CT*, January 2, 1898, 26.

203   "It ought to be": "Tear Out Loop, Advice of Mayor," *CT*, November 9, 1908, 2.

203   as this list illustrates: The list is based on Chicago-L.org, "Frequently Asked Questions: 3.7," accessed January 31, 2019, https://www.chicago-1.org/FAQ.html#3.7 and Hauser and Kitagawa, *Fact Book*, 134, as well as the following *Tribune* stories: "Budd Plan to Extend CTA!" *CT*, February 16, 1954, 1; "Mayor Submits Superhighway Transit Plan," *CT*, January 27, 1957, 1; Thomas Buck, "Raising Loop Elevated Still Is Aim of CTA," *CT*, November 18, 1962, A1; "Daley Asks More Mass Transit as 3d Term Begins," *CT*, April 18, 1963, 1; Thomas Buck, "CTA's Big Goal: New Subway," *CT*, January 19, 1965, 16; Thomas Buck, "Daley Names Committee to Plan Subway," *CT*, February 16, 1966, A5.

204   Mayor Daley unilaterally ordered: The original story and the fallout afterward is detailed in Paul Gapp, "Razing of 'L' Now Opposed by Experts," *CT*, January 3, 1974, 1; Paul Gapp, "New Subway Given Priority: City Hedges Plan to Raze 'L' Now," *CT*, January 4, 1974, 5; Paul Gapp, "How Pressure Ended Daley's 'L' Proposal," *CT*, January 6, 1974, 1. See also "Plans for New Subways Revised," *CT*, December 31, 1973, 1.

206   Sears Tower: Huth, "Chicago's El," 3.

207   Deep Tunnel Project: Casey Bukro, "A 'Rocky' Future for Deep Tunnel," *CT*, July 17, 1975, B1; Schein, "Deep Tunnel"; "McCook Reservoir to Open Soon, Holding Sewage and Runoff until Storms Pass," *CT*, December 4, 2017, https://www.chicagotribune.com/news/local/breaking/ct-deep-tunnel-mccook-reservoir-met-20171204-story.html; "McCook Reservoir to Greatly Boost Flood Storage Capacity," *Tunnel Business Magazine*, January 16, 2018, https://tunnelingonline.com/mccook-reservoir-greatly-boost-flood-storage-capacity/; Metropolitan Water Reclamation District of Greater Chicago, "Tunnel and Reservoir Plan," accessed April 30, 2020, https://mwrd.org/tunnel-and-reservoir-plan.

207 "the downtown Big People": Fletcher, "The Loop El," 205.
207 "steel noose": Paul Gapp, "How Pressure Ended Daley's 'L' Proposal," *CT*, January 6, 1974, 1.
207 "girdled": "They Want No Loop," *CT*, January 13, 1895, 13.
207 "Chinese Wall": Hoyt, *One Hundred Years*, 183.
207 "strangled": Street, *Abroad*, 185.
207 "choke-chain": Letter of Charles G. Gardner, October 3, 1978, in City of Chicago, "Reasons."
208 "The el is a liability": Quoted in Fletcher, "The Loop El," 201.
208 "It never": Letter of Arthur K. Muenze, October 11, 1978, in the files of the Illinois Historic Sites Advisory Council (IHSAC), which, when examined in December 2012, were somewhat in disarray.
208 "Chicago's Loop elevated structure": Letter of Jack H. Cornelius, October 4, 1978, in City of Chicago, "Reasons."
209 "I know": Letter of H.(?) J. McCormick to Harry Weese, August 28, 1978, in Weese, "Chicago Loop Elevated."
209 "The basic thinking": Fletcher, "The Loop El," 205.
209 "Some critics": "Loop Proposal Startles Chicago," 6.
209 "His City Hall": Cohen and Taylor, *Pharaoh*, 10.
210 "Central Business District Slum": Quoted in Cohen and Taylor, *Pharaoh*, 174.
210 "Unless something drastic": Quoted in Cohen and Taylor, *Pharaoh*, 175.
210 "itching to build": Paul Gapp, "Let's Not Enshrine the 'L,'" *CT*, November 12, 1978, A1
210 "Chicago's Loop": Weese and Kiriazis, "Nomination." Note: An erroneous statement in this paragraph that the elevated was "symmetrical (1/2 mile each side)" has been omitted here.
211 "We have to": Quoted in Paul Gapp, "Don't Take the 'L' out of Loop, Plead Chicago Architects," *CT*, August 15, 1978, 3.
211 Fleischman and Murtaugh letters: City of Chicago and Chicago Transit Authority, "Master Plan," bottom two paragraphs on page IV-I.
211 In an interview: Author interview with Edward R. Fleischman on January 28, 2014.
211 eligibility determination: This section on the protection provided to a structure by eligibility for or inclusion on the National Register benefited greatly from my interview with Fleischman, as well as my interview with Anne Haaker, deputy state historic preservation officer, on January 9, 2013.
211 "If the good": Memo written by Carroll William Westfall, dated December 14, 1978, to other members of the IHSAC, found in the council's files.
212 "moot point": Skramstad made this assertion in a letter on September 13, 1978, to Dan Malkovich, chairman of IHSAC, and Westfall during the December 14, 1978, meeting of the council, according to the meeting minutes. Both documents are found in the files of the IHSAC.

213   "We, at the CTA": Author interview with Harold Hirsch on October 22, 2013.

213   A hyperactive child: This thumbnail description of Weese is based on Sharoff, "Harry Weese," 2, 9; Bruegmann, *Harry Weese*, 28; Blair Kamin, *Tribune* architecture critic, "Harry Weese, Visionary Architect Known as 'Chicago's Conscience,'" *CT*, November 1, 1998, 9; author interview with architect Walker Johnson, January 31, 2013.

214   "aesthetically pleasing": Quoted in DeZutter and Fahey, "Learning to Love the El."

214   sixty-eight-page statement: City of Chicago, "Reasons for Not Listing." See in particular pages 1–8.

215   Hoyt and Lind: See Hoyt, *One Hundred Years*, 142–48; Lind, *Chicago Surface Lines*, 9.

215   "That was language": Author interview with Stephen E. Roman on October 9, 2012.

215   The headline: Paul Gapp, "Landmark Unit Opposed to Saving of 'L' Structure," *CT*, December 6, 1978, E1.

216   "its appalling ugliness": "Who Says the 'L' Is a Landmark?" *CT*, December 10, 1978, A4.

216   The LPC decision: This section is based in part on documents provided by Landmarks Illinois, including minutes of the November 16 programs and policy committee meeting, the November 22 executive committee meeting, and the November 29 board meeting, all in 1978.

216   Maurice Forkert memo: This November 28, 1978, document was provided by Landmarks Illinois.

216   Tangora and Westfall: Author interviews with Martin Tangora on November 12, 2012, and Carroll William Westfall on December 17, 2012. The vote total is from the Westfall interview; Landmarks Illinois declined to provide the number of board members voting in the majority.

217   National Trust: Letter from Mary C. Means to Robert J. Piper, December 12, 1978, found in the files of the IHSAC.

217   "It is strange": Author interview with Lisa DiChiera on October 16, 2012.

217   "Now, the general public": Email to author from Bonnie McDonald on December 4, 2012.

217   "Would anyone": Memo from Titus Karlowicz, December 14, 1978, in the files of the IHSAC.

218   "The elevated loop": Statement of George Krambles at a public hearing conducted by the Chicago Urban Transportation District, August 18, 1978, 1. See also memos from Karlowicz and Westfall, December 14, 1978. All in the files of the IHSAC.

218   "This staff": Undated staff statement in the files of the IHSAC.

219   Sculle letter: Letter from Keith A. Sculle to George Krambles, December 19, 1978, in the files of the IHSAC.

219   surprise decision: F. Richard Ciccone and Daniel Egler, "Byrne,
       Thompson to Eliminate Franklin St. Subway, Crosstown," *CT*, June 22,
       1979, 1.
219   "Nobody was getting out": Author interview with Anne Haaker, deputy
       state historic preservation officer, on January 9, 2013.
219   Resulting plan and refinements: See City of Chicago and Chicago Tran-
       sit Authority, "Master Plan," particularly the first item in the section titled
       "Conditions for a Determination of No Adverse Effect for the Chicago
       Loop Elevated Rehabilitation Project."

16. The Loop, New Year's Day 2019

221   "most distinctive": Carl Smith, *American Literary Imagination*, 103.
221   "heady experience": Huth, "Chicago's El," 7.
221   "How could I": Mrs. Bailey (Marion) Shearer in a letter to the editor,
       Chicago Daily News, January 18, 1978.
222   Nowhere else in the world: See "36-Month Miami-Dade Transit Rider
       Loss Worsens," *Miami Today*, May 2, 2018, https://www.miamitoday
       news.com/2018/05/02/36-month-miami-dade-transit-rider-loss-worsens/;
       Miami-Dade County Department of Transportation and Public Works,
       Ridership Technical Report, September 2018, https://www.miamidade
       .gov/transit/library/rtr/2018-09-Ridership-Technical-Report.pdf; "Detroit
       People Mover," City-Data.com, accessed January 14, 2019, http://www.
       city-data.com/articles/Detroit-People-Mover-Detroit-Michigan.html;
       "Metro Rings and Loops," Metrobits, accessed January 14, 2019, http://
       mic-ro.com/metro/metrorings.html.
222   "I would estimate": Quotes from James Harper are from a series of author
       interviews and email exchanges in 2015 and 2018.
224   "one of [Chicago's] most": Mayer and Wade, *Metropolis*, 210.
224   "major tourist attraction": Conzen, "Changing Character," 235.
224   "Who could have": Bronsky and Samors, *Downtown Chicago*, 38.
224   "As time wore on": Quoted in Bronsky and Samors, *Downtown Chicago*,
       194.
224   "pride of the city: DeGroote, "Riding the Rails," 86.
224   "extraordinary piece": Author interview with David Bahlman in July
       2004.
224   "People like": Author interview with Carroll William Westfall, December
       17, 2012.
224   catnip to generations of moviemakers: I am indebted, again, to Greg
       Borzo for a brochure he created on many of the movies made in Chicago
       that have used the elevated system. See also Borzo, *The Chicago "L."*
224   "As the cable car represented": Huth, "Chicago's El," 7.
225   "I shudder": Denise Blankenship, "Hey, Hollywood! Films Are Reelin'
       toward Illinois," *Suburban Trib*, April 28, 1978.

226   100,000: See "100,000 Jam Loop to Say Hello to '71," *CT*, January 1, 1971, 1; Steve Johnson, "Chicago Toddles Its Way to '87," *CT*, January 1, 1987, A2.

226   "At 10 minutes": "City Intelligence," *CT*, January 1, 1886, 3.

226   "Chicago's Down-Town Streets": "With Horn Blowing," *CT*, January 1, 1893, 1.

226   "Moist Hilarity": "Moist Hilarity Greets 1929," *CT*, January 1, 1929, 1.

226   Byrne: "Thousands Jam Mall to Greet '80s," *CT*, January 1, 1980, 3.

226   150,000: Steve Johnson, "Chicago Toddles Its Way to '87," *CT*, January 1, 1987, A2.

227   "downright dangerous": Author interview with Tim Samuelson, the city of Chicago's cultural historian, on April 28, 2014.

228   hip place: See John Giuffo, "America's Best Downtowns," *Forbes*, October 14, 2011, https://www.forbes.com/sites/johngiuffo/2011/10/14/americas-best-downtowns/#3c8485492f64; Yuqing Pan, "Top 10 Cities Where Downtown Is Making a Comeback," Realtor.com, March 20, 2017, https://www.realtor.com/news/trends/top-10-downtowns-that-have-made-a-comeback/; Alyssa Ochs, "12 of America's Most Beautiful Downtown Areas," Trips to Discover, last updated February 5, 2020, https://www.tripstodiscover.com/americas-most-beautiful-downtown-areas/; "Top 10 Best American Downtowns," TopTenz, January 16, 2012, https://www.toptenz.net/top-10-american-downtowns.php.

228   Since then: The Census Bureau 2014–18 estimates for individual census tracts are aggregated for each of Chicago's seventy-seven community areas, including the Loop, in the table "Chicago Community Area Data," Rob Parel & Associates, accessed April 29, 2020, https://robparal.com/chicago-data/.

228   nearly fifty-eight million visitors: "Mayor Emanuel, Choose Chicago Release 2018 Annual Tourism Report," Office of the Mayor, City of Chicago, April 18, 2019, https://www.chicago.gov/city/en/depts/mayor/press_room/press_releases/2019/april/2018AnnualTourismReport.html.

229   "Manhattan has no center": Traub, "Reflection," 85.

229   "literally, as well as metaphorically": Chatfield-Taylor, *Chicago*, 27.

229   "the city's rusty heart": Algren, *Chicago*, 77.

229   "broken nose": Algren, *Chicago*, 23.

229   "Why did": McClelland, *Nothin' but Blue Skies*, 189.

⬅ Bibliography

Abrams, Charles. *The Language of Cities: A Glossary of Terms.* New York: Viking, 1971.

Ade, George. *Stories of the Streets and of the Town: From the Chicago Record, 1893–1900.* Edited by Franklin J. Meine. Chicago: Caxton Club, 1941.

Alexiou, Alice Sparberg. *The Flatiron: The New York Landmark and the Incomparable City That Arose with It.* New York: St. Martin's, 2010.

Algren, Nelson. *Chicago: City on the Make.* 50th anniversary ed. Chicago: University of Chicago Press, 2001.

———. *The Neon Wilderness.* 1947. Reprint, New York: Seven Stories, 1986.

Andreas, Alfred Theodore. *History of Chicago: From the Earliest Period to the Present Time.* Vol. 1, *Ending with the Year 1857.* Salem, MA: Higginson, 1884.

Andrews, Wayne. *Battle for Chicago.* New York: Harcourt, Brace, 1946.

Archer, William. *America To-Day.* London: William Heinemann, 1900.

Banfield, Edward C. *Political Influence.* New York: Free Press, 1961.

Bennett, Lerone, Jr. *Forced into Glory: Abraham Lincoln's White Dream.* Chicago: Johnson, 2000.

Binford, Henry. "Multicentered Chicago." In Keating, *Chicago Neighborhoods,* 41–54.

Bobeda, Tricia, and Alyssa Edes. "Gulp! How Chicago Gobbled Its Neighbors." WBEZ.org. January 27, 2014. https://www.wbez.org/shows/curious-city /gulp-how-chicago-gobbled-its-neighbors/15490e14–5c5c–4b93-b4c2 –74b592bfe11a.

Bobrick, Benson. *Labyrinths of Iron: A History of the World's Subways.* New York: Newsweek Books, 1981.

Bolotin, Norman, and Christine Laing. *The World's Columbian Exposition: The Chicago World's Fair of 1893.* 1992. Reprint, Urbana: University of Illinois Press, 2002.

Borzo, Greg. *Chicago Cable Cars.* Charleston, SC: History Press, 2012.

———. *The Chicago "L."* Charleston, SC: Arcadia, 2007.

Brandon, David. *London and the Victorian Railway.* Stroud: Amberley, 2013.

Bronsky, Eric, and Neal Samors. *Downtown Chicago in Transition.* Chicago: Chicago's Book Press, 2007.

Bross, William. *History of Chicago.* Chicago: Jansen, McClure, 1876.

Brown, Kathi Ann. *Diversity by Design: Celebrating 75 Years of Howard, Needles, Tammen & Bergendoff, 1914–1989.* New York: Howard, Needles, Tammen & Bergendoff, 1989.

Bruegmann, Robert. *The Architecture of Harry Weese.* With building entries by Kathleen Murphy Skolnik. New York: Norton, 2010.

Bullard, Thomas R. *Illinois Rail Transit: A Basic History.* Self-published, 1987.

Burchard, John, and Albert Bush-Brown. *The Architecture of America: A Social and Cultural History.* Boston: Little, Brown, 1961.

Burke, Edward M. "Lunatics and Anarchists: Political Homicide in Chicago." *Journal of Criminal Law and Criminology* 92 (Spring 2002). http:// scholarlycommons.law.northwestern.edu/cgi/viewcontent.cgi?article =7106&context=jclc.

Burnham, Daniel H., and Edward H. Bennett. *Plan of Chicago.* 1909. Reprint, Chicago: Great Books Foundation, 2009.

Butler, Ruth. *Rodin: The Shape of Genius.* New Haven: Yale University Press, 1993.

Callwell, Robert, and Walter E. Rice. *Of Cables and Grips: The Cable Cars of San Francisco.* 2nd ed. March 2005. http://www.cable-car-guy.com/html /ccocg.html.

Carey, Heidi Pawlowski. "Prairie Avenue." In Reiff et al., *Encyclopedia of Chicago.* http://www.encyclopedia.chicagohistory.org/pages/1003.html.

Caton, John Dean. *The Last of the Illinois and a Sketch of the Pottawatomies: Read before the Chicago Historical Society, December 13, 1870.* Chicago: Rand, McNally, 1870.

"Charles Yerkes: Conquistador of Metroland." *The Economist,* December 20, 2014. http://www.economist.com/news/christmas-specials/21636509 -how-vision-and-cunning-unknown-american-changed-shape.

Chatfield-Taylor, Hobart. *Chicago.* Boston: Houghton Mifflin, 1917.

"The Chicago Union Elevated Loop," *Railway Age,* July 23, 1897, 602–5.

City of Chicago. "The Chicago Union Loop Elevated Structure: Reasons for Not Listing upon the National Register; Submitted to the Illinois Historic Sites Advisory Council." October 13, 1978. Cc P97W9 1978c. Municipal Reference Collection, Harold Washington Library Center, Chicago Public Library.

———. "Quincy Elevated Station, 220 South Wells Street: Final Landmark Recommendation Adopted by the Commission on Chicago Landmarks, September 7, 2017." Department of Planning and Development.

City of Chicago and Chicago Transit Authority. "Master Plan for the Loop Elevated Rehabilitation and Historic Preservation." September 1981. Cc P97W9 1981e. Municipal Reference Collection, Harold Washington Library Center, Chicago Public Library.

Cohen, Adam, and Elizabeth Taylor. *American Pharaoh: Mayor Richard J. Daley; His Battle for Chicago and the Nation.* Boston: Little, Brown, 2000.

Conzen, Michael P. "The Changing Character of Metropolitan Chicago." *Journal of Geography* 85, no. 5 (1986): 224–36.

———. "Themes in Greater Chicago's Morphological Development." In *Prairie Urbanism,* edited by Zachary R. Borders, 39–44. Chicago: Congress for the New Urbanism, 2004.

Cox, Ted, Lizzie Schiffman Tufano, Paul Biasco, and Mark Konkol. "CPS Closings: Board Votes to Close 50 Chicago Schools." *DNAinfo*, May 23, 2013. https://www.dnainfo.com/chicago/20130522/downtown/cps-closings-school-board-decide-schools-fates-today/.

Crane, Hart. *The Bridge*. Paris: Black Sun, 1930.

Cudahy, Brian J. "Chicago's Early Elevated Lines and the Construction of the Union Loop." *Chicago History* 8, no. 4 (1979-80): 194–205.

——. *Destination: Loop; The Story of Rapid Transit Railroading in and around Chicago*. Lexington, MA: Stephen Greene, 1982.

Cutler, Irving. *Chicago, Metropolis of the Mid-Continent*. 4th ed. Carbondale: Southern Illinois University Press, 2006.

Daly-Bednarek, Janet R. *The Changing Image of the City: Planning for Downtown Omaha, 1945–1973*. Lincoln: University of Nebraska Press, 1992.

Danckers, Ulrich, and Jane Meredith. *A Compendium of the Early History of Chicago to the Year 1835 When the Indians Left*. River Forest: Early Chicago, 2000.

Danzer, Gerald A. "The Loop." In Reiff et al., *Encyclopedia of Chicago*. http://www.encyclopedia.chicagohistory.org/pages/764.html.

Darrow, Clarence. *The Story of My Life*. New York: Da Capo, 1996.

Dedmon, Emmett. *Fabulous Chicago*. New York: Random House, 1953.

DeGroote, Raymond. "Riding the Rails." In *Chicago in the Fifties: Remembering Life in the Loop and the Neighborhoods*, edited by Neal Samors and Michael Williams, 86–87. Chicago: Chicago's Neighborhoods, 2005.

D'Eramo, Mario. *The Pig and the Skyscraper: Chicago; A History of Our Future*. London: Verso, 2002.

DeZutter, Hank, and Patrick Fahey. "Learning to Love the El with Architect Harry Weese." *Chicago Reader*, September 1, 1978, 3, 34.

Donaldson, Scott. "'A Very Short Story' as Therapy." In *Hemingway's Neglected Short Fiction: New Perspectives*, edited by Susan F. Beegel, 99–105. Tuscaloosa: University of Alabama Press.

Dreiser, Theodore. *Dawn: A History of Myself*. New York: Horace Liveright, 1931.

——. *Sister Carrie*. Norton Critical Edition. Edited by Donald Pizer. New York: Norton, 1991.

Duis, Perry. "The Shaping of Chicago." In *AIA Guide to Chicago*, edited by Alice Sinkevitch, 3–24. New York: Harcourt, Brace, 1993.

Dunne, Finley Peter. *Mr. Dooley: In the Hearts of His Countrymen*. Boston: Small, Maynard, 1899.

——. *Mr. Dooley and the Chicago Irish: The Autobiography of a Nineteenth Century Ethnic Group*. 2nd ed. Edited by Charles Fanning. Washington, DC: Catholic University of America Press, 1987.

Ebner, Michael H. "Suburbs and Cities as Dual Metropolis." In Keating, *Chicago Neighborhoods*, 29–40.

Edmunds, R. David. *The Potawatomis: Keepers of the Fire*. Norman: University of Oklahoma Press, 1978.

Edwards, Dennis, and Ron Pigram. *London's Underground Suburbs*. London: Baton Transport, 1986.

Ehrenhalt, Alan. *The Great Inversion and the Future of the American City*. New York: Knopf, 2012.

Elevated Railway Employees, Division 308. *The Story of the Chicago Rapid Transit Lines: The "L" System*. Chicago: Chicago Transit Authority, 1940.

Fairchild, Charles Bryant. *Street Railways: Their Construction, Operation and Maintenance (Trams); A Practical Handbook for Street Railway Men*. New York: Street Railway, 1892.

Fanning, Charles. *Finley Peter Dunne and Mr. Dooley: The Chicago Years*. Lexington: University Press of Kentucky 1978.

Finch, James K. "John Alexander Low Waddell." In *Dictionary of American Biography*, Supp. 2, edited by Harris E. Starr, 685–86. New York: Charles Scribner's Sons, 1944.

Fletcher, Connie. "The Loop El: Love It or Lose It." *Chicago* 26, no. 11 (November 1977): 192–206.

Fleury, Albert. "Picturesque Chicago." *Brush and Pencil* 6, no. 6 (1900): 273–77, 279–81.

Fogelson, Robert M. *Downtown: Its Rise and Fall, 1880–1950*. New Haven, CT: Yale University Press, 2001.

Franch, John. "Opposite Sides of the Barricade." *Chicago History* 24, no. 2 (1995): 38–57.

———. *Robber Baron*. Urbana: University of Illinois Press, 2006.

Frieden, Bernard J., and Lynne B. Sagalyn. *Downtown, Inc.: How America Rebuilds Cities*. Cambridge, MA: MIT Press, 1989.

Fuller, Henry Blake. *The Cliff-Dwellers*. New York: Harper & Brothers, 1893.

Garland, Hamlin. *A Son of the Middle Border*. New York: Grosset & Dunlap, 1928.

Garrison, William L., and David M. Levinson. *The Transportation Experience: Policy, Planning, and Deployment*. New York: Oxford University Press, 2014.

Geo. P. Rowell and Co.'s American Newspaper Directory. New York: Geo. P. Rowell, 1872.

Giedion, Sigfried. *Space, Time and Architecture: The Growth of a New Tradition*. Cambridge, MA: Harvard University Press, 1941.

Gober, Patricia. *Metropolitan Phoenix: Place Making and Community Building in the Desert*. Philadelphia: University of Pennsylvania Press, 2006.

Gorsuch, Edwin N. "The City's Functions: A Historical and Cultural Perspective." In *The Future of Atlanta's Central City*, edited by Edwin N. Gorsuch and Dudley S. Hinds, 12–13. Atlanta: Georgia State University, 1977.

Grandin, Madame Leon. *A Parisienne in Chicago: Impressions of the World's Columbian Exposition*. Translated by Mary Beth Raycraft. 1894. Reprint, Urbana: University of Illinois Press, 2010.

Gray, Robert. *A History of London*. New York: Taplinger, 1978.

Halley, William. *The Centennial Year Book of Alameda County, California*. Oakland, CA: William Halley, 1876.

———. *Halley's Pictorial Oak Park*. Oak Park, IL: William Halley, 1898.

Halliday, Stephen. *Underground to Everywhere: London's Underground Railway*. Stroud, UK: History Press, 2001.

Halpern, Kenneth. *Downtown USA: Urban Design in Nine American Cities*. London: Watson-Guptill Publications, 1978.

Hanscom, W. W. *The Archaeology of the Cable Car*. Edited by Walt Wheelock. Pasadena, CA: Socio-Technical Books, 1970.

Harris, Neil. *Building Lives: Constructing Rites and Passages*. New Haven, CT: Yale University Press, 1999.

Harrington, John Lyle. "Biographical Notes." In Waddell, *Principal Professional Papers*, 1–11.

Harrison, Carter H. *Stormy Years: The Autobiography of Carter H. Harrison, Five Times Mayor of Chicago*. Indianapolis: Bobbs-Merrill, 1935.

Hauser, Philip M., and Evelyn M. Kitagawa, eds. *Local Community Fact Book for Chicago, 1950*. Chicago: Chicago Community Inventory, 1953.

Hemingway, Ernest. "A Very Short Story." Internet Archive. January 25, 2016. https://archive.org/stream/AdvRAVeryShortStoryByErnestHemingway/Adv+R+A+Very+Short+Story+by+Ernest+Hemingway_djvu.txt.

Hilton, George W. *The Cable Car in America: A New Treatise upon Cable or Rope Traction as Applied to the Workings of Street and Other Railways*. Berkeley, CA: Howell-North, 1971.

———. *Cable Railways of Chicago*. Chicago: Electric Railway Historical Society, 1954.

Hooker, George E. "Congestion and Its Causes in Chicago." In *Proceedings of the Second National Conference on City Planning and the Problems of Congestion: Rochester, New York, May 2–4, 1910*, 42–57. Boston: University Press, 1910.

Hoyt, Homer. *One Hundred Years of Land Values in Chicago: The Relationship of the Growth of Chicago to the Rise of Its Land Values, 1830–1933*. Chicago: University of Chicago, 1933.

Hungerford, Edward. *The Personality of American Cities*. New York: McBride, Nast, 1913.

Huth, Tom. "Chicago's El Rattles On—and Outlasts Its Critics." *Historic Preservation* 32, no. 1 (1980): 2–9.

Hutson, Wendell. "Roseland Elementary School Renamed after Jesse Owens." *DNAinfo*. March 28, 2014. https://www.dnainfo.com/chicago/20140328/roseland/south-side-elementary-school-renamed-after-jesse-owens/.

Ickes, Harold L. *The Autobiography of a Curmudgeon.* New York: Reynal & Hitchcock, 1943.

Industrial Chicago: The Building Interests. Vol. 1. Chicago: Goodspeed, 1891.

Jackson, Alan A., and Desmond F. Croome. *Rails through the Clay.* London: George Allen & Unwin, 1962.

Jackson, Kenneth T. *Crabgrass Frontier.* New York: Oxford University Press, 1985.

Jacobs, Jane. *The Death and Life of Great American Cities.* New York: Random House, 1961.

Johnson, Curt, and R. Craig Sautter. *Wicked City Chicago: From Kenna to Capone.* Chicago: December Press, 1994.

Johnson, Earl Shepard. "The Natural History of the Central Business District with Particular Reference to Chicago." PhD diss., University of Chicago, 1941.

Johnston, James L. "Free Market Walking Tour of Chicago's Loop." Heartland Institute. January 1, 2004. https://www.heartland.org/publications-resources /publications/free-market-walking-tour-of-chicagos-loop.

Jones, Emrys. *Metropolis.* Oxford: Oxford University Press, 1990.

Junger, Richard. *Becoming the Second City: Chicago's Mass News Media, 1833–1898.* Urbana: University of Illinois Press, 2010.

Keating, Ann Durkin. *Chicago Neighborhoods and Suburbs: A Historical Guide.* Chicago: University of Chicago Press, 2008.

———. *Rising Up from Indian Country: The Battle of Fort Dearborn and the Birth of Chicago.* Chicago: University of Chicago Press, 2012.

Kent, Elizabeth Thacher. *William Kent, Independent: A Biography.* N.p., 1950.

Kimbrough, Emily. *Through Charley's Door.* New York: Harper & Brothers, 1952.

King, Charles. "The City of the World's Fair." *Cosmopolitan,* November 1891.

Kipling, Rudyard. *From Sea to Sea: Letters of Travel.* New York: Doubleday, Page, 1907.

Kogan, Herman, and Robert Cromie. *The Great Fire: Chicago 1871.* New York: G. P. Putnam's Sons, 1971.

Lake Shore & Michigan Southern Railway. *The Union Elevated Loop in Chicago.* Cleveland: Forman-Bassett-Hatch, 1898.

Lang, Robert E. *Edgeless Cities: Exploring the Elusive Metropolis.* Washington, DC: Brookings Institution, 2003.

Latrobe, Charles Joseph. *The Rambler in North America.* R. B. Seeley & W. Burnside, 1836.

Lemon, James T. *Liberal Dreams and Nature's Limits: Great Cities of North America since 1600.* Toronto: Oxford University Press, 1996.

Le Normand-Romain, Antoinette. *Rodin: The Gates of Hell.* Paris: Musee Rodin, 1999.

Lerner, Max, and Mary F. Holter. "Charles Tyson Yerkes." In *Dictionary of American Biography,* vol. 10, edited by Dumas Malone, 609–11. New York: Charles Scribner's Sons, 1957.

Leslie, Thomas. *Chicago Skyscrapers, 1871–1934.* Urbana: University of Illinois Press, 2013.

Lewis, Arnold. *An Early Encounter with Tomorrow: Europeans, Chicago's Loop, and the World's Columbian Exposition.* Urbana: University of Illinois Press, 1997.

Lewis, Lloyd, and Henry Justin Smith. *Chicago: The History of Its Reputation.* New York: Harcourt, Brace, 1929.

Liebling, A. J. *Chicago: The Second City.* 1952. Reprint, Lincoln: University of Nebraska Press, 2004.

Liedtke, Walter. "Dutch Paintings in America: The Collectors and Their Ideals." In *Great Dutch Paintings from America,* edited by Ben Broos, 37–38. Zwolle, The Netherlands: Waanders Publishers, 1990.

Lind, Alan R. *Chicago Surface Lines: An Illustrated History.* Park Forest, IL: Transport History, 1974.

"Loop Proposal Startles Chicago." *Planning,* October 1978, 6–8.

Malloy, Betsy. "A Cable Car Tour of San Francisco." *TripSavvy.* Last updated August 3, 2019. http://gocalifornia.about.com/cs/sanfrancisco/a/cablecartour.htm.

Martin, Andrew. *Underground Overground: A Passenger's History of the Tube.* London: Profile Books, 2013.

Masters, Edgar Lee. *Across Spoon River.* Urbana: University of Illinois Press, 1936.

———. *Songs and Satires.* New York: Macmillan, 1916.

———. *Spoon River Anthology.* 2nd ed. New York: Macmillan, 1916.

Mayer, Harold M., and Richard C. Wade. *Chicago: Growth of a Metropolis.* Chicago: University of Chicago Press, 1969.

McBriarty, Patrick T. *Chicago River Bridges.* Urbana: University of Illinois Press, 2013.

McBrien, Judith Paine. *Pocket Guide to Chicago.* New York: Norton, 2004.

McClelland, Edward. *Nothin' but Blue Skies: The Heyday, Hard Times, and Hopes of America's Industrial Heartland.* New York: Bloomsbury, 2013.

McShane, Clay, and Joel A. Tarr. *The Horse in the City: Living Machines in the Nineteenth Century.* Baltimore, MD: Johns Hopkins University Press, 2007.

Meeker, Arthur. *Chicago, with Love: A Polite and Personal History.* New York: Alfred A. Knopf, 1955.

Melosi, Martin V. "'Out of Sight, Out of Mind': The Environment and Disposal of Municipal Refuse, 1860–1920." In *The Physical City: Public Space and the Infrastructure,* edited by Neil L. Shumsky, 331–50. New York: Routledge, 1995.

Merchant, Carolyn. *American Environmental History: An Introduction.* New York: Columbia University Press, 2007.

Miller, Donald L. *City of the Century: The Epic of Chicago and the Making of America.* New York: Simon & Schuster, 1996.

Miller, John Anderson. *Fares, Please! A Popular History of Trolleys, Horse-Cars, Street Cars, Buses, Elevateds, and Subways.* New York: Dover, 1941.

Miller, Ross. *American Apocalypse: The Great Fire and the Myth of Chicago.* Chicago: University of Chicago Press, 1990.

Millstein, Cydney. "An Historical Perspective of Kansas City's Twelfth Street Trafficway Viaduct 1911–1915." Architectural & Historical Research. 2013. http://www.ahr-kc.com/reports/12th_street_trafficway_viaduct/.

Moffat, Bruce G. *The "L": The Development of Chicago's Rapid Transit System, 1888–1932.* Chicago: Central Electric Railfans' Association, 1995.

Moody, Walter D. *Wacker's Manual of the Plan of Chicago.* 1911. Reprint, Chicago: Calumet, 1912 and 1915; revised 2nd ed., 1916.

Motter, H. L., ed. *The International Who's Who.* New York: International Who's Who, 1912.

Murray, Thomas Hamilton. *The Journal of the American Irish Historical Society.* Vol. 3. American Irish Historical Society, 1900.

Noguchi, Yone. *The Story of Yone Noguchi.* Philadelphia: George W. Jacobs, 1914.

Norton, Charles D. "The Merchants Club and the Plan of Chicago." In *The Merchants Club of Chicago 1896–1907,* 95–103. Chicago: Commercial Club of Chicago, 1922.

Nyman, William E. "Dr. J. A. L. Waddell's Contributions to Vertical Lift Bridge Design." Presented at the Ninth Biennial Symposium of Heavy Movable Structures, Daytona Beach, FL, October 23–26, 2002. https://heavy movablestructures.org/wp-content/uploads/2017/12/0092.pdf.

Old Tippecanoe Club of Chicago. *Dedication to Benjamin Harrison, Christian Gentleman; Patriotic Citizen; Brave Soldier; Wise Statesman and 23d President of the United States.* Chicago: Press of the Peerless, 1889.

Pacyga, Dominic A. *Chicago: A Biography.* Chicago: University of Chicago Press, 2009.

Parker, C. W., ed. *Who's Who and Why: A Biographical Dictionary of Men and Women of Western Canada.* Vol. 3. Vancouver: International, 1913.

Passingham, W. J. *Romance of London's Underground.* New York: Benjamin Blom, 1972.

Philadelphia and Its Environs. Philadelphia: J. B. Lippincott, 1873.

Pierce, Bessie Louise, ed. *As Others See Chicago.* Chicago: University of Chicago Press, 1933.

——. *A History of Chicago.* Vol. 1, *The Beginning of a City, 1673–1848.* Chicago: University of Chicago Press, 1937.

Platt, Harold L. *The Electric City: Energy and the Growth of the Chicago Area, 1880–1930.* Chicago: University of Chicago Press, 1991.

——. "Gas and Electricity." In Reiff et al., *Encyclopedia of Chicago.* http://www.encyclopedia.chicagohistory.org/pages/504.html.

——. *Shock Cities: The Environmental Transformation and Reform of Manchester and Chicago.* Chicago: University of Chicago Press, 2005.

Poole, Ernest. *Giants Gone: Men Who Made Chicago*. London: Whittlesey House, 1943.

Ralph, Julian. "Chicago: The Main Exhibit." *Harper's New Monthly Magazine*, February 1892.

Rand, McNally & Co.'s Bird's-Eye Views and Guide to Chicago. Chicago: Rand, McNally, 1893.

Randall, Frank A. *History of the Development of Building Construction in Chicago*. Urbana: University of Illinois Press, 1949.

Reardon, Patrick T. "The Burnham Plan as Literature." *Burnham Blog*. The Burnham Plan Centennial, University of Chicago Library, November 30, 2009. http://burnhamplan100.lib.uchicago.edu/node/2565/.

———. "David Michael Reardon (1951–2015)." *Pump Don't Work* (blog). November 29, 2015. https://patricktreardon.com/david-michael-reardon-1951 -2015/.

———. "The Man Who Envisioned Chicago: Daniel Burnham's 'Plan' for the Windy City Celebrates a Century." *Illinois Heritage*, September 2009. https://patricktreardon.com/the-man-who-envisioned-chicago-daniel -burnhams-plan-for-the-windy-city-celebrates-a-century/.

———. Review of *The Plan of Chicago*, by Daniel H. Burnham and Edward H. Bennett. *Pump Don't Work* (blog). October 1, 2018. https://patricktreardon .com/book-review-the-plan-of-chicago-by-daniel-h-burnham-and-edward -h-bennett/.

Reiff, Janice L., Ann Durkin Keating, and James R. Grossman, eds. *The Encyclopedia of Chicago*. Chicago Historical Society, 2005. http://www. encyclopedia.chicagohistory.org.

"A Riveting Squad at Work at John Brown's Shipyard, Glasgow in 1949." National Library of Scotland. February 1, 2010. https://www.youtube.com /watch?v=CVjS1DsqYvo.

Roberts, Gerrylynn K. *American Cities & Technology: Wilderness to Wired City*. London: Open University, 1999.

Roberts, Sidney I. "Portrait of a Robber Baron: Charles T. Yerkes." *Business History Review* 35, no. 3 (1961): 344–71.

"Rosie, Pass the Rivets aka Ship Building." British Pathé. April 13, 2014. https:// www.youtube.com/watch?v=oqfYHmmhDvg.

Rowell's American Newspaper Directory. New York: Geo. P. Rowell, 1893.

Rowsome, Frank, Jr. *Trolley Car Treasury: A Century of American Streetcars; Horsecars, Cable Cars, Interurbans, and Trolleys*. New York: McGraw-Hill, 1956.

Royko, Mike. *Boss: Richard J. Daley of Chicago*. New York: Dutton, 1971.

Russell, Herbert K. *Edgar Lee Masters: A Biography*. Urbana: University of Illinois Press, 2001.

Samors, Neal, and Michael Williams. *Chicago in the Fifties: Remembering Life in the Loop and the Neighborhoods*. Chicago: Chicago's Neighborhoods, 2005.

———. *The Old Chicago Neighborhood: Remembering Life in the 1940s.* Chicago: Chicago's Neighborhoods, 2003.

Sandburg, Carl. *Always the Young Strangers.* New York: Harcourt, Brace, 1952.

Sande, Theodore Anton. *Industrial Archeology: A New Look at the American Heritage.* Brattleboro, VT: Stephen Greene, 1976.

Schaaf, Barbara C. *Mr. Dooley's Chicago.* Garden City, NY: Anchor, 1977.

Schaffer, Kristen. *Daniel H. Burnham: Visionary Architect and Planner.* New York: Rizzoli, 2003.

Schein, David L. "Deep Tunnel." In Reiff et al., *Encyclopedia of Chicago.* http://www.encyclopedia.chicagohistory.org/pages/504.html.

Schneer, Jonathan. *London 1900: The Imperial Metropolis.* New Haven, CT: Yale University Press, 1999.

Schneirov, Richard. *Labor and Urban Politics.* Urbana: University of Illinois Press, 1999.

Seeger, Nancy. *The People's Palace: The Story of the Chicago Cultural Center.* Chicago Department of Cultural Affairs, 1999. http://www.cityofchicago .org/city/en/depts/dca/supp_info/the_people_s_palacethestoryofthe chicagoculturalcenterpage2.html.

"The Shaping of Towns, II." *American Architect and Building News* 2, no. 79 (1877): 203–4.

Sharoff, Robert. "On the Life and Work of Chicago Architect Harry Weese." *Chicago Magazine,* July 7, 2010. https://www.chicagomag.com/Chicago -Magazine/July-2010/On-the-Life-and-Work-of-Chicago-Architect-Harry -Weese/.

Sherwood, Tim. *Charles Tyson Yerkes: The Traction King of London.* Stroud, UK: Tempus, 2008.

Shumsky, Neil L., ed. *The Physical City: Public Space and the Infrastructure.* New York: Routledge, 1995.

Sinclair, Upton. *The Jungle.* 1906. Reprint, New York: Barnes & Noble, 1995.

Skogan, Wesley G. *Chicago since 1840: A Time-Series Data Handbook.* Urbana: Institute of Government and Public Affairs, University of Illinois, 1976.

"Skyscrapers of New York 1906 (Part 1)." American Mutoscope and Biograph Company. December 11, 1906. https://www.youtube.com/watch?v=M -QFGC0wi7c.

Smith, Carl. *Chicago and the American Literary Imagination, 1880–1920.* Chicago: University of Chicago Press, 1984.

———. *The Plan of Chicago: Daniel Burnham and the Remaking of the American City.* Chicago: University of Chicago Press, 2006.

Smith, J. Bucknall. *A Treatise upon Cable or Rope Traction, as Applied to the Working of Street and Other Railways.* 2nd ed. with additional material by George W. Hilton. Philadelphia: Owlswick, 1977.

Spinney, Robert G. *City of Big Shoulders: A History of Chicago.* DeKalb: Northern Illinois University Press, 2000.

Stead, William T. *If Christ Came to Chicago.* 1894. Reprint, Evanston, IL: Chicago Historical Bookworks, 1990.

Steevens, George Warrington. *The Land of the Dollar.* New York: Dodd, Mead, 1897.

Steinberg, Ted. *Down to Earth: Nature's Role in American History.* Oxford: Oxford University Press, 2002.

Strauss, Anselm L. *Images of the American City.* New York: Free Press of Glencoe, 1961.

Street, Julian. *Abroad at Home.* New York: Century, 1914.

Thomas, R. H. G. *London's First Railway: The London & Greenwich.* London: B. T. Batsford, 1986.

Thompson, James. "Thompson's Plat of 1830." In Reiff et al., *Encyclopedia of Chicago.* http://www.encyclopedia.chicagohistory.org/pages/11175.html.

Tietjen, Randall. "Clarence Darrow & Edgar Lee Masters." *Green Bag* 13 (Summer 2010): 411–25. http://www.greenbag.org/v13n4/v13n4_tietjen.pdf.

Towle, George Makepeace. *American Society.* London: Chapman & Hall, 1870.

Towner, Wesley. *The Elegant Auctioneers.* New York: Hill & Wang, 1970.

Trachtenberg, Alan. *Brooklyn Bridge: Fact and Symbol.* 2nd ed. Chicago: University of Chicago Press, 1979.

Traub, James. "Reflection." In *The Greatest Grid: The Master Plan of Manhattan, 1811–2011,* edited by Hilary Ballon, 85. New York: Columbia University Press, 2012.

"Union Elevated Railroad, Union Loop, Wells, Van Buren, Lake Streets & Wabash Avenue, Chicago, Cook County, IL." *Historic American Engineering Record,* HAER ILL,16-CHIG,108. Library of Congress Prints and Photographs Division, Washington, DC. https://www.loc.gov/pictures/item/il0389/.

Waddell, John Alexander Low. *Economics of Bridgework: A Sequel to Bridge Engineering.* New York: John Wiley & Sons, Inc., 1921.

———. *The Principal Professional Papers of Dr. J. A. L. Waddell, Civil Engineer.* Edited by John Lyle Harrington. New York: Virgil H. Hewes, 1905.

———. *A System of Iron Railroad Bridges for Japan.* Tokyo: Tokio Daigaku, 1885.

———. "To the Graduating Class in the Engineering Department." (Rensselaer) *Polytechnic* 19 (1903): 201–11.

Walker, Robert A. "Chicago" In *Great Cities of the World: Their Governance, Politics and Planning,* edited by William A. Robson, 191–228. London: George Allen & Unwin, 1957.

Warner, Sam Bass, Jr. *The Urban Wilderness.* New York: Harper & Row, 1972.

Weber, Robert David. "Rationalizers and Reformers: Chicago Local Transportation in the Nineteenth Century." PhD diss., University of Wisconsin, 1971.

Weese, Harry. "The Chicago Loop Elevated, Presentation to the Illinois Historic Sites Advisory Council for Nomination to the National Register of Historic Places." With the assistance of Judith Kiriazis and Douglas Schroeder. September 15, 1978. Illinois Historic Sites Advisory Council, Springfield.

Weese, Harry, and Judith Kiriazis. "National Register of Historic Places Inventory: Nomination Form" for Chicago Loop Elevated. July 14, 1978. Illinois Historic Sites Advisory Council, Springfield.

Weingardt, Richard G. "John Alexander Low Waddell: Genius of Moveable Bridges." *Structure* (February 2007): 61–64.

Wendt, Lloyd, and Herman Kogan. *Bosses in Lusty Chicago: The Story of Bathhouse John and Hinky Dink.* Bloomington: Indiana University Press, 1971. Originally published in 1943 as *Lords of the Levee.*

——. *Give the Lady What She Wants: The Story of Marshall Field & Company.* South Bend: Marshall Field, 1952.

White, Charles Henry. "Chicago." *Harper's Monthly Magazine* 118 (April 1909): 729–35.

Whyte, William H. *City: Rediscovering the Center.* New York: Doubleday, 1988.

Willis, Carol. *Form Follows Finance: Skyscrapers and Skylines in New York and Chicago.* New York: Princeton Architectural, 1995.

Wilson, Mark R. "Farwell (John V.) & Co." In Reiff et al., *Encyclopedia of Chicago.* http://www.encyclopedia.chicagohistory.org/pages/2660.html.

——. "Field (Marshall) & Co." With contributions by Stephen R. Porter and Janice L. Reiff. In Reiff et al., *Encyclopedia of Chicago.* http://www.encyclopedia.chicagohistory.org/pages/2663.html.

——. "Sears, Roebuck & Co." With contributions by Stephen R. Porter and Janice L. Reiff. In Reiff et al., *Encyclopedia of Chicago.* http://www.encyclopedia.chicagohistory.org/pages/2840.html.

Windsor, H. H. *Souvenir: A Short Description of the Cable System as Operated by the Chicago City Railway Co.* Chicago: Chicago City Railway, 1889.

Wolmar, Christian. *The Subterranean Railway: How the London Underground Was Built & How It Changed the City Forever.* Chicago: Atlantic Books, 2012.

The World Almanac and Encyclopedia 1912. New York: Press Publishing, 1911.

Young, David M. *Chicago Transit: An Illustrated History.* DeKalb: Northern Illinois University Press, 1998.

——. "Street Railways." In Reiff et al., *Encyclopedia of Chicago.* http://www.encyclopedia.chicagohistory.org/pages/1207.html.

Young, Philip. *Ernest Hemingway: A Reconsideration.* University Park: Pennsylvania State University Press, 1966.

Zorbaugh, Harvey Warren. *The Gold Coast and the Slum: A Sociological Study of Chicago's Near North Side.* Chicago: University of Chicago Press, 1929.

Index

Page locators in italics refer to figures and tables.

For more than three decades, Patrick T. Reardon was an urban affairs writer, a feature writer, a columnist, and an editor for the *Chicago Tribune*. In 2000, he was one of a team of reporters who won a Pulitzer Prize for explanatory reporting. Now a freelance writer and poet, he has contributed chapters to several books and is the author of eight other books, including the poetry collection *Requiem for David*. His website is https://patricktreardon.com/.